# Old School Ties

## Educating for Empire and War

John Oakes & Martin Parsons

First Published 2001
by DSM
The Studio
Denton
Peterborough
Cambs PE7 3SD

**British Library Cataloguing in Publication Data**
A catalogue record of this book is available from the British Library

ISBN 0 9536516 6 5

Produced by
DSM
The Studio
Denton
Peterborough
Cambs PE7 3SD

Cover design and maps by Marc Lowen

Printed in Finland by WS Bookwell

This book is dedicated to

## Flight Lieutenant Ted Wright, RAF

*'In Memoriam'*

(John Oakes)

and

## Rex Bowley
History Master, Reading School

## John Martell
Senior Lecturer, Borough Road College, University of London

*'For initiating my interest in historical research'*

(Martin Parsons)

# About the Authors

**Martin Parsons**

Dr. Martin Parsons is Deputy Head of the School of Education and Director of the Secondary Post Graduate Certificate of Education course at the University of Reading.

He was a student at Reading School from 1963 to 1970.

Formerly a Senior Teacher at Theale Green Community School in West Berkshire, Martin moved to the University in 1990 to become Head of PGCE History and now lectures on both undergraduate and post-graduate courses.

Since 1992 he has been heavily involved in researching evacuation at the Micro level spending a great deal of time investigating a variety of sources within the former reception areas and relating his findings to the national situation. As a result his PhD thesis examined the perpetuation of the myths and images inherent in text book and media depiction of Evacuation and Air Raid Precautions.

Martin is Chairman of the Executive Committee of the Evacuee Reunion Association, has lectured and organised workshops on the topic at various Universities in the USA, Finland and Poland for students and teachers and has presented papers at a number of international conferences. In the UK he has given lectures to various groups and gave the Key-note address at the Imperial War Museum Evacuation Day. He has been listed in 'Who's Who in the World' for his work in this area.

He has completed a series of text books and worksheets related to his research for Key Stage 2 pupils. These were published by 'Wayland' in 1999. He is also collaborating with Homerton College Cambridge on their research project into Wartime Education and with colleagues in the Community Studies Department at the University of Reading who are researching into the effects of evacuation on babies. He has also established an Evacuation Archive at the University of Reading library on the Bulmershe Court campus.

He was joint historical advisor for the Sony Gold Award Winning BBC Radio 4 Series, The Evacuation the True Story.

**Other works by Martin Parsons published by DSM:**

*I'll Take That One - Dispelling the Myths of Civilian Evacuation 1939-45*
Times Educational Supplement Book of the Week.

*Waiting to Go Home - Letters and Reminiscences from the Evacuation 1939-45.*

*The Evacuation - The True Story* (In association with BBC Radio 4)
The Radio Series was the winner of the Sony Gold Award.

*Friendly Foe - The Letters of Leo Schnitter, a German POW in England.*


**John Oakes**

John was educated at Probus School in Cornwall and St. Luke's College, Exeter. He joined the Royal Air Force in 1955. After a tour of duty in the UK on the staff at the RAF Air Signallers School, he spent eight years in Libya, working in both military and civil aviation.

Prior to Colonel Ghadaffi's take over, he left Libya and worked for two years for Pacific Island Traders in Fiji and Papua New Guinea. He was severely injured in a traffic accident in Suva, Fiji and took up school teaching.

He taught Biology at Reading School in Berkshire for 25 years. During this time he was Contingent Commander of the Combined Cadet Force for eight years, Housemaster of a Boarders House for ten years and Chairman of the Staff Common Room for four years.

He is now Honorary Secretary of the Old Redingensians Association and Editor of its magazine 'The Old Redingensian'.

# Preface

In 1900 Reading School established a Cadet Corps. The idea had been suggested by Lieutenant C.C.R. 'Paddy' Murphy of the Suffolk Regiment at the Old Boy's Dinner at the Queen's Hotel in November 1897. The Editors of the Reading School Magazine reported that Paddy Murphy had at one time been a member of the Chitral Relief Column (see page 62). He had not and Paddy wrote to them from the Andaman Islands on October 26th 1895 to correct the misunderstanding. It was this single letter which led us to look for others. We found them in abundance. Letters from the Tirah Campaign, the Boer War, the Canadian Prairies and other parts of the Victorian and Edwardian Empire were published in editions of the magazine spanning the 19th and 20th centuries. They were written at a time when there was little other communication and they leave behind a written legacy of the life of many ORs who had found careers, both civil and military, in remote outposts of the Empire.

It was only natural that we took this one step further and examined the role of ORs in the First World War and traced those whose names now appear on the War Memorial in the Chapel. Although this took a great deal of micro-research it proved to be a worthwhile exercise because we not only managed to find the graves and memorials of those who had died but found two omissions, H.Louth and C.B.Major. If the book achieves nothing else, it will at least enable the names of these ORs to receive their rightful place on the memorial tablet.

The publication of this book coincides with the ORs appeal for money to restore the old major classroom and assembly hall in the School known as 'Big School'. John has pledged the royalties of this book to this appeal. Martin has pledged his to establish a research fund for pupils wishing to initiate their own historical research.

# Acknowledgements

We are indebted to a number of people who in some way have helped us with this project. In particular we wish to thank Andrew Linnell, Headmaster of Reading School, for allowing us freedom of access to school records and pictorial archives and providing the encouragement; A.R.Waring JP, President of the Old Redingensian Association in 2000, and its current Chairman, under whose auspices the authors were brought together to collaborate on this book; Denis Moriarty, present President, for his interest in the project; Kerr Kirkwood, the Honorary Archivist of the Old Redingensians Association, without whom the Reading School Archives would have ceased to exist long ago; Beverly Taylor, the Reading School Librarian, to whom we offer our thanks and apologies for past and future misdemeanours. There is no doubt that it was her selective amnesia about the dates books were due back which allowed us to start and finish this project. To Michael Naxton whose book on the History of Reading School, now sadly out of print, was a great source of background information. We would urge Mike to think of reprinting it as copies are highly sought after and those of us who have one refuse to lend it out.

Thanks are also due to Jan Keohane, Assistant Curator at the Fleet Air Arm Museum, Yeovilton for providing details of the ORs who were members of the RNAS, and for explaining the issue of shore-based cost centres which saved us a great deal of time in what would have been fruitless investigations into ships which did not in fact exist; Colin Brooks, a close friend of Martin's now retired to Yorkshire, who carried out graveyard searches in that area on the authors' behalf and saved us a great deal of time; likewise Jenny Ellis who took the photos of the Plymouth memorial and saved us a trip.

For reading parts of the manuscript and for making constructive comments we would also like to thank Michael Griffin, Jan Hamblin and Stephen Haley.

It goes without saying that we are greatly indebted to Paul Holness of DSM Publishing, by coincidence another RAF man, for seeing the potential in this book and being extremely patient as deadlines came and went!

Finally our wives, who put up with us being locked away in our studies for the duration. For Jo Parsons, this has been an annual experience for sometime, although it does not get any easier, but for June Oakes, as a 'first-timer', living with a 'temperamental' author must have been rather difficult, a situation not helped by an illness which affected her during the time we were writing the book and from which she is now thankfully recovering.

Martin Parsons & John Oakes

# Further Research

We have provided details of where almost all of the ORs who died in the First World War are buried or commemorated. As many people now visit the battlefields of the Western Front and Gallipoli we would welcome copies of any photographs of the sites, tombstones or memorial panels of those listed in order to put them in the archive.

Any other resource material from families etc. would also be welcome and will be returned once copied.

Any such material can be sent to us at either:

c/o Reading School, Erleigh Road, Reading, Berks.

or

c/o DSM Publishing, The Studio, Denton, Peterborough, Cambs PE7 3SD.

# Publishers Note

Many of the pictures of the individuals featured in this book have been extracted from school team photographs, some of which, due to the ravages of time, are of poor quality. Where possible we have done our best to improve the quality during reproduction.

Throughout the book Reading School old boys, known as Old Redingensian(s), are referred to as OR(s), a method commonly used by Public School old boys.

*'The noble voices of the past*
*Are clearly to us calling;*
*Examples of such men as they*
*Prevent the weaker falling.*
*Come, let us in their footsteps tread,*
*And make this our ambition,*
*That men may say when we are dead,*
*'They kept their School's tradition'.*
*So let her song rise loud and strong*
*'Look to the light*
*Strive for the right*
*Floreat Redingensis!'*

School Song. Verse 2. J. Boorne, 1898

**Mr. C. Outen Fullbrook gave the toast:**
*'The Army, Navy and Auxiliary Forces'*

*'In looking through the list of Old Boys he said that although none of them had reached a high position in the two services, he was glad to say that one of them had won the Victoria Cross. At the same time Reading had great demands to make on the future; they wanted someone to rise who should be greater than all his predecessors, they wanted an Admiral or General who should be in his time what Wellington or Nelson had been in theirs'.*

**Old Boy's Dinner, November 19th 1897.**

# Contents

# Maps

# Chapter 1

## THE IDEA OF AN EMPIRE, READING SCHOOL, IMPERIALISM AND WAR

On June 22nd 1897, Lord Roberts of Kandahar rode his grey Arab 'Vonolel" in the parade to celebrate Victoria's Diamond Jubilee. How proud that diminutive soldier must have been riding before the tiny Queen for whom he had fought so fiercely. She had dominion over an Empire which covered a quarter of the Earth, and her ships ranged the oceans without challenge. How did she exert such power? How could the people of a few small islands off the north coast of Europe rule so many? Why did so few question the morality of such rule?

On May 8th 1915, 2nd Lieutenant Giles Frederick Ayres of the 3rd Battalion, the Dorset Regiment closed a letter to his parents with the words 'I am going over the top of the parapet with the shout of 'School' on my lips and then pray that God's will be done'. He was killed leading his men in an attack on the German trenches the following day. What made men like this? What gave them the strength of character to offer their lives for King and Country? We examine that question at length in a later part of this book and look for the unifying principle which motivated such men as the Subaltern on the Western Front, the pioneer rancher in Saskatchewan and the civil engineer in the Indus Valley.

In the expansion of the British Empire profit, and hope of profit, was an obvious driving force. The attraction of spices, sugar, slaves, cotton, rubber, silver, tin and gold over the centuries is ample testimony to that, but there was more to imperialism and colonialism. There was something that allowed decent men and women to accept that distant territories and their indigenous populations could, and should, be subjugated. The Empire was carved out and maintained under harsh and adverse conditions often in circumstances where there was a great disparity in numbers between the colonisers and the subjugates. For example, in India, in the 1930s, 4,000 British Civil Servants assisted by 60,000 soldiers and 90,000 civilians, in trade or the church, imposed themselves on a country of 300 million people.

# The British Empire, 1914

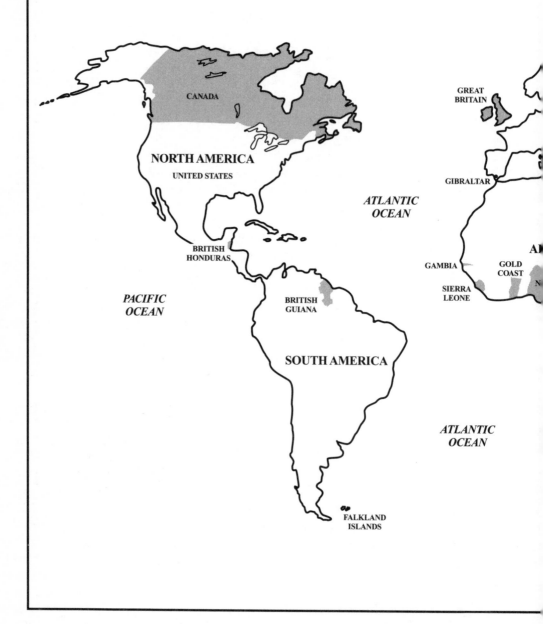

CANADA

**NORTH AMERICA**

UNITED STATES

GREAT
BRITAIN

GIBRALTAR

*ATLANTIC
OCEAN*

BRITISH
HONDURAS

GAMBIA

GOLD
COAST

SIERRA
LEONE

*PACIFIC
OCEAN*

BRITISH
GUIANA

**SOUTH AMERICA**

*ATLANTIC
OCEAN*

FALKLAND
ISLANDS

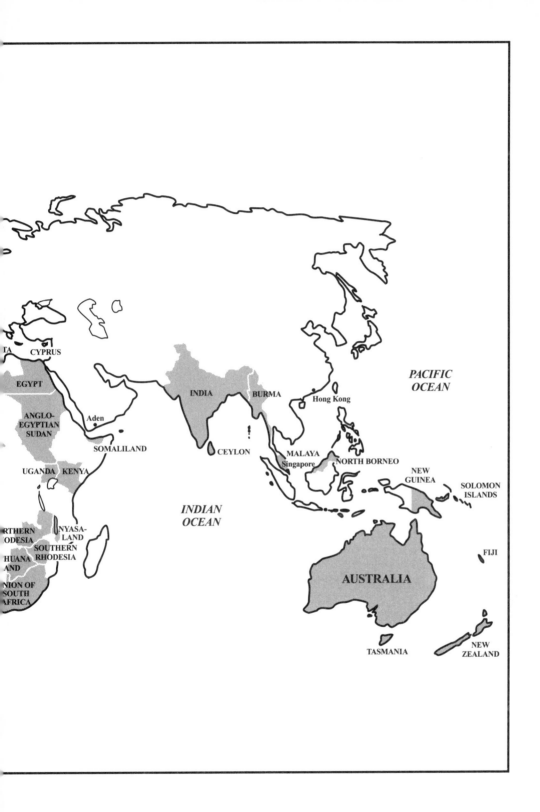

The clear and startling conclusion is that the concept of empire was the most powerful weapon at the disposal of the imperialist and that it came to be accepted by both the proponents of such a concept and their subjects. However, when the 'ruled' began to realise that the 'rulers' were vulnerable, for example when the weakness of the tactics employed by the British Army in the Boer War was exposed, it spelt the beginning of the end of colonial rule!

The basis of imperial authority was in the mind set of the colonists and of the colonised. How was this possible? In order to partly answer this question one must first ask how the agents of Victoria's rule were selected and trained. For example, what sort of person would become a District Commissioner and rule alone in a remote fort in Uganda? Who could build a road in the Himalayas whilst being shot at by determined Afridis? Why should someone wish to build canals in the Sind or guard a penal colony on a remote island in the Indian Ocean? What motivated men to grow tea in the hills of Assam or train camels to pull artillery pieces in Somalia. There had to be some driving force.

Victoria's Empire was ruled over by members of a male Imperial Elite. They were the products of what the British call the Public School system, a network of private residential schools which were the nurseries of the Empire. Together they had evolved a code of conduct, which permitted its 'old boys' to govern a quarter of the world's landmass. These Schools followed the Prefectorial system devised by Thomas Arnold, Head Master of Rugby School between 1828 and 1841. It was this method which encouraged the emergence of a class of capable and devoted administrators to meet the needs of the growing Empire.

It was a selective system in which the senior boys, even from 'scholarship' or 'freeplacer' backgrounds were admitted to a ruling elite, given responsibilities and accorded special privileges. They were called Prefects who adopted titles such as House Captain or School Captain and filled specific executive roles. They often wore subtle modifications of school uniform as an indication of their status, and had their own common room to reinforce their power and insularity from the rest of the school. They could punish their juniors, often being able to use the cane, and prescribe tasks or extra drills or detentions. They acted as leaders, heroes, guides and mentors for their juniors. The effect of the system reached right down into the lower school and helped shape the behaviour of the great majority who aspired to succeed to its ranks. In bad schools it was open to abuse. In good ones, like Reading School, it was a remarkable success.

Successes on the games field, especially in team games, was rewarded, and by the turn of the twentieth century Cadet or Officer Training Corps had been formed and Head Masters were reporting that the incidence of ill-discipline and subsequent punishment had gone down. The schools were largely cut off from the outside world during term time. It is worth reminding ourselves, that TV did not exist and there were no radios or telephones. The supply of newspapers was likely to have been monitored. It was easy for the typically muscular Christian Head Masters to support the prefect system, as Arnold did, with frequent moralising sermons. The days were well regulated and selected lecturers, some of whom were old boys, gave talks in the evenings on the subject of behaviour, patriotism and the Empire. The School Magazines, 'The Wellingtonian', 'Cliftonian' etc etc., were full of propaganda for the Empire and letters from old boys ensconced in prestigious jobs in far-flung parts of the world.

The Prefectorial system was a very powerful method of control with a dual purpose. It allowed each school to promote its aims by selecting those pupils who epitomised its ideals and in return it gave training in the art of leadership. In boarding schools, during term time, prefects were never off duty. They learned to live with responsibility even when they were asleep.

There were a number of factors which were common to the Old Boys of schools which adopted this system. They kept up 'appearances' and maintained 'stiff upper lips'. They knew when a rule was to be kept and when it was to be broken. They never curried favour with their subordinates and they could turn their hand to anything. They did not need the companionship of women and they did not need luxuries. They loved the outdoors and they loved danger and they liked to hunt wild animals. The best of them were highly motivated, totally flexible, unencumbered, well-trained, highly disciplined, literate, numerate, unselfconscious leaders of the Empire. They were not consciously arrogant but they were insular. They saw the world as being theirs by right and themselves as being uniquely selected to rule. Many argue that they were psychologically damaged but it is too facile to see them through the prism of today's mores. It is a fair bet that few would put up with the job nowadays.

However, there was a problem. The late Victorian and Edwardian schoolboys were encouraged to be selfless and loyal to institutions. As a consequence they did not question their elders and betters and to a certain extent this allowed the management and administration of the Empire to ossify. The imaginative, innovative, exuberance of the early Victorians was replaced by a reverence for statistics and status. Where, at one time, the emphasis was on the man not the system; the system became more important than the man. In the end the Empire became tangled in precedence and protocol. It's administrators and soldiers lived more and more in tight little English suburbs cut off from the world around them. Many of the inhabitants of these little colonial enclaves were unable to believe that the natives could have possibly desired to run their own country. It was sadly the case that many of the British refused to meet the natives apart from their own household staff.

A number of Public Schools were founded in the decade of the 1870s in imitation of Arnold's Rugby. They were given a fillip by a significant change in entrance requirements to the public services which had hitherto, been somewhat skewed in the hereditary direction. The Indian Civil Service was recruited from successful candidates in an examination in 1855 and the home Civil Service followed suit in its recruiting in 1870. Gladstone was strong enough to challenge the 'last bastion of privilege' when he abolished the purchase of officers' commissions in the army in 1871. It became the aim of the new public schools to get candidates into the Military Academies by examination and Army Classes were set up in public schools for this purpose.

Reading School is particularly interesting in this context since it reinvented itself in the latter part of the 19th century. At just about the time that other schools were developing a tradition, the Head Masters of Reading School could already cite a long and illustrious history. It had been founded in 1486, (but there is evidence that it was in existence before 1125). It had a number of eminent pupils. Its recent history was particularly important because it had achieved fame in Georgian times during the era of Richard Valpy (Headmaster 1781-1836)[1]. Therefore, there was a history on which any good Head Master could found and develop the idea of 'his' school.

For a school to work well there must be commonality of aims between the parents who send their children to the school, its Head, its staff, its governors and its pupils. At the time when most of our contributors were writing to the School Magazine, Reading School was a Public School. Its Head Master was the Reverend Charles Eppstein, one of the breed of Head Masters who did so much to promote the Public School System and the idea of Empire. He was a good publicist as well as a good teacher and he set out to marshal the key assets at his disposal and to promote them vigorously.

He had a glorious building designed by that great Victorian architect Waterhouse. It was, and remains, an architectural poem to the late Empire and it still looks the very model of an English Public School.

Eppstein had a number of alumnae who were eminent in their various fields who he could allude to. He advertised their names in the main classrooms and corridors and took every opportunity to extol their virtues and achievements. One such, H.G. Clinch epitomised the perfect Reading School pupil of the time (see page 99).

---

1   Valpy had been 'head-hunted' by Rugby, but Mrs Valpy did not want to move because she felt that the enterprise
    would be unprofitable. Valpy himself would have thought the job description to be too restrictive. Unlike Arnold,
    Valpy's system did not have the Prefectorial arrangement but was based more on personal 'intervention'. The fact that
    he was known as 'Flogger Valpy' gives some indication of how this philosophy was implemented. However, despite,
    or even because, of this he was highly regarded by his pupils and peers.
    (Ref. Personal correspondence R. Valpy.)

The New Buildings, opened 11 September 1871.

Eppstein quickly established the Old Boy's Association and saw to it that they met frequently. Something he also did in the School Magazine, which in itself simply became an extension of this self-fulfilling public image making. Like Arnold before him, Eppstein's speeches and sermons were reproduced in full within its pages and he too, brought speakers and 'experts' into school to reinforce his ideas. He established a Cadet Corps and turned it into an effective means of training pupils to accomplish shared tasks and learn leadership skills and traits which were to prove invaluable to some of its members in later life.

He maintained careful links with Oxford University and cultivated the local University College, then under the auspices of London University, so that he could support his pupils' academic aspirations. To get one's name on the Honours Board in school became the aim and driving force for many pupils.

Eppstein was, as much as any general, proconsul or bishop, a maker of empires and leader of men in war, if only because his philosophy and principles were always in the minds of his pupils as they governed various parts of the empire or led their men over the parapet in time of conflict.

In this book we offer the letters and obituaries of numerous pupils of Reading School in the period leading up to and including the First World War, until the time of the unveiling of the War Memorial in the Chapel in 1922. By reading them we may attempt to understand their motives and share their enthusiasms. Now we would certainly find some of their language racist in the extreme and, with some justification, question their beliefs. However, we must remember we have the benefit of hindsight and it is very easy to place 21st Century values on a 19th and early 20th Century society, so much different from our own.

Earl Roberts visits Reading School, December 14th 1906.

# Chapter 2

## LETTERS FROM AFRICA

At the time our contributors to the Magazine were writing about their adventures, the British were consolidating their grip on great tracts of Africa. Most of the rest of that continent was divided between the major European powers, France, Germany, Italy and Portugal. In all, 110 million Africans were subjugated by the then colonial powers.

Slavers had taken their toll on the human population and Rinderpest on the animal. The latter had devastated the domestic herds of cattle and, in consequence, in many parts of Africa the loss to this terrible cattle plague led to the disintegration of societies and wide-spread starvation. It also resulted in ecological changes and allowed the wild game to take over great regions of tsetse-fly-infested tropical savannah. The great National Parks of today, such as the Serengeti, the Masi Mara, the Selous and others, are examples of this effect.

Brutality was a common theme. In the Sudan, the Mahdi had hurled thousands of his followers against the British guns. At the Battle of Omdurman in 1898, 10,000 Mahdists had been killed and at least 15,000 wounded and abandoned. In South West Africa, the Germans drove out 20,000 people into the Omaheke desert to die. The early history of the Congo Free State is one of unmitigated atrocity. This was the 'Heart of Darkness' and the past was not forgotten in 1960 when Patrice Lamumba ejected the Belgians from what the latter thought was a model colony.

In South Africa, diamonds and gold had been found in fabulous quantities and the wealth, which flowed for them, did much to provoke the Boer War, although it would be too simplistic to suggest that this was the only, or even the main cause. There were distinct similarities between the 17th century Puritans in England with the Boers of the 1890s. Both 'carried' the teaching of the Bible in their left hand, but the latter had as a weapon the Mauser rifle rather than the two-edged sword in their right.

In common with many of their contemporaries our contributors enjoyed killing animals for sport. Our African hunters had the courage to face fierce animals on foot. One became a much-admired 'white hunter' and another a Colonial

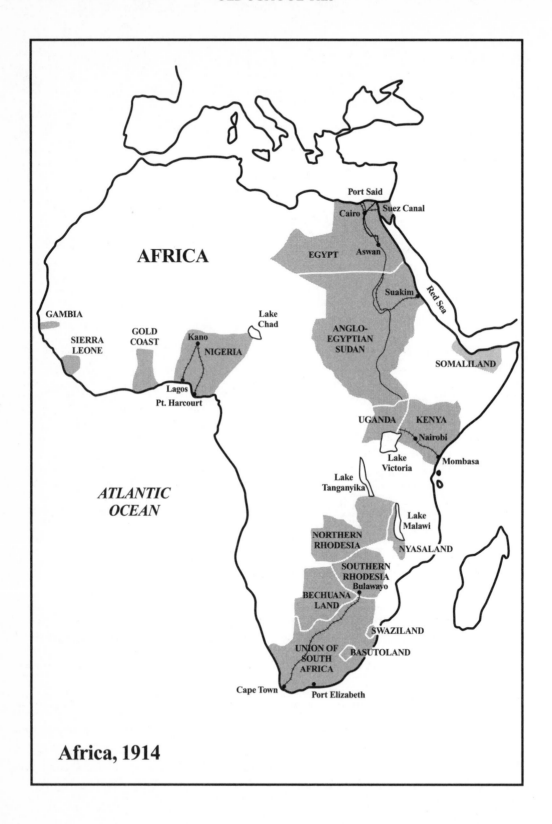

Africa, 1914

Governor. We should not hurry to condemn them on moral grounds for a pastime which was the norm for their day. Nowadays it is the indiscriminate poaching of animals for their parts; rhino for their horns, elephants for their tusks etc. which distresses us. In the 19th and first half of the 20th centuries such pursuits were common-place for those who could afford it.

Our contributors were 'of their time' and, because they were immersed in the day to day business of running an empire or fighting a war, were not given to philosophising a great deal. They thought they were bringing civilisation to the Africans. It is a measure of the changes we have experienced that we are rightly shocked by the raw racism of some of their remarks. The Africans increasingly saw colonial powers as conquerors and began to fight back but it took fifty years for many nations to rebuild their strength and regain their independence. It should come as no surprise that there is still resentment amongst them at the traces of colonialism and conquest.

### Cecil John Rhodes 1853 - 1902

It is Cecil John Rhodes, who looms large in the lives of a number of our contributors who ventured to Africa. Rhodes was an excellent businessman who suffered from the delusion that he could arrange a British controlled Africa from Cairo to the Cape of Good Hope and he went some way towards doing so. It was Rhodes who caused the Cape to Cairo telegraph to be built, no mean feat in the light of the formidable obstacles he overcame to do so.

Cecil Rhodes was a clergyman's son, born in Bishop Stortford in England, who went to South Africa for his health. At the age of 17 he arrived in Kimberley where he succeeded in the diamond business, forming the De Beers Consolidated Mines Company with his friend Barney Barnarto. He later went to Oxford University whilst Barnarto looked after the business in South Africa.

Rhodes became one of the youngest self-made millionaires and set about building a white empire in Africa. He was concerned that the Dutch South African Republics, the Transvaal and the Orange Free State, might have ambitions to expand northwards. There was evidence that they were making common cause with Germany whose colonisation of what is now Namibia, threatened a link up of powers in South Africa. Rhodes thought that together they would block the northward expansion of British interests so, in order to limit this, he persuaded the British to declare Bechuanaland a Protectorate.

Rhodes purchased the mineral rights for the territory of the Matabele Chief Lobengula and formed the British South African Company to exploit them, obtaining a Royal Charter for it in 1889. He sent groups of settlers, formed up as the Rhodes Pioneer Column, into Matabeleland and Mashonaland from Motloutsi on the Bechuanaland border on June 27th 1890. Among them were 200 hopeful settlers lead by Frank Johnson to whom he had promised £87,000. The settlers were protected by 500 of the newly formed Charter Company police (later to become the British South Africa Police) and had at their disposal 117 wagons pulled by 2,000 oxen. Rhodes' personal friend, Dr. Leander Starr Jameson[1], accompanied the Pioneers although Rhodes himself never joined the column. They trekked to a place they were to call Salisbury from where they dispersed and claimed 3,000-acre farms for themselves. In this way Rhodesia was born.

Rhodes became the Prime Minister of the Cape Colony, an office he held between 1890 and 1896. He attempted to persuade the Transvaal into a confederacy with the Cape Colony but its President, Kruger, would have none of it. The British in the Transvaal, known as the Uitlanders, were denied civil rights and were restive. The goods and supplies for the gold mines of the Rand were controlled by Boer monopolies and this did not please the mine owners so Rhodes and some of the 'Gold Bugs' decided to incite the Uitlanders to rise and seize the Transvaal. He financed an armed uprising, which he attempted to synchronise with a raid from Bechuanaland by 400 Charter Company police led by Jameson. Both the uprising and the raid failed, as we see from the extract of a letter from one of our contributors, Trooper Mousely, and as a result Rhodes was forced to resign as Prime Minister of the Cape Colony. He spent much of the rest of his life developing Rhodesia and in philanthropic pursuits. He is buried in Rhodesia.

The force involved in the Jameson Raid set out from Bechuanaland on December 29th 1895. It was stopped and beaten by the Boers on January 2nd 1896 in a battle at Doornkop, within sight of Johannesburg. By the time Jameson had raised the white flag 16 of his troops had been killed. The Boers had lost only one man.

The Boers were going to take Jameson to be hanged but the Transvaal President Kruger intervened and had him returned to England for trial. Joseph Chamberlain, the Colonial Secretary, appeared to be implicated in the fiasco in that he was privy to the plans made by Rhodes. The German Kaiser sent a telegram of congratulations to Kruger which allowed Chamberlain to play on the British fears of an alliance between German Imperial expansionists and the Boer Republics.

Jameson helped with the negotiations with Lobengula, the Matebele chief, and successfully conducted the Matebele Wars, which eventually led to the formation of Rhodesia. He later became the Prime Minister of the Cape Colony between 1904 and 1907 and it was he who served as the inspiration for Kipling's poem 'If'.

---

1    Dr. Leander Starr Jameson was in medical practice in Kimberly when he first met Rhodes. He was his close friend and right hand man until the latter died. He led the infamous Jameson Raid for which he was tried in England and sentenced to eighteen months imprisonment.

## 1896 - SOUTH AFRICA

### TROOPER MOUSLEY AND FRIENDS ATTEMPT TO TAKE OVER THE TRANSVAAL

### TROOPER MOUSLEY OF B COMPANY, THE UITLANDERS' ASSOCIATION

The following appeared in the April 1896 edition of the Reading School Magazine:

*"No self respecting School Magazine could appear at the present time without a letter from some Old Boy at or near Johannesburg. Fortunately, although we cannot claim for Reading any of the members of Dr. Jameson's famous troop, we have received permission to quote from a letter dated Johannesburg, January 6th 1896 by Trooper Mousley of the B Company of the Uitlanders' Association, who spent New Year's Eve and the early hours of New Year's Day on sentry-go".*

*Johannesburg*
*6th January 1896*

*"We got up at 5 o'clock in the morning, on the go all day, on guard all night, as the Boers were expected. I don't think they will do much against us as we are too well sheltered and 400 strong."*

Later he writes: *"We are surrounded by Boers and prepared for a two months' siege; we expect troops from Bechuanaland. A man went mad on sentry duty the other night and shot the sentry next to him .......... The Boers have sent word to say that if we lay down our arms all will be right; they give us until four o'clock tomorrow to decide. If we refuse they will give the women and children six hours to get out of Johannesburg, then down they come upon us"*

This small fragment of a letter is rare because it adds to the evidence about the infamous Jameson Raid, an event generally seen as one of the precursors of the Boer War.

## THE BOER WAR

Overview:

**1899** British Army defeated by Boers at:
**10th December**      Magersfontein
**11th December**      Stormberg
**15th December**      Colenso
                         Siege of Ladysmith

**1900**
**27th February**      Relief of Ladysmith
**17th May**           Relief of Mafeking
                         Battle of Kimberley
**6th September**      Battle of Lyndenberg
                         Kronje, leader of the Boers, surrendered

**1902** War ended with Peace of Vereeniging

On October 11th, 1899, Britain went to war with the Transvaal and the Orange Free State, the two Boer Republics in South Africa. The War lasted until May 31st 1902 and it cost the British Government £210 million.  448,895 British soldiers served in it with a total of 20,721 casualties of whom 7,582 were killed in action or died of wounds. Far and away the largest number of fatalities, 13,139, succumbed to disease. On the Boer side it is thought that a total of 87,365 men took up arms and that 7,000 of them were killed. The British incarcerated Boer families, a total of somewhere between 18,000 and 20,000 people, in concentration camps. (These must not be confused with the German Death camps used later in the century. The former were used to 'concentrate' the prisoners in one place, although they were still not pleasant places in which to be imprisoned.) The involvement of African natives is difficult to quantify but it is said that there were 10,000 armed Africans and up to 40,000 labourers and drivers on the British side. Estimates of native African casualties vary from between 7,000 to 10,000.
*(Ref. M.Carver. The Boer War. P252)*

The medical services on the British side were bad. There was little or no attention paid to basic hygiene. Food, clothing and shelter were inadequate and water was drunk from rivers without any due care and attention, causing many deaths from Enteric Fevers. The Medical Officers in charge were spectacularly incompetent and there were not enough nurses. In 1900 there were only 850 doctors with the British troops. It is clear that the top commanders should have taken the ultimate responsibility for the failures in the medical services, as it is apparent that although they were presented with reasonably accurate figures of sick and wounded they failed to act.

The Senior Officers of the British Army were split into factions. So-called 'Rings' had formed around the two most senior generals, Field Marshal Lord Roberts of Kandahar and Field Marshal Lord Wolseley, the Commander-in-Chief of the British Army. Roberts had been fobbed off with command in Ireland, from whence he intrigued with Landsdowne, the Secretary for War, to replace Wolseley. In the meantime, General Sir Redvers Buller, a Wolseley man, was conducting the war against the Boer Republics in South Africa.

By the end of September 1899 Buller had presided over a number of defeats. The British had been used to easy victories against weak opposition and they did not take well to the fact that the Boers had besieged British troops in Ladysmith, Kimberley and Mafeking. Nor did they react well to Black Week when Gatacre was defeated at Stormberg on December 10th 1899, Methuen at Magersfontein on December 11th 1899 and Buller at Colenso on December 15th 1899. Field Marshal Lord Roberts, from his backwater in Ireland, was stung by all this into sending a telegram to Landsdowne in which he proposed himself as Buller's replacement.

As a result the diminutive 67-year-old Lord Roberts had himself appointed Commander-in-Chief in South Africa above Buller. He took Kitchener, the hero of the Sudan, along as his Chief of Staff and the two of them arrived in Cape Town on January 10th 1900. 45,000 men, being the main part of the British Army, including much of the Militia, were shipped out to take part in the War, leaving Britain poorly defended. (Buller took the news of his demotion with complacency and during the weeks he remained in place while waiting for Roberts arrival, he had plenty of opportunity to demonstrate his incompetence as a General).
*(Ref. Battles of the Boer War. W. Baring Pemberton. p147)*

General Sir Redvers Buller
(Radio Times Hulton Picture Library)

With this army at his disposal, Roberts devised a plan that would allow him to use the main railway line from Cape Town right through the Boer Republics to Komati Poort on the border between the Transvaal and Portuguese East Africa. He would bring overwhelming force to bear on the Boer capitals whilst Buller remained in Natal to raise the siege of Ladysmith and soak up as much Boer war effort as he could. The plan was simple, direct and flawed as it failed to take account of the history and psychology of the Boers. Some of their commanders, notably Prinsloo, surrendered, but many, Botha and Oliver for example, did not.

The British infantry was not suited to the war in South Africa. It was ineffective when too far away from a railway line, whereas the Boers, who were expert horsemen and knew the country, had developed a superb mounted infantry which could move over great distances and appear and disappear disconcertingly. Buller realised this after the Battle of Colenso and sent the following telegram to Wolseley.

*"Would it be possible to raise eight thousand irregulars in England? They should be equipped as mounted infantry, be able to shoot as well as possible and ride decently. I would amalgamate them with the Colonials".*
(Ref. Packenham. The Boer War p252)

George Wyndham, Landsdowne's junior minister, embraced the idea and thus the Imperial Yeomanry was born, recruited partly from the hunting farmers and horsemen. Much of the cost of raising it was found by private subscription, a good sum having been donated by Wernher-Biet, the Rand millionaire. It was amateurish but the calibre of recruit was better than that of the regular infantry. The British press and the people liked the idea of an elite corps and several thousand 'Gentleman Rankers' enlisted, including stockbrokers, journalists and an MP.

On February 11th 1900 Roberts launched his 'great flank attack' with five divisions, about 40,000 men, on the main Boer centres of Bloemfontein, Pretoria and Johannesberg. In 1900 he took Bloemfontein on March 13th, Johannesburg on May 31st and Pretoria on June 5th, but allowed much of the Boer Army to escape.

Meanwhile on February 27th 1900 Buller raised the siege of Ladysmith and later broke through the Boer positions on the Drakensberg. He took Lydenburg on September 6th 1900 and sailed for England on October 24th, 1900. Roberts then annexed the Boer Republics into the British Empire and also went home.

On November 27th, 1900 Kitchener succeeded Roberts as Commander in South Africa and presided over the guerrilla phase of the war against the Boers which the latter had failed to subdue. The campaign was long and disgracefully bloody. The British commenced to burn Boer farms and put the families into concentration camps. They built lines of blockhouses joined by barbed wire fences to divide up the country into sections and commenced to hunt the Boer commandos within them. With their wives and families incarcerated in the camps and dying at an alarming rate, the Boer commandos were worn down. They signed an armistice and the war ended on May 31st 1902.

The British extricated themselves from the War without really achieving their aims. The Command of the British Army, hitherto so patently riven with petty jealousy, was reorganised before the First World War, but many of the tactical lessons learned in the Boer War were not applied in time to save countless lives. It is said that the files containing the crucial reports that might have helped, had been lost in the War Office.

General Cronje (right) surrendering to Lord Roberts. February 27th 1900.

(Radio Times. Hulton Picture Library)

## HAWLEY F.H.

*'F.H. Hawley has also got a commission and has gone to the front to join the other ORs who are fighting for their country'*
May 1900

Football XI.  1898-1899

*'....one prominent feature of the year had been the starting of the Engineer Cadet Corps in the School. This had been undertaken with no intention of irritating our Continental neighbours;.....but because the Boer war has emphasised the importance, nay, the necessity, of every man being able to take up arms for his country and Empire and because this seemed to be the only way to avoid conscription, which would always remain abhorrent to not a few people, they had thought it wise to give their boys the opportunity of having a thorough knowledge of what would be required, should they, at any time be called upon to serve their country'.*
Headmaster. Speech Day. October 26th 1900:

*'ORs serving at the Front have our sympathies and encouragement in their tiresome task. We wish them truly 'God-speed'.*
April 1901

## 1900 - SOUTH AFRICA

### FIGHTING BOERS WITH THE 58th IMPERIAL YEOMANRY

### D.E.L. HOLMES - IN MEMORIAM

Dennis Edward Lane Holmes was born at Eastheath, Wokingham, in 1886. He attended Boxmore Grammar School, Hertfordshire, before entering Reading School in September 1891. He left in May 1893 and sailed for Canada to try farming. In December 1899 he returned to England intending to go to South Africa to farm, but the Boer War having broken out, he joined the 58th Imperial Yeomanry and sailed to the Cape on the "Norman" in February 1900. The 58th Company was to form part of the 5th Battalion Imperial Yeomanry in South Africa.

The following extracts from his letters, which he wrote from that time until he died of enteric fever, were published in the School Magazine in December 1903. A stained glass window was erected in his memory next to the Boer War Memorial in Reading School Chapel.

8th March 1900
Queenstown

*We are still in camp; we arrived last Monday and expected to leave on Tuesday, but have had no orders yet, although there is a rumour that we leave on Monday for Naupoort, and from there to Mafeking. We got our horses and had them out for drill the last two days. Mine is one that was captured from the Boers; they are all very small horses and fairly quiet. The weather is very hot in the daytime, and as there are 13 of us in a tent, we are generally very warm at night. Today we are having an awful dust storm. The food we get is not so bad; the meat is very tough, as it is only killed the night before. There is a canteen, where they sell tinned meat and lemonade. Pineapples we can get at 2d. and 3d. each. Captain Ricardo took most of us down to the baths in Queenstown yesterday afternoon. Our horses have been shod this afternoon. We have very little spare time, as we are obliged to take our horses 1 mile three times a day for water.*

2nd April 1900
Near Kimberley

*I have not tasted butter for a month, and no bread for 10 days, only biscuits just like puppy cakes. We have been on the march again. And have just come back from a 10 days' march beyond Berkeley West; we came under Lord Methuen, and we got quite close to a lot of Boers, but the order came from Lord Roberts to go back to Kimberley by forced marches, and here we are just now, but we are likely to move any day, perhaps to Boshof, and then on to Bloemfontein. We had about six nights out in the rain with only a blanket over us, and a pool of water under us. We are now under canvas, and a good thing too, for the nights are very cold, and such heavy dews! Lord Methuen seems very pleased with us. I think we shall join Lord Roberts soon. About 12 Yeomanry here are now on their way to Pretoria as prisoners. I am glad I am not one of them. I am sitting on the ground with a bully beef tin to write on.*

### 29th May 1900
### Kroonstad

*We got here yesterday after two weeks' march, and expect to start again tomorrow. The Boers were going to make a stand but we entered the place without firing a shot. Our Company is now reduced to 70; all the others have dropped out from fever and dysentery, and some are now on their way home.*

### 4th June 1900
### Lindley

*We had some fighting; we drove the Boers back and took the town, but arrived two hours too late to relieve the Yeomanry Regiment, which had to surrender. It was very hard luck, as we heard that they could hold out until Saturday afternoon, and we got here on Friday morning by a lot of forced marching. There are a lot of Boers still about; as I am writing I can see them about four miles away, and our outposts keep having a few shots. We only had two men slightly wounded. We were in two very hot corners. We expected to stay here for a day or two as our horses want rest; we have had three weeks on the move, a lot of forced marching, and left the Infantry and convoy a long way behind, and only Artillery and Yeomanry are in the fight; we had four horses shot, seven had a wash yesterday, the first in twelve days; and last night my boots were off for the first time for a month, and then only because my feet are sore.*

### 5th July 1900
### Bethlehem

*We are just going into Bethlehem. I do not know if we shall be opposed or not. We have had our camp shelled this morning, but the enemy have been in full retreat for two days, so I don't think they will make much of a stand, as we have General Clements on one side and I think General Hunter is not far away. We are with General Paget, and part of our Regiment is with Lord Methuen. The last two weeks we have been on short rations.*

**16th July 1900**
**Lindley**

*They tell us the war is nearly over, but we are busy still as there are lots of Boers all round us here; they have sent in twice to ask us to surrender, but there is no danger of that, for we have a good position but not much food left; we have been on three-quarter rations for some time, and expect them daily to be cut down to half. We had a long ride last Monday, about 70 miles; we started about 7 p.m. and were in the saddle 10 out of 24, and two hours of the other on guard; we were mending telegraph posts, etc, which the Boers kept cutting. Last night the Boers shelled us for the first time; we got up at 3 a.m. and saddled and then went back to bed.*

**17th August 1900**
**Heilbron**

(the last letter)

*I think it is the 17th, but I am not sure about it, and nobody seems to know. I have had no letters since April. I think we are stopping here for a few days. We are now attached to Generals Hunter and Macdonald; we were with the latter when Prinsloo surrendered. It took a whole week's fighting to catch that lot. We had a bit of a fight with Oliver when we came in here. We have been three months on biscuits, and all the time have been on the move without tents. I have just had my hair cut for the first time for four months, a shave the first time in three months, a wash the first time for over a month, so feel quite 'smart'.*

Shortly after writing this letter, Dennis Holmes was taken ill with enteric fever and ordered back into Hospital at Norval's Point, where he died on September 5th 1900. The two main operations in which Dennis Holmes was involved caught the interest of the British at home. They were the failure to save the 13th Battalion of the Imperial Yeomanry at Lindley and the surrender of Prinsloo at Verliesfontein in the Brandwater Basin.

## 29th MAY 1900
## TRYING TO SAVE THE 13th BATALLION, IMPERIAL YEOMANRY

On the May 28th 1900 Major-General Colvile with the Highland Brigade was on the way to Heilbron under orders from Lord Roberts. He was to be joined by the 13th Battalion Imperial Yeomanry under Col Spragge. It did not join him but he received this message.

*'Col Spragge to General Colvile – Found no one at Lindley but Boers – have 500 men but only one day's food, have stopped three miles back on the Kroonstadt Road. I want help to get out without great loss.*
*B. Spragge, Lieutenant Colonel. 27-5-1900'*

Colvile was in a hurry to get to Heilbron. In fact his troops marched 130 miles in eight days to reach it, often under fire from the Boers. The aim was to occupy the area before the Boers under De Wet could do so. In the event Colvile did not go to save the 13th Batallion. For this omission he was eventually invited to return to England by Roberts.

Spragge had arrived in Lindley at about midday on May 27th expecting to find the Highland Brigade. It had already left and the Boers had reoccupied the town. Instead of following Colvile immediately, he decided to stay where he was.

There were 500 men in the 13th Battalion. For mounted infantry to make a stand there must be grazing for their horses and pack animals so Spragge chose a defensive position in a valley, 460 metres (500 yards) wide, containing a dam and a farmhouse. He kept his horses and his transport in the valley and defended the high points surrounding it.

Spragge's Battalion was particularly interesting. It had been recruited in Ireland and consisted of four companies; the Duke of Cambridge's Own, the Irish Hunt and two Ulster Companies. The troopers of the Duke of Cambridge's Own, and to some extent, the Irish Hunt Company, were said to be of 'gentle birth and wealthy'. Many had purchased their own equipment and handed their Army pay over to a military charity.

Bragge could have extracted his battalion right up until May 30th. Until then the Boers were mainly interested in getting him out of Lindley. On the 31st Piet de Wet and Prinsloo arrived on the scene with gun reinforcements for the Boers. Spragge was surrounded and subject to artillery bombardment. His number was up. He surrendered on May 31st.

Roberts ordered Lord Methuen, who was at Kroonstadt, to try to save Spragge. On May 28th he despatched the 3rd, 5th and the 10th battalions of the Imperial Yeomanry and some artillery to make a dash for Lindley. They arrived on June 2nd only to find that Colonel Spragge had surrendered two days earlier. The Boers took a number of Irish aristocrats as prisoners of war. There was considerable interest in the affair in England and Ireland.

## JULY 30th 1900
## THE SURRENDER OF PRINSLOO IN THE BRANDWATER BASIN

On July 5th, 1900 Dennis Holmes writes from Bethlehem. From that date until he writes again he was in action, helping to drive a great host of Boers under Piet De Wet into the Brandwater Basin.

The Brandwater Basin is a valley formed by a great horseshoe of mountains of the Wittenbergen range and the Roodebergen Range. The circumference of the horseshoe is about seventy-five miles and the base line of the valley is formed from a forty-mile length of the Caledon River that separates the Orange Free State from Basutoland.

There are a number of passes through the mountains and the Boers defended them for a while. One of these was called Slabbert's Nek and another, a difficult one, was called the Golden Gate. Eventually the British pushed into the Basin and blocked the passes through the Ranges, but not the Golden Gate.

De Wet and a number of Boers managed to escape through Slabbert's Nek on July 15th leaving a remnant of 5,000-6,000 men behind in the Basin. This large remnant, cooped up within the horseshoe of mountain ranges, began to panic. There was an argument as to who was in command. On July 27th Prinsloo was voted in as commander. It was then decided, though not unanimously, to ask the British for an Armistice but the British insisted that the Boers surrender.

Prinsloo, who was somewhat past his prime, agreed and the surrender took place at Verliesfontein on July 30th, but not before some of the best soldiers amongst the Boers had escaped through the Golden Gate.

In all 4,313 men surrendered and the British collected 3 guns, two of which had been captured from them in the first place, 2,800 cattle, 4,000 sheep, 5,000 - 6,000 horses and about 2,000,000 rounds of ammunition. The surrender was said to be one of the great sights of the war.

The following list of those serving at the front appeared in the December 1900 issue of the magazine:

| | |
|---|---|
| **A.H.P. Austin** | Imperial Light Horse |
| **W.E .Booker** | Hampshire Volunteers |
| **C. Collins** | Natal Police. (Died of Enteric Fever) |
| **F.H. Hawley** | Derbyshire Regiment. |
| **R. Holmes** | Berkshire Yeomanry. (Died of Enteric Fever. Pretoria) |
| **R.C. Hurley** | King's Royal Rifles |
| **T.F.H .James** | Thorneycroft's Horse |
| **H.F.Lawrence** | Berkshire Yeomanry |
| **A. Morris** | Paget's Horse |
| **Captain Murphy** | Suffolk Regiment |
| **C. Pallant** | Berkshire Yeomanry |
| **M. Percival** | Imperial Light Horse |
| **B.G. Ruddock** | Natal Police |
| **E. Walker** | Natal Police |
| **W. Walker** | Natal Police |
| **W.W. Williams** | Berkshire Volunteers. |

*'Three of our Old Boys fell in the war*[1]. *In this respect we have been much more fortunate than other schools in losing so small a fraction of our old members, for ever Old Boys were fighting at the front. It is hoped that something will be done to preserve their memory. One suggestion is that windows be placed in the School Chapel by past and present members of the school' in quiam memoriam.'*
December 1902

*'R.Wilkin, OR has had some trying experiences at the Front with Paget's Horse. Obtaining with difficulty a berth in the hospital owing to a bad leg, he contracted scarlet fever from the bedding and had to be invalided home'.*
December 1902

---

1    **Charles William Collins.** Natal Mounted Police.
     **Percy Bernard Cooper.** 28th Company. Imperial Yeomanry.
     **Dennis Edward Lane Holmes.** 58th Company. Imperial Yeomanry.

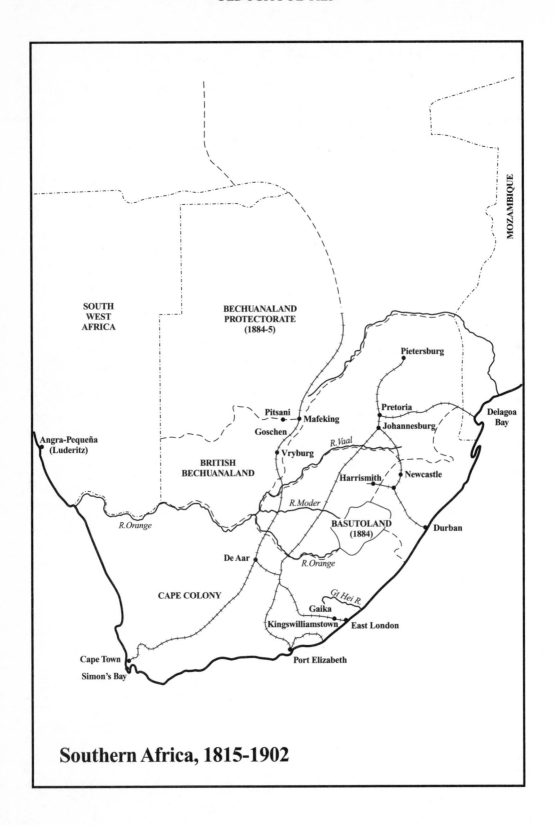

**Southern Africa, 1815–1902**

# 1901 - SOUTH AFRICA

## A LETTER FROM THE FRONT - A NIGHT ATTACK BY THE BOERS

### 'LINESMAN'

The author of this letter is at some pains to remain anonymous. 'Linesman' was the nom de plume of Lt. Maurice Grant, a serving officer in the British Army, who wrote numerous articles for the national press from the Boer War front. Maurice Grant went on to become one of the official historians of the Boer War. However, there is no record of such a person on the Reading School lists.

The battle at Bothwell village on the north shore of Lake Chrissie is well documented in Volume V of the Times History of the War in South Africa. In it the Sussex Regiment is placed firmly in the battle and, significantly, in the outposts, on the night of March 6th 1901.

The Reading School Magazine records the presence of an Old Boy of the School called Captain C.C.R Murphy of the Sussex Regiment amongst those serving in South Africa during the Boer War. The Sussex Regiment was praised for its work in the out post during the battle and Captain Murphy may have been exercising that modesty which was common amongst British Officers of his day in wanting to remain anonymous.

The evidence supports the hypothesis that the "Linesman" of our letter was Captain C.C.R. Murphy of the Sussex Regiment. He appears as a contributor in this book in the chapter on India with his letter from Port Blare in the Andaman Islands dated October 25th 1895. He served in India and Burma and recorded much of his adventurous life in the seven books he wrote. He was promoted to brevet Lieutenant Colonel in the First World War for bravery in the field while with 30th Punjabis.

*Piet Retief*
*9th April 1901*

*Dear Mr. Editor,*

*The December number of the School Magazine reached me at Assegai River, about three miles from here where I had been sent with two companies to guard a bridge the engineers had made, as owing to heavy rains the river had become impassable.*

*I was glad to learn to what extent the School is represented in the war, and to see that a list of Old Boys at the front is being compiled.*

*We are nearly seventy miles from the railway line, our nearest point being perhaps Volkshurst. All our supplies and mails have therefore to come to us by convoy, so there is a good deal of escort duty to be done, and the small parties of Boers hovering about near the road along the route would soon collect and attack if the wagons were not strongly guarded.*

*The Boers have lately been going in for night attacks and many of them have been successful. It has now become necessary for a force whenever it halts, to surround itself with a chain of enclosed works each being protected by a barbed wire entanglement. Entrenching is the sound thing from a tactical point of view, but there are limits to the endurance of soldiers, and after a long march, when perhaps, there is night outpost duty to follow, this is a thing to be got over as soon as possible.*

*The Boers made one of their typical night attacks at Lake Chrissie on February 6th. Three days before we had left Wonderfontein, a small place on the Dalgoa Bay Railway about thirty miles east of Middleburg. The force which consisted of three infantry regiments, one cavalry regiment, some guns and mounted infantry, all under Major-General Smith-Dorrien, DSO, was able to carry out the first two marches without interruption, but on the third day our rear-guard was considerably harassed getting into camp. My company, which formed part of the rear-guard that day, was for outpost duty that night, and so as soon as we had taken up positions for the night we began to entrench. The enemy was evidently in considerable numbers round us and had used a pom-pom against us on the way into camp. They had seen us march in with three 5-inch guns and several others of smaller calibre, and had resolved on a night attack so that we should not be able to use these against them. At half-past three in the morning they attacked and desperately too did they carry it out. Our outposts however held on and after a while the Boers retired. They lost nearly thirty killed and fifty-four wounded, and nearly all the horses of the 5th Lancers stampeded or were killed. The Boers were led by Louis Botha and numbered about two thousand, and amongst their casualties were two Commandants, one killed and one wounded and two Field Cornets, both killed. You could see the flashes of the Boer rifles in the dark, and that was all, but the enemy came on with such dash that numbers of them got between our outposts and the main body. It was the one time above all for fire discipline, and it was this, combined with our entrenchments, which eventually turned the scale in our favour.*

*After this adventure we had very little fighting, although the day we crossed over the border into Swaziland, they sniped us with such good effect that an officer and several men were hit, the majority of casualties occurring at a range of 2,400 yards.*

*In a few days we hope to leave the line when we expect to hear that the war is at all events within a measurable distance of termination.*

*Believe me,*
*Dear Mr. Editor,*
*Yours very truly,*
*'LINESMAN'*

## THE FIREFIGHT AT LAKE CHRISSIE

Kitchener was about to begin his scheme of 'devastation and depopulation'. The British were to clear the country systematically of supplies, horses, cattle, crops, transport-vehicles and non-combatant families. Bakeries and mills were to be destroyed. Every farm was to be visited and the families sent away to concentration camps. The action at Lake Chrissie occurred during the first 'drive' to accomplish Kitchener's aims.

The drive commenced near Pretoria and aimed to push the Boer fighting commandos up onto the Swaziland and Zululand borders to the east of the Transvaal. The columns involved were to operate between diverging railway lines, the one to Komati Poort to the north and the other to Newcastle in the south. They would get further and further from the railways as they pushed on. In all there were seven columns in the field together containing about 14,000 men with 58 guns and pom-poms. However, the feeding strength also included the Army Service Corps, Engineers, medical and telegraph units as well as drivers. The total strength came to 21,000 men, 11,500 horses and 9,000 mules.

Smith-Dorrien's column, in which 'Linesman' served, was to bring a large convoy of supplies down to Lake Chrissie from the railway in the north, sufficient to feed his own column and three others for twenty days. With Smith-Dorrien, according to the Times History of the War in South Africa, were 300 members of the 5th Lancers; 320, 2nd Imperial Light Horse; 400, 3rd Mounted Infantry; 600, 1st Suffolks; 600, 2nd West Yorkshires; 750, 1st Cameron Highlanders and Artillery with 8 guns; two 5 inch guns and two pom-poms. (Note that 'Linesman' writes that there were three 5-inch guns). This column was amongst the last to join the drive and vital because it was to supply the forces operating far away from the railway lines.

Botha had previously intended to invade Natal but this great drive by Kitchener put a stop to his plan. He had about 2,000 men in all with him and decided to break back through the British lines, leaving a light screen of fighters to protect the families as they retreated before the British columns. Smith-Dorrien's column was isolated and, as it was accompanied by an enormous quantity of supplies, it presented an irresistible target. Botha decided to attack it at night, using surprise to win the firefight and then to plunder the supplies for his own use.

Lake Chrissie, where the night fight took place, was little more than a glorified pan, partially dry in times of drought. The village of Bothwell was close on the north shore where the roads from Ermlo, Carolina and Swaziland meet. It was here that Smith-Dorrien halted. He made a good choice of a campsite and he set out his defences with skill. In the centre were the horse lines and the transport, whilst three regiments of infantry under Colonel Spens were disposed around them, each finding good outposts. The Cameron Highlanders took the South, the West Yorks the Northwest and the Suffolks, in which we suspect that 'Linesman' had a command, the Northeast. As 'Linesman' says, all were strongly entrenched and in place by sunset. There had been little intimation of an attack by the Boers but Smith-Dorrien was a prudent officer.

Botha came up by road skirting the western shore of the lake and fetching up in front of the West Yorks outposts on the night of Saturday, February 6th 1901. At 2.50 a.m. ('Linesman' says 3.30 a.m.) his troops commenced to fire a tremendous fusillade and it was then that the horses of the 5th Lancers and the Imperial Light Horse stampeded causing great confusion.

It was pitch dark and misty. The Suffolks were severely tested by determined attacks by the Boers. It was time, as 'Linesman' says, for fire discipline. Botha turned the stampeding horses back on the British and sent his men in under their cover. The Suffolks were returning the enemy fire with steady volleys, a sound which spread confidence in the camp behind. After about 45 minutes the Boer fire eased off. Botha realised he had lost the element of surprise and there was no point in continuing the fight. The British losses were slight mainly because the enemy never penetrated their outposts in sufficient numbers to bring fire to bear on the main camp. By 4.30 a.m. the Boers were in full retreat. In total there were 75 casualties on the British side and the Boers lost 80.

It was the 300 horses stampeded or killed which put Smith-Dorrien's column temporarily out of action. He was prevented by fog the next morning from stopping Botha's troops breaking back to the north and south of his lines. He eventually based himself at Piet Retief.

## 1906 - UGANDA

### RULING A LARGE PIECE OF UGANDA

### F.M. IREMONGER

### OR 1886-1894

Francis Maxwell Iremonger and his twin brother, Fredrick Charles, were born on July 5th 1876 and were at Reading School between 1886 and 1894. The brothers were educated at Miss Martin's, a Dame School in Reading, and both won Boarding Scholarships valued at £30 per annum at Reading School.

Francis became a District Commissioner in Uganda in 1906, having worked for six years in Borneo for the British North Borneo Company.

British influence in Uganda commenced in 1860 with the arrival of John Hanning Speke, who discovered the source of the Nile. In 1888 the British East African Company took over the country which had been under Arab control. It was hoped that the Company would make the territory pay for itself but, as usual, it did not and the British Government took over Uganda as a Protectorate in 1894.

Under the British the country was divided into Districts, which were ruled by Commissioners. The Districts were then divided into Counties, which in turn were subdivided into Sub-counties and further into Parishes and Sub-parishes.

In March 1906 F.M. Iremonger wrote a letter from Makasa, which was published in the Reading School Magazine in April of that year. Makasa is 137 kilometres by road south west of Kampala, the present capital of Uganda.

*Makasa*
*Uganda*
*March 1906*

*There are at least two O.R's out here. I met the one in Head Quarters a year ago, but I did not find out, until he and his wife stayed with me here a month ago, that he was at the old School. It was good to meet this Dr. Lowsley and to talk over old times.*

*I got the appointment out here under the Foreign Office last year. I got it suddenly, so I chucked British North Borneo and came out here at once. The work – administrative – is similar to what I had in Borneo, but the climate is better. To counterbalance this the nigger is not half so interesting as the Malay, nor is his country so pretty. However, it was most interesting to come 600 miles up into Africa, from Mombassa to the famous Lake Victoria, and to cross the lake in a swagger electric-lighted steamer to Entebbe (or Port Alice as it is sometimes entered on the maps, but never called). I called in at Jinja, where the only outlet from the huge lake goes over the Ripon Falls, and starts the Nile. After nine months in Entebbe as Assistant Secretary to the Commissioner I got a District. This was luck, as I have had to be content to start from the bottom of the list, and might well have got an Assistant Collector's billet under a man my senior in service and junior in years. Here I am my own master and responsible for a district of four counties – living by myself but always getting visitors as I am on a main road. If any place could excel all others for foreign languages, this does. There are French missionaries all around me at a distance of 8 miles; the Germans share a boundary with me; Italian, Indian, and Greek traders earn a living in the district; my official language is Swahili; native tongue Luganda; my cook is Malay. I only 'run' to Malay, French and Swahili myself.*

*The climate in this particular district is remarkably cool, ranging from 56 degrees to 78 degrees – a great difference from Borneo with a temperature never below 75 degrees, and generally over 82 degrees from 8 a.m. to 4 p.m. Yet this is called an unhealthy country on the whole – and some of it is – so leave is given after one year and eight months if wanted, whereas in the East we had to do five years. What is more I start pay at more than I got after six years in the British North Borneo Co., and I get pension ten years counting from fifteen.*

*There are more dangers to life out here with lions, elephants, black-water fever, sleeping sickness – that fearful disease brought into the country by Emin Pasha's porters. Now, wherever there are infected belts of the Tsetse-fly, the country has been swept clean of natives, and unfortunately Europeans have got it before it was known that the Tsetse-fly was the transmitter of it. As the Tsetse only live near water, and then only in certain parts, the disease can easily be avoided.*

*Masaka is a fort perched on an iron-stone hill, and I am guarded by sentries as if there was war abroad. However, the police guard my cash, not me. The hunting of game is quite an attraction, and I have had good sport with zebra, hartebeest, water-buck, bush-buck, and other kinds.*

F.M. IREMONGER

## THE SLEEPING SICKNESS PROBLEM

Iremonger was mistaken about how sleeping sickness was brought into Uganda. In fact, the Tsetse fly, the vector of the parasite called Trypanosomas, was endemic to the area. Its habitat is thornbush, which abounds in certain parts of Uganda if not checked.

Uganda was cattle country and the huge domestic herds controlled the spread of the thornbush thickets by eating the seedlings as they grazed. In 1889 the Italians colonised Massawa on the Horn of Africa and imported cattle from India, Russia and the Yemen to feed their troops. They brought Rinderpest, the highly contagious cattle plague, into Africa. It is a viral disease and it spread throughout the continent killing 90 to 95 per cent of all the cattle between 1899 and 1900. This was a natural disaster of huge proportions to the cattle herding economy of Uganda.

With fewer cattle eating the seedlings, the thornbush spread widely, giving the tsetse fly more habitats in which to increase its numbers. The Tsetse fly eats mammalian blood and ingests the Trypanosomas parasite in the blood of wild animals. If it then feeds on humans it injects the parasite into their blood, in which case the individual contracts the fatal disease called sleeping sickness. More thornbush means more tsetse fly. More tsetse fly means more humans are infected. Thus it was that sleeping sickness became more prevalent. It was first reported in Uganda in 1901 and by 1906 it had killed 200,000 people.

Iremonger's suggestion that Emin Pasha's porters brought the disease into Uganda is now known to be a fanciful but interesting hypothesis. Emin Pasha was the name used by a German medical doctor called Edward Shnitzer. He was a convert to Islam having worked in Albania for an Ottoman Pasha with whose wife he had an affair. He married the lady after the sudden death of the Pasha. He also had an Ethiopian wife.

Emin Pasha took a post with the Egyptians and was recruited as Governor of Equatoria under Gordon of Khartoum. Equatoria was the province in the South of the Sudan bordering on the Congo Free State and Uganda. After the Mahdi killed Gordon in 1885, Emin Pasha continued to rule his province for a while but he was cut off from his masters in Cairo and threatened by the Mahdi's forces. He therefore sent an urgent message requesting a rescue.

Henry Morton Stanley, himself a colourful and ruthless figure, led the 'Emin Pasha Relief Expedition'. He drove it through the Congo Free State leaving a bloody path in its wake. In 1889 he brought Emin Pasha and some 600 followers, together with 360 of his own, out of Equatoria. They all moved around the southern end of Lake Victoria into the German colony of Tanganyika.

It was presumably this group, led by Stanley, which is credited by Iremonger with bringing sleeping sickness into Uganda!

The bloody and protracted rescue ended in farce. The German colonists feted Emin Pasha. He got drunk and fell from a balcony whilst celebrating his arrival in Tanganyika!!

## 1906 - SOMALILAND

### HUNTING LIONS AND TRAINING CAMELS IN SOMALILAND

### CAPTAIN A.S. LAWRANCE DSO

Arthur Salisbury Lawrance was born on November 6th 1880 and was at Reading School between 1890 and 1895. He had been prepared for Reading School at the establishment of a Mr. Blount. He became a distinguished soldier and colonial administrator.

He was with the 106th Squadron, 4th Regiment of the Imperial Yeomanry in the Boer War and news of his winning the DSO was published in the School Magazine in December 1902. Lawrance appears to have suffered some health problems after his service in the Boer War and remained in England until 1905. In that year he 'returned' to East Africa from where he wrote the letter of which an extract is published here. Most of his career was devoted to service in Somalia.

In December 1910 there is news of his transfer to Northern Nigeria where he took up an "important administrative post". By 1913 he had been promoted to Major in the King's African Rifles and returned to Somaliland as Commandant. He spent the years of World War 1 with the Somali Camel Corps.

In 1937, by this time Governor General and Commander in Chief of British Somaliland, he was awarded the KCMG in the Coronation Honours List to add to his KBE, awarded in 1934, and his CMG, awarded in 1920. He retired in 1938 and became President of the Old Redingensians Association in 1959.

Arthur Lawrance was devoted to his old school and donated the three silver caskets he had been given on relinquishing office as Governor of British Somaliland to the three Boarders' Houses. (See Appendix 4) His medals are on display in the Reading School Combined Cadet Force Orderly Room.

The following is an extract from a letter written by Captain Lawrance in Somaliland which was published in the April 1906 edition of the Old Boy's Club News in the Reading School Magazine.

BRITISH SOMALILAND
APRIL 1906

*"I have just returned after twenty-four hours hard going after lion; we were hot on his tracks most of the time, but lost them and had to return here: now he has followed us up and is quite near in the jungle. I heard a lion early this morning and hope to get another go at him, but I think I shall wait until I know of a kill; this ground is so hard that tracking is very difficult.*

*Am having grand times most days trying to make four camels draw a nine-pounder gun about; have only home-made rope harness, and the animals have never done anything like this before, we have some most exciting times. A few days ago the gun ran away, nearly killing the wretched camels and a dozen Somalis, and finished up taking a piece out of the fort wall.*

*About two weeks ago I had to help dig up the remains of two officers who had been buried about two years ago; we have to send the remains to Berbera to be reburied in the Cemetery there, since we may be leaving this part of the country altogether, and some of the Somalis are not too good to the English graves.*

*We had a village on fire a night or two ago; it was a great burn since all the huts are made of wood and grass. Of course the Somalis, at a time like this, are always quite helpless, and were quite content to let the whole thing burn down. After some time we got it under control by cutting a passage through the huts and throwing sand on the flame – there was no water to spare for fires.*

*We are to have specially enlisted Indians in this Battalion; all the Somalis will be turned into Militia. I shall be sorry to exchange my Company, since I have grown very fond of the men; but of course Somalis would never make good regulars and one can hardly expect them to fight well against their own people. We may get a more exciting time when the Indians do arrive."*

A.S. LAWRANCE

## THE SOMALIS – A PEOPLE WITHOUT A STATE

The Somalis are a largely nomadic Muslim people who live in what is known as the Horn of Africa. Their territory was at one time divided between the British, French and Italians who disputed for spheres of influence. In 1880 the Somali chiefs petitioned Britain for protection and British Somaliland was created, with arbitrary boundaries, enclosing around 68,000 square miles. There were said to be around 2,500,000 Somalis in all, of which about 650,000 lived roughly within the boundaries of British Somaliland. The bulk of the people lived in Italian Somaliland.

At first the British administered their protectorate from Aden, which was itself controlled from India but in 1905 the administration was taken over by the Foreign Office in London. They did not control much of their Colony since they were constantly at war with Mohamed bin Abdulla, known to the British as the 'Mad Mullah', but in reality a freedom fighter of an early vintage. Bin Abdulla fought the British from 1901 until they could spare enough troops to put him down in 1920.

In 1855 Sir Richard F. Burton, the renowned explorer, thought its port, Berbera in the Gulf of Aden, would have been a more suitable coaling and victualling station for the British in India than Aden on account of its more fertile hinterland. He had been there during his famous journey to the forbidden Ethiopian city of Harrar. On his return, a force of Somalis attacked his expedition at night when it was encamped on a beach near Berbera. He was wounded with a spear thrust right through from one cheek to the other. He had caught syphilis from a Somali lady at some time during his journey and suffered some bad health as a result of his wounds, both warlike and amatory. Berbera was a great slaving port when Burton was there, exporting most of its produce to the Ottoman Empire, which was still in some ramshackle state of existence. At the very least the Royal Navy and the Pax Britannica put a stop to most of the slave trade.

## 1907 - ALEXANDRIA

### AN ACCOUNT OF HIS LIFE IN THE RAS-EL-TIN SCHOOL, ALEXANDRIA.

#### H.A.TURNER (School Magazine 1907)

*"I am glad I am here and not at Cairo, there is nearly always a nice little sea breeze to be got here, except when the Khamsin is blowing, which means no air at all, but this is very rare, and I have so far only had one good dust storm. That was distinctly unpleasant. I was coming back by tram from one of the suburbs where everyone lives, when the storm began, in some way it stops the circulation of the electricity, so that the current does not pass into the ground at all but makes beautiful fireworks round the wheels, and eventually the car stops. The sand is most painful to the eyes and takes a long time to get rid of it.*

*There are nineteen Englishmen on the staff; the boys are most awful liars and cheats, they all have their midday meal at the School, so that the great punishment, and the one they dislike, is to put them on a bread and water diet. We have an Egyptian Head Master with the result that the discipline is better in our school than in those at Cairo, the difficulty is to get hold of a good native, but given one, the results are better under him than under the Englishman.*

*I got a letter from Sandy Colvin the other day, he is up, or rather down, about 900 miles south of Khartum, and is enjoying himself as he generally does anywhere. I met Edwards (major) today at the Athletic Sports, where the Duke of Connaught was giving away the prizes; and lunched with him on the 'Minerva'. He was looking very fit, I thought, and we had a long talk over old school life. The 'Minerva' is ordered off to Port Said tomorrow, but we hope to see them again soon as they are due to stay here for two or three months."*

## 1909 - SOUTH AFRICA

### "THINGS THAT BELONG ONLY TO THE WORLD OF ROMANCE AND ADVENTUROUS LITERATURE".

#### W.E. SIMPSON

The following letter was sent to the Head Master who had it published in the Old Boys section of the Reading School magazine in July 1909. W.E. Simpson was not an active member of the club. His letter is rather sad and there is some doubt if he or the School was aware of the moral implications of his association with the German colonists of South West Africa.

*Gordonia*
*Cape Colony*
*South Africa*
*10ᵗʰ April 1909*

*"One gets awfully homesick here, and there is absolutely no compensation whatever for a man to live in this Colony. Since I came to Africa, I have been doing many things, such things as I had thought belonged only to the world of romance and adventurous literature. But all things are possible in this country and it is reserved always to the home-born Englishman to take up the more strenuous paths of life, indeed, it is the only thing he is permitted to do. My dear Headmaster, when you hear at home of new countries opened up and a colony praised for its enterprise, do you ever think that in nearly every instance it is the old public schoolboy, who has not perhaps made a success in life – come the proverbial "mucker" in fact – who has really borne the brunt of the attendant hardships, leaving the kudos for others?*

*As I have said, I have done many things from superintending camel-transport under the German Government to teaching Dutch children at a country farm. Scouting for the German Army against the Hottentots, leading a party to capture freebooters on the Kalahari, raiding Chinese gambling dens, all these and many other things I have done, enjoying the excitement immensely whilst it lasted, and always with the old longing to get clear of it all and 'come into my own again.' And there are many such as I, who go into the thick of things, carrying their lives in their hands, but always with one feeling deep down in their hearts, which others are not privileged to know of, and which amounts at times to sheer despair.*

*W.E. SIMPSON*

## SCOUTING FOR THE GERMANS AGAINST THE HOTTENTOTS

It would be likely that nowadays we would call W.E. Simpson a mercenary, as he appears to have given his services to the German government of South West Africa, now Namibia. It is a generally arid country to the north of the Cape Colony and to the south of Portuguese West Africa, now known as Angola. To the east was Bechuanaland in which the Kalahari Desert is found.

Two semi-nomadic, pastoral people competed for the thin brown grass of the central plateau of German West Africa, the Nama, otherwise known as the Hottentots, and the Herero. They were at war with each other until 1892. In 1884

Bismarck had taken advantage of the preoccupation of the Hottentots with the Herero and pounced on the territory for Germany.

In autumn 1903, there were 5,000 German settlers in the colony and not many troops to defend their interests. Colonel Theodor von Leutwein, the colonial governor, had taken two thirds of the soldiers off to the south to put down a rebellion of the southern Hottentot tribes known as the Bondelswarts. Whilst von Leutwein was away the Herero, noting the weak garrison in the capital Windhoek, decided to revolt. Von Leutwien could not get back from the south to deal with the rebellion effectively and was deemed to have failed by his masters in Germany.

The Kaiser sent General Lothar von Trotha out to crush the revolt. On October 2nd, 1904 the latter issued an extermination order which condemned 20,000 Herero to death in the Omaheke desert. By October 13th of that year the Hottentots rebelled again, the Germans finally defeating them in October 1905. There were plenty of opportunities for W.E. Simpson to superintend camel transport or deploy his tracking skills.

# 1910 - KENYA

## GAME HUNTING IN BRITISH EAST AFRICA

### PHILIP H. PERCIVAL

*'Pop slept quietly too, you could see his soul was close to his body. His body no longer housed him fittingly. It had gone on and changed, thickening here, losing lines, bloating there, but inside he was young and lean and tall and hard as when he galloped lion on the plain below Wami.'*

Ernest Hemingway on observing Philip Percival, his 'White Hunter', asleep during a safari in Kenya in 1933.
*(From 'The Green Hills of Africa'. Ernest Hemingway.)*

Philip Hope Percival was born on May 10th 1884 and was at Reading School between 1896 and 1901. His family lived near Brent Knoll in Somerset and he was prepared for Reading School at a Prep School in Burnham in Somerset. On leaving school he is noted as joining the 3rd Somerset Light Infantry as a 2nd Lieutenant. He went to British East Africa and became a famous white hunter with a farm at Machakos near Nairobi in Kenya, not far from the Kaputei Plains (Kapiti in Percival's letter).

He wrote from Limoru, near Nairobi, to Marcus Love, the Secretary of the Old Boy's Club, who published the letter in the Reading School Magazine of July 1910.

*Limoru, British East Africa,*
*15th June 1910.*

*Dear Love,*

*Many thanks for your letter. I was pleased to hear from you again. You asked about life out here, so here goes for a few of my hunting experiences, though I am afraid they are hardly interesting enough for the School Magazine.*

*I killed my first lion very easily: at the time I was ostrich catching with a friend, he and I being the first to try ostrich farming in British East Africa.*

*The country had then (five years ago) only recently been thought of as a white colony, and no one had worried themselves about the wild ostriches, which were and still are very plentiful in many parts of the country.*

*Our camp was away on the Kapiti plains and I found the life ideal. The plains swarm with game, and we had it all to ourselves; so with a couple of ponies and a pack of mongrel dogs, you may guess we had a top-hole time. We were out by dawn and usually in bed by 7.30 at the latest.*

*Our work consisted of riding round visiting old nests to see how many eggs there were, and, if enough, bringing them in to the incubators, watching birds with glasses to try to mark them into new nests, and often an exciting round up of a brood of new chicks. "Oh, the hardest day was never too hard!"*

*Riding home one day we saw some vultures, and turned out of our way to see what the "kill" was; a hyena slunk off as we rode up, and I tried a snap at him as he hurried away. I missed him clean, but at the shot two lions jumped up, and after looking at us for a minute turned and bolted.*

*My partner was without a rifle, so I started off in pursuit alone: after a gallop of about a mile over bad ground, one of them laid down in a patch of grass. I knew almost to a foot where the beast was, but although I rode round several times, not a sign could I see; finally I started firing feelers; at the third shot she jumped up snarling, and I began to think I was too close to be pleasant; however, she lay down again, and this time I could just make her out, so promptly let drive; by some extraordinary chance I not only hit her, but I hit her mortally, she sat up like a dog on her haunches, gasping and pivoting round on her front paws. Wildly excited I fired twice more, one shot grazed her forearm and the other her neck. Luckily, the first shot had been sufficient and she soon rolled over on her side and died.*

*My friend had meanwhile marked the second one down, but although we searched the place thoroughly she must have sneaked off somehow without our seeing her.*

*I remember another time I was out by myself riding round when I came on three lions, two fine-maned lions and a very bad-tempered lioness. I was off my pony (who had not seen or winded them), and was trying to see something definite to shoot at (they were all lying asleep in a heap), when one looked up and seeing me, gave a grunt and bolted: the second lion followed suit, but the lioness started walking slowly towards me growling and lashing her tail about. Jumping on my pony I was soon on terms with one of the runaways, who finding running useless, lay down and awaited developments. The fun began, my poor pony got the fidgets, wouldn't let me shoot off his back, went mad when I tried shooting holding the reins over my arm, and was generally a nuisance. To make a long story short, I spent a very exciting two hours, was charged three times, and the last time I was in such a hurry to get on, and the pony in such a hurry to get away, that I abandoned my rifle and climbed on anyhow, fairly fled with the old lion growling behind. Once I was on the way the lion lost no time in getting into long grass, and I was able to go back and get my rifle.*

*A real good shooting pony is worth his weight in gold, but preserve me from bad ones.*

*On another occasion, when out with two other men, we found three fine lions in the open, and all being mounted, rounded them up: in twenty minutes from the first view, they had bagged the lot without trouble. Sometimes they die very easily, but at others, they take an awful lot of lead, and a wounded lion in long grass is about as nasty as can be, they lie like stones and when they do come with their head down and tail straight up, growling fiendishly, its about as exciting as one can wish. Personally, I think a wounded leopard can be worse; they almost invariably charge and offer a much smaller mark than a lion.*

*I have never had serious trouble with a Rhino or Elephant, in both cases "wind" is the thing to watch. In the long grass Rhino are rather beastly, as one often walks on to them unexpectedly, and they come snorting and blundering at one like a runaway engine, giving one quite a start to say the least of it. Fortunately, as a rule, they are easily turned by a shot at the nose.*

*Quite recently I got well scared by elephants. I had followed up the spoor of a herd into thick forest and came on to them all scattered out feeding; a mob of about twenty-five cows and calves got my wind and came to investigate, making a most appalling noise as they crashed along. I was devoutly thankful when I was well out of it.*

*I have not long returned from a trip with the Duke of Connaught's party, when I was hunter to Prince Arthur; we had a very successful time, the party's bag including elephant, rhino, buffalo, lion, cheetah and hippo, as well as most of the buck found in this country. Certainly as the home of big game, East Africa has no equal; it is truly a Sports-man's Paradise, as the advertisements say!*

*Apologising for the very poor attempt at an article.*

*I remain,*
*Yours sincerely,*
*Philip Percival*

## BRITISH EAST AFRICA

The British rather fell into British East Africa in their usual haphazard way. The area had been largely under Arab influence. The Imperial British East Africa Company commenced operations on the coast around Mombassa in1887 and a railway from Mombassa to Uganda was built at great cost and completed in 1901. It opened up the Kenyan farming country to the settlers, which the British Government encouraged. When Philip wrote his letter to Marcus Love the white settler population was under 3,000.

The Germans had colonised Tangyanika, known as German East Africa, and when World War I broke out in Europe, the British in Kenya and Uganda went to war with the Germans. Philip Percival served in this campaign as a Captain in the Intelligence Corps.

## THE 'PERCIVAL' – 'HEMINGWAY' CONNECTION

Philip Percival was Ernest Hemingway's white hunter during the two safaris the latter made in Kenya in 1933 and 1953. Hemingway admired courage and he was clearly in awe of the white hunter from whom he derived so much inspiration. Ernest immortalised Percival in his book, 'The Green Hills of Africa', written soon after the 1933 expedition.  This small book is a record of the safari through Ernest's eyes, though he used the technique of changing the names of the participants to make it read as fiction. For example, he calls his second wife Pauline, 'POM', short for Poor Old Mama, and Philip Percival 'Pop' or 'Jackson Phillips'.

Ernest's short story, 'The Snows of Kilimanjaro', in which a dead leopard is found in the snows at the top of the mountain, is an elaboration of one of Percival's own campfire stories with which he charmed and educated Ernest whilst they were in camp. It is likely, if the extract at the head of this chapter from 'The Green Hills of Africa' can be taken as evidence, that Percival had developed the story he told in his letter to Marcus Love of hunting with a pony, as a tale with which he regaled his safari clients.

## 1914 - RHODESIA

### 'THE FURTHER WE GOT FROM CAPE TOWN THE LESS THE NATIVES HAVE ON'

### L.E. BARRY

Laurence Edward Barry was born on October 8th 1894, entered Reading School from Private Education in May 1906 and left in July 1912. He served in World War One as a Captain in the RAF.

*Headquarters.*
*B.S.A.P.*
*Salisbury*
*Rhodesia*
*April 1914*

*Dear Sir,*

*As, I suppose, you will have heard by now, I have obtained what I applied for, and am now a member of the B.S.A.P. (British South African Police). At present we recruits here are getting it pretty hot in Salisbury, for they have lately made the Police the first line of defence for Rhodesia, so they are giving us military training as well as police training, beside which we have to attend lectures on medical and veterinary work.*

*Altogether we do eight parades a day, reveille at 5.15, the first parade at quarter to six, and in our spare time we have to clean our saddles etc.*

*But taking it all round it is not bad at all, even though, as everyone confesses, the recruits training is the worst part; and there is a great deal to look forward to, for when you go out on patrol you have a great time, you take two 'Black Watch' boys out with you and they do all the work, such as cleaning your kit, grooming the horse or mules, whichever it happens to be, and all you have to do is investigate complaints, see that the taxes are paid, serve summonses etc. and the great thing is that a policeman does not have to obtain a permit or a licence to shoot game, so that they mostly live off the game they shoot and save two shillings a day scoff allowance, beside which the kaffirs are only too glad to give you anything in the way of chicken, milk, feed for the horse, so as to keep on the right side of the 'arm of the law'. But of course that is a little way ahead yet and the sooner it comes the better; for living is very expensive* here, and although we have scoff and quarters found, all the little extras cost a good deal and make a big hole in the month's pay.

There are about fifty recruits in the camp at present, some of whom are going out on their first patrol, and ten more are expected up on Tuesday (tomorrow).

The police camp is about two miles out of Salisbury, and is composed of scattered bungalows or barrack-rooms called 'kyres' (I am not quite sure if that is the way to spell it, but it is pronounced in that way anyhow), each one holding ten men, but at present the camp is so full we (the last squad) are lodged in tents until there may be room in the kyres.

I have not as yet had much chance to see the country, except during the train journey up from Cape Town, which took four days; the first part of it was through very mountainous country, and therefore very interesting. We saw many spots marked by half-ruined block-houses, collections of graves etc., where there had been engagements during the war, but the latter part of the journey was through the Karoo Desert, very uninteresting and flat, beside which we nearly got choked with sand and dust. One thing I noticed was that the further we got from Cape Town (except of course in the towns) the less the natives seemed to have on.

We stopped at several interesting towns on the way, Kimberley, Bulawayo for example, but did not have much time to look round us, as our train was an "Express de Luxe" (and it did do nearly fifteen miles per hour) up to Salisbury which is a very scattered town possessed of very wide streets, some very good shops and cafés with two or three picture palaces, at which theatrical companies occasionally perform. The place on the whole is very clean and well kept and apparently devoid of poverty.

Coming back to myself, I am very sorry I was unable to see you and the other Masters, and thank you for all you had done for me before I left, but as I had only nine days' notice to quit, and you were all away, it was impossible; but I do thank you very much now and assure you that I am very grateful for all the kindness to me while at School and after I left.

Now I must close as it is nearing "Lights Out." Please give my kindest regards to Mrs. Eppstein, and remember me to Mr. Newport, Mr. Silo-Jones, Capt. Crook, and the other Masters.

I remain,
Yours very sincerely,
L.E Barry.

*P.S. – I wish the team every success this season and only wish I were there to play with them. I shall look forward with great eagerness to the coming of the Mag. – L.E.B.*

When Laurence Barry wrote his letter, just before 'Lights Out' one day in April 1914, the white population of Southern Rhodesia was 34,000. There were 732,000 natives of which half were living in special areas which we would nowadays call reservations. The white colonists had a House of Assembly through which they ruled the colony and the instrument of that rule was the British South African Police.

# Chapter 3

## THE SUB-CONTINENT - INDIA AND THE FAR EAST

### THE EAST INDIA COMPANY 1600–1857

In order to contextualise the role of later ORs in the Indian sub-continent we need to look briefly at the development of the East India Company, which was first established in London in 1599 by 80 London Merchants. Queen Elizabeth I gave it a charter on December 31$^{st}$ 1600 and from this point it rapidly began to set up trading posts in India. It was in conflict with the French for some time and it was only after the Peace of Paris in 1763 that the British ambitions in India outdid the French.

The Battle of Plassey in 1757, in which Robert Clive defeated the Nawab of Bengal, was decisive in that it established the power of the British East India Company. The Mogul Emperor legally recognised the Company and granted the management of the Revenue of Bengal, Behar and Orissa to Lord Clive. Henry Vansittart OR, and a friend of Clive, was made Governor of Bengal in 1759. He remained in post until 1764 when he returned to England.

The East India Company failed to manage the provinces effectively and was driven to near bankruptcy. Questions were raised in Parliament and a Council of Reform, under the Chairmanship of Vansittart was set up. He sailed for India in the HMS Aurora, which unfortunately sank in the Mozambique channel in 1771 with the loss of everyone on board.

Acts of Parliament resulted in the appointment of a Governor-General of all the Company's three provinces, Calcutta, Bombay and Madras overseen by a President of the Board of Control in London. Warren Hastings, the first Governor, followed by Lord Cornwallis, consolidated British control and made the Company's administration of its growing Empire more efficient.

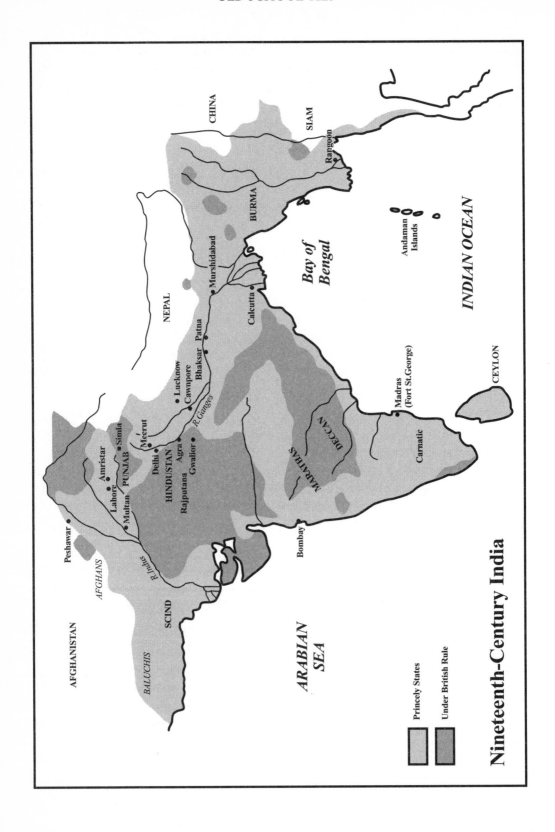

Nineteenth-Century India

Lord Wellesley, later to be the Duke of Wellington, defeated Tipu Sultan of Mysore. The Nizam of Hyderabad was also defeated and a great deal of other territory was annexed. Sind was absorbed and by 1852 so too were the Punjab, Kashmir, Assam, Chittagong and Lower Burma. British supremacy had been established.

The East India Company expanded its interests to the whole of the sub-continent. It also looked eastwards towards Malaysia and Indonesia and westwards towards Aden and Abyssinia. It needed to protect its lines of communication to England to the West and China to the East. The latter route was required to maintain the opium trade and therefore the passage through the Sundra and Malacca Straits were of strategic importance. The Company took over Java for a while, under the control of Sir Stamford Raffles, and through him established a port on an island off the southern tip of the Malay Peninsular called Singapore.

Ceylon, now Sri Lanka, had been ruled continuously by Europeans since 1507 when the Portuguese settled on the west and south-west coasts. They were dispossessed by the Dutch in 1656 who in turn were evicted by the British in 1756. At first the British held the so-called Maritime Provinces but they expanded into the interior and took over the Kandyan Kingdom in 1815. Ceylon was governed under the Raj as a separate entity with its own Civil Service.

There has always been trouble on the mountainous northern frontiers of India. In fact the effort to stem Russian ambitions to expand its empire into India, coupled with the war-like nature of the tribes such as the Pathans and the Afghans, employed a great deal of British military effort and money! For his part in the First Afghan war 1838-42, John Keane OR was created Baron Keane of Ghuznee. The town of Ghuznee was sacked and razed to the ground by the British 'pour encourage les autres' and it may well have been this action which resulted in Keane being honoured.

Eventually the cost of maintaining the Company in India, where a number of British soldiers had been posted, far outweighed the profit. The Indian Mutiny, or the First War of Indian Independence, all but sealed the Company's fate. The Mutiny started with a rising of Indian soldiers at Meerut on May 10th 1857, the cause being that cartridges for the new Enfield rifles were lubricated with "cow and pig grease" thus upsetting both Muslim and Hindu soldiers. It ended when the Siege of Lucknow was raised in 1857. During this engagement Lieutenant Hastings Harrington OR won the School's one and only Victoria Cross.

Lt. Harrington V.C.

In some despair the British Government abolished the governing powers of the Company in 1858 and assumed direct rule with a Viceroy of India to oversee the administration on its behalf. However, the situation of having a Secretary of State in England and a Viceroy in India created a scenario ripe for administrative 'mischief'!

## THE RAJ 1857–1947

As well as the Civil Services and the Army, another route for potential career development was Engineering. There were many British Civil Engineers who took their expertise to India, their work being romanticised and fictionalised in Kipling's "The Bridge Builders" which was said to have been inspired by the opening of the Sutlej Bridge in the Punjab whilst Kipling was working for the Civil and Military Gazette.

By 1891 new canal systems built under the British Raj had made 10 million acres available for cultivation and one eighth of the population was dependent on them for food. It could be argued that they would have been built without the British. To do so would ignore the obvious point that large civil engineering works that cross political and linguistic boundaries require an administrative machine of considerable power and sophistication before they can be undertaken. The unifying effect of the British Raj produced great progress in this regard if in no other. What is more, the British civil engineers brought the benefits of the industrial revolution and its educational concomitants to bear in India very quickly.

Up to 1870 engineers for the Public Works departments were found from the Corps of Royal Engineers and from Civil Engineers appointed in England by competitive examination and from qualified students of the Indian Engineering Colleges. It was decided to improve and reorganise the recruiting of civil engineers for Indian service with the formation of a dedicated College in England for which entry was to be by competitive examination.

To meet this need, the Royal Engineering College at Cooper's Hill was established in 1871. It was a college specifically for the education of civil engineers for service in the Indian Public Works department. The age of admission was seventeen to twenty one and the course lasted three years. In 1906 the residential college at

Cooper's Hill was abolished as too expensive as it became possible to get qualified engineers from other colleges which had developed courses of sufficient standard.

However, while these peaceful pursuits were being followed, within 30 years of the Indian Mutiny, the history of the British in India was essentially a struggle against the inevitability of independence. The Indian National Congress was established in 1885 and grew in strength and by 1905 it had adopted Indian Independence as its political aim. The All India Muslim League started in 1906 and began demanding separate Muslim representation.

Lord Curzon, a colourful and romantic figure, was Viceroy of India for two terms. He began his second term of office in 1904 by sending the ill-fated Younghusband expedition to Lhasa in Tibet. Both Curzon and Younghusband were convinced that the Russians were attempting to establish a hold over the Tibetans. They were wrong and the expedition found no evidence of Russian occupation when they arrived. This set Curzon at odds with London and Younghusband was withdrawn with only a Trade Treaty to show for the massive expenditure of both blood and money spent on the expedition. Younghusband's use of machine guns against the indigenous peoples resulted in a great number of fatalities (see page 93).

During World War 1, the British conflict with the Sultan of Turkey upset the Muslims of India because he was their Khalifa, or spiritual head, and this led to a number of Muslims being drawn to the Home Rule League. Mohandas Karmchad Gandhi returned from South Africa where he had been campaigning against the white government and expounded his ideas of passive resitance to some effect. In 1947, Lord Mountbatten, the last Viceroy, drew the long struggle for independence to its inevitable conclusion. By this time Britain had much to be sad about but a lot to be proud of.

However, what we can also say is that the British were positively lethal with a gun in their hands and a wild animal in their sights and there can be no doubt that they wreaked havoc among the duck population in the Sind!

# 1895 - PORT BLAIR, ANDAMAN ISLANDS

## 'SOME OF THE TRIBES ARE STILL PERFECTLY SAVAGE'

## LIEUTENANT C.C.R. MURPHY

Lt. Murphy had been in England on leave and had given a speech at an Old Boys dinner during which he advocated the idea of a Cadet Corps in Reading School. It was in the report on this speech that the Editors of the Old Boys Club News mistakenly stated that Lieut. 'Paddy' Murphy had been a member of the Chitral Relief Expedition. The Chitral Relief Expedition in 1895 was a punitive campaign against rebel Pathans in the Northwest Frontier region of India.

The following appeared in the December 1895 edition of the Reading School Magazine:

*'On the authority of a usually reliable correspondent it was stated in our last issue that Lieut. C.C.R. Murphy, 2nd Battalion Suffolk Regiment, was with the Chitral Relief Expedition, but he has written to disclaim the honour wrongly assigned to him. We print his letter.'*

*Port Blair,*
*Andaman Islands*
*October 26th, 1895*

*To the Editor*

*Dear Sir,*

*In the last edition of the School Magazine, which has reached me, I see that I am credited with having been on the Chitral Expedition. I am sorry to say I was not there, possibly because the authorities value an "OR" so much, that they did not think the expedition was of sufficient importance to allow any of them to risk their lives in it. My regiment is one of the first on the roster for active service, but the expense of moving troops is too great to send a regiment to Chitral from Madras when there are always plenty of troops in the North of India. The honour of being on the expedition is one which I must therefore disclaim.*

*The British Regiment at Rangoon furnishes a detachment of 140 men at Port Blair, and that is my reason for being here. The Andamanese are the most extraordinary people, both their race and their language are quite distinct, and cannot be classified as belonging to any other. They are small, absolutely black, and live in dense jungle. They build no houses and wear no clothes of any description, and of course do not use money. They fight with bows and arrows, and some of the tribes are still perfectly savage. The Adamanese Islands are used by the Government of India as a Penal Settlement and there are nearly 14,000 convicts here, including a great many of the Dacoits from Burmah and some rebel leaders from Manipur. There are one or two old convicts still remaining who were sent here for taking part in the mutiny of 1857.*

*C.C.R. Murphy*
*2nd Batt. Suffolk Regt.*

## THE PENAL COLONY IN THE ANDAMAN ISLANDS

The 200 Andaman Islands form an archipelago in the Bay of Bengal some 1,000 kilometres off the east coast of India. In 1777 a British Lieutenant, Blair, chose the South Andaman harbour, now known as Port Blair, for a penal colony. South Andaman Island is very unhealthy. The many swamps around it are habitats for the Anopheles species of mosquito, which act as the vector of the malarial parasite. The colony was soon abandoned. It was reopened to receive the deported political activists who were said to have fuelled the Indian Mutiny of 1857. They were made to clear land and build their own prison. Of the 773 deportees, 292 of them died, escaped or were hanged in the first two months. By 1896, presumably whilst C.C.R. Murphy was there with 140 troops and 14,000 prisoners, work began on the South Andaman prison and tiny solitary cells were built to confine political prisoners. They were last used in 1945 and the cells that remain are now a tourist attraction.

The Dacoits from Burma are likely to have been deported after the British toppled the regime of King Theebaw in 1885. After that there were a number of anti British uprisings. The British called the insurgents 'Dacoits' but freedom fighters might have been the better name. The campaign against them was prolonged and difficult. Operations in Burma against the Dacoits, did not finish until 1892.

Manipur was one of the 'Princely States'. These were ruled over by hereditary princes of whom there were 675 at the beginning of the twentieth century. Together they ruled over 822,000 square miles of territory and 72.5 million inhabitants. Each Princely State had signed a treaty with the old East India Company and the British needed their goodwill. A British resident was posted to each state and he reported to the Viceroy's government. Governor-Generals and Viceroys turned a blind eye to affairs within these states but intervened if they thought that they would prove dangerous to British interests elsewhere. The State of Manipur neighboured Burma and it had been most useful in 1885 during the operations against that country. But in 1890 there was a palace coup and a populist regime took over. This did not suit the British and a badly organised attempt to capture the new rulers was botched. It resulted in bloodshed and all signs of British influence were attacked. The British had to suppress the affair and sent the Gurkhas and some mountain guns to do the job. No doubt there were some deportations as a result of the punitive moves after the event. It is said that Queen Victoria was upset by the severity of the punishments.

In 1856 there were thought to be about 5,000 aborigines on the islands divided into twelve native tribal groups. Where they came from is a puzzle. The black people of which Lt. Murphy writes, appear to have been African in origin but there are also inhabitants of the Nicobar Islands, to the south of the Andamans, who are perhaps of Burmese origin. In the Andamans the population is divided into the 'eramtaga' (those living in the jungle) and the 'ar-yuato' (those living on the coast).

It was probably members of the Jarawas tribe, who were observed by Paddy Murphy. They moved into the forest when the land around Port Blair was cleared for the penal colony. Their numbers have been severely reduced by being cut off from their traditional hunting grounds and by diseases such as syphilis brought in by colonists.

## 1897 - THE TIRAH CAMPAIGN

### CAPTAIN F.F. WEEDON

There is no record of the date at which F.F. Weedon commenced or finished at Reading School, however, there is a record of a Weedon in the Classical Third Form in 1880. Capt. Weedon attended the Old Boy's Dinner in 1889 together with another Old Boy of the School, Captain Cooper of the 2nd Punjab Infantry, who was also in the Tirah Campaign[1]. It is reasonable, and pleasing, to assume that they attended the dinner together as members of the same cohort at School and fellow campaigners with the Tirah Field Force.

Captain F.F. Weedon was an officer in the Queen's Own Sappers and Miners in Bangalaore when he was posted to the Tirah Expeditionary Force on September 5th 1897. He clearly survived the Tirah Campaign and was posted to Mandalay in December 1903. By April 1905 he was promoted to Major. During World War 1 he served as a Lieutenant Colonel in the Royal Engineers.

The Editor of the Reading School Magazine published in December 1897 wrote:

---

1    Lieutenant-Colonel Lewis Ernest Cooper. Joined the army in 1879 and passed into the Bengal Staff Corps from the South Lancashire Regiment in 1882, becoming a Captain in the Staff Corps in 1890, Major in 1899 and a Lt-Colonel in the Indian Army in 1904. He served in the first Miranzai expedition of 1891, and between 1897-98 with the 2nd Punjab Infantry, forming part of the Kohat-Kurram Field Force, in the campaign on the North-West frontier of India under Sir William Lockhart. In this campaign he took part in the engagement at the Ublan Pass on August 27th 1897, his conduct there being mentioned in despatches, and in the operations on the Samana in August and September 1897, including the defence of the Samana posts and the relief of Gulistan. He also served with the Tirah Expeditionary Force and took part in the march down the Bara Valley. He commanded the 57th 'Wilde's Rifles' Frontier Force from February 1903. He died in Caversham in 1905 aged 44.

*"The following extracts are taken from the diary of an Old Boy, Capt. F.F. Weedon; we hope they will prove interesting to our readers[1]":*

(N.B. The spelling of place names has not been changed. Some of F.F. Weedon's spelling is at odds with that which appears in maps and official publications. This is a diary extract and, no doubt, the Editor followed the spelling in the script he received.)

*BANGALORE, September 5th, 1897. Just received a telegram directing me to proceed at once to Jullendur for orders. I think and hope I am destined for the big expedition against the Afridis.*

*REST CAMP, KUSHULJARH, September 12th. Arrived here after travelling for five days and nights. This is the last station on the Railway, and the hottest place I ever was in. My charge is the Malerholla Imperial Service Sappers. I am the only British officer with the company, and none of them talk English.*

*September 14th Still here; can't get away till our ammunition arrives. The heat is tremendous, and such dust I never saw. Hundreds and thousands of transport animals are continually passing through, and dying camels are all over the place.*

*KOHAT, September 17th. Reached here after two night marches. We have been placed under the orders of General Yeatman Biggs, and are to go to the front, road-making.*

*HANGU, September 20th. Arrived here yesterday after a fearful march of 27 miles, which took us nearly 132 hours. The men have never done a longer march than five miles. With all this night marching one gets scarcely any sleep, as the days are too hot to think of it.*

*SHINWARI, September 23rd. Here we are perched on a little hillock right beyond the frontier. This is really a police post, but the Afridis raided it about a fortnight ago, took it and dismantled it, and now there is nothing but the bare walls standing. There are three companies of Gurkhas here, who were all through last week's fight; they said they were often surrounded by hundreds of Afridis, who came up within ten yards of them, but never actually close quarters. At present our orders are to improve the roads up to Chagru Kotal; then we shall probably have to make a new track down the valley on the other side.*

---

1   In the December 1897 issue of the Magazine there is a note which states: Capt. F.F. Weedon has been so kind as to send 'A full account of the Risings of the North West Frontier 1897-8'. This has now been placed in the school library.

SHINWARI, *September 26th*. We passed rather an anxious time last night, as news was brought that the enemy was meditating an attack. All the possible preparations were made, and the men paraded and slept in the places they would occupy in case of an attack. We waited on the qui vive all night, but nothing happened. Our work will consist chiefly of road-making, as beyond the Chagru Kotal the tracks are said to be very indifferent, but no one knows much about them, as only two Europeans have ever been into Tirah. We have to do a lot of digging and blowing up of trees and rocks with gun cotton and dynamite. Altogether it is a delightful life.

SHINWARI, *October 3rd*. The first real holiday we have had since we started. I have celebrated the occasion by giving my men a sheep.

*October 7th*. To-morrow we shift camp to Chagru Kotal, it will be a great relief to get there, as we have a stiff climb of two hours to our work each day.

*October 10th*. Still here, as our move to Chagru Kotal was postponed.

*October 13th*. A really exciting time yesterday. We went up to work where we stopped on the 9th, our covering party consisting of 300 infantry. All was quiet until 12.30, when the enemy appeared in force above us and began firing. They got the range perfectly, and it got so warm that I thought it prudent to withdraw the men from that part of the road. The enemy then kept pretty quiet until we began to pack up; we were then all crowded together on the narrow road, and they began coming down the hill and dropping shots at comparatively short range. Any amount of bullets fell quite close to me, and two men near me were hit. We moved off as fast as we could, and of course, being the only British officer present, my position was in the rear; and I was very relieved when we got safely round the corner. They could not follow us as our covering party was in position. My men did very well.

KAI, *October 20th*. Suddenly got orders last night to march back here this morning. I was quite sorry to leave Shinwari, as I had become the oldest inhabitant.

SHINWARI, *October 20th*. Back again. There has been a big affair today. They have signalled for 80 more stretchers to be sent in addition to about the same number they took with them. The Kotal is only six miles from here; and to give you an idea of the length of the baggage, the column started at 4 a.m. and the last baggage has not yet started at 7 p.m.

*October 21st*. A most mournful procession is just passing my tent – yesterday's killed and wounded; some of the latter look ghastly. I have just received orders to march to Karaffa at 5.15 to-morrow, en route for Tirah.

## THE TIRAH CAMPAIGN

Tirah is the 'elevated tract' to the south west of the Peshawar Valley on the North West Frontier of what was British India. It is, or was in 1897, the summer home of two great Pathan tribes, the Afridis and the Orakzais. It is roughly oval in form and is 45 miles long in the east-west direction and 20 miles long on the north-south axis. It is surrounded by high mountains and the passes into it were, and maybe still are, less than easy to negotiate, especially for a large body of troops.

In 1897 the Afridis and Orakzais were restive. Between them they could field 55,000 fighting men who were equipped with modern rifles. They were excellent mountaineers, could subsist on a small amount of rice for a long time and were masters of camouflage and fieldcraft. They had taken the Khyber Pass, a strategic route into Afghanistan and one which the British government of India was loathe to lose. There had been attacks on some of the outposts maintained by the Indian Army on the North West Frontier, notably those of the Samana Forts 30 miles to the south of the Khyber Pass. Weedon would have been interested to note that Captain, later Lt. Colonel Lewis Ernest Cooper OR, was also involved in the defence and the eventual relief of the Samana Posts.

It was decided to mount a military expedition in strength, which would enter the Tirah and demand the submission of the Adfridis and the Orakzais. The Army Headquarters in Simla issued the following proclamation:

*'The general object of this expedition is to exact reparation for the unprovoked aggression of the Afridi and the Orakzais tribes on the Peshawar and Kohat borders, for the attacks on our frontier posts, and for the damage to life and property which has been inflicted on British subjects and those on British service. It is believed that the object can best be attained by the invasion of Tirah, the summer home of the Afridis and Orakzais, which has never before been entered by a British force'.*

The expedition was to be undertaken by the Tirah Field Force. The force, comprising about 31,000 all ranks, with some 18,000 followers, was first to be concentrated at Shinwari on the border with Pathan Country. It was to be moved in by rail to Khushalgurh and Peshawar, and marched on into Shinwari via Kohat. The transport for the Main Column and its line of communication troops amounted to about 29,000 mules and 13,000 camels and bullock carts. This large and intimidating body of men was to push into the Tirah over the Chagru Kotal ('Col' in English) and Karappa on the Kotal River.

Whilst the main body of the Expeditionary Force made its way into camp at Shinwari, the troops, which had been on the spot for some time, largely Pioneers, Sappers and Miners, were engaged in clearing and improving the tracks from Shinwari to Karappa.

Their labours had been restricted to the six miles or so between Shinwari and the Chagru Kotal because of the presence of hostile tribesmen. The official report of this action notes that from the 11th to the 17th October the working parties "were fired upon daily, and the supporting troops indulged in some smart brushes with the Orakzais". Captain Weedon gives us eyewitness accounts of these skirmishes.

By October 17th Captain Weedon and his colleagues had improved the six miles of track, which steadily ascends up to the Chagru Kotal and a few miles on the other side. The concentration of the Field Force at Shinwari was nearly complete so a considerable force began to advance up Captain Weedon's road. The significant force of Orakzais who had been harassing him were holding the Dargai Bluff just to the west of the Chagri Kotal. They were in the way of the advance into the Tirah so General Yeatman Briggs ordered that the Dergai Bluff be taken "at all costs".

As a result, one of the most widely publicised battles of the North West Frontier was to take place on October 20th 1897. The force attacking the Dergai heights contained the Ghurkas, and significantly the Gordon Highlanders. Throughout the morning regiment after regiment, even the Ghurkas, had tried to take the heights but could not advance over the open ground before them.

When Colonel Mathias of the 1st Gordons arrived he launched his troops against the Pathans with this clear, unequivocal order. *"The General says this hill must be taken at all costs. The Gordon Highlanders will take it."* As General Lockhart, the commander of the Tirah Field Force, would later recall *"The Gordon Highlanders went straight up the hill without check or hesitation"* and *"This splendid Battalion marched across the open. It dashed through murderous fire and in forty minutes it had won the heights"*.

It was the wounded and exhausted soldiers coming back from this battle that had so excited Captain Wheedon's sympathy on October 20th 1897. It is clear that he went on with the Filed Force into the Tirah.

The Tirah Field Force eventually received the submission of the Pathans and returned to their various posts in India. It seems, to quote Col. C.E. Calwell, the historian of the Campaign, that in January 1898 "Swarms of wild hillmen gathered together around Sir W. Lockhart's House in Peshawar. ... they vowed that in future they would fight on the side of the British, no matter who the enemy might be, and not against them".

# 1903 - TUMKUR DISTRICT, MYSORE, INDIA

## ILLUSTRATING THE THEORY THAT THE PANTHER (OR TIGER) CANNOT SCENT A HUMAN BEING

### H.D. RICE 1885-87

*Tumkur, 11th November 1903*

*Sir,*

*The following is an experience I had lately, and I trust you will kindly insert it in your valuable paper as it may be of interest to sportsmen and those who study the habits of wild animals:*

*On the night of the first instant a panther killed a pony close to the fort wall at Devaroy Droog, in the Tumkur District\*. On the 2nd instant he returned to the kill and partook of a big feed. I was informed of the fact on the 3rd instant, and after seeing the kill I ordered a pit to be dug about ten yards from it, in some bushes, as there was no tree in the vicinity in which to erect a machan. On the right and left of the pit, stones were fixed and planks were placed on them so as to cover the pit and protect me from the rain. Another plank was fixed on the edge in front with a hole in it, so that when I sat on the stool in the pit I could see the kill in front of me through the hole in the plank. I took up my position at 6 p.m. with a D.B. 12 bore gun loaded with No. 2 shot, as I had no ball cartridges. My men then placed some thorns and twigs so as to conceal the hole. At 11 p.m. the panther suddenly appeared on my left and sat down five feet from me facing the kill. In raising the gun, which was on the floor of the pit, I made a very slight noise and the panther deliberately turned round and looked straight at the hole through which I was peering, but apparently saw nothing to excite his suspicion as he remained where he was and proceeded to lick his shoulders. (It was a beautiful moonlight night so that I could see everything clearly). I then kept perfectly still and did not again attempt to bring up the gun while he was so close. After three or four minutes he went to the kill, snatched it up bodily in his mouth, shook it once or twice, then dropped it and strolled away a short distance. He came back within two minutes and as he was sniffing at the kill and was nearly broadside on, I fired at the shoulder. With a tremendous roar he rushed straight at me, but swerved to one side as he saw me draw the gun into the pit, jumped over the corner of the pit and straight down the fort wall, the height of which was about 25 feet vertical. I then got out, went to the village and fetched the men, but we decided to leave him till the morning. In the morning we discovered him dead near the foot of the wall. Whether he intentionally took a 25 feet vertical jump I cannot say, but he died within a few yards of where he landed.*

*I think this is a striking illustration of the truth of the theory that a panther (or tiger) cannot scent a human being. It also shows the deadly effect of small shot at close range.*

*The panther was a very fine one, measuring 7ft 9in., and when skinning him I found an old bullet just under the skin on his back.*

*H.D. RICE.*

*\* Tumkur, not far out of Bangalore.*

## 1906 - THE PUNJAB

### WE GOT PIG STICKING AND ANY AMOUNT OF SHOOTING

### N.F.C. MULLOY

Valete 1903

N.F.C Mulloy left Reading School in 1903. He reached form VI M., and turned out for the 2nd XV. Rugby and the 2nd XI Cricket in 1902.

The following appeared in the April 1906 edition of the Reading School Magazine:

'N.F.C Mulloy, who was attached for the last year to the 85th King's Light Infantry, has been appointed to the 15th Lancers. He met with good success as a cricketer in his late regiment and gained the first spear at the sport of Pig-sticking'.

"I have just joined the 15th Lancers ... I did my year attached to the KLI down at Fazabad, which as regards sport was a much better place, as we got pig-sticking and any amount of shooting; here of course there is nothing of that sort, though at present I don't miss it as, in addition to the rudiments of polo, I am trying to learn to drive the break. Out in this country every Cavalry Regiment and most batteries have a break instead of the coach one sees at home. I find the reins a trifle complicated and difficult to handle, besides being fearfully heavy after driving for half an hour.

"I am thankful to say that, as far as parades went, I avoided the Prince and Princess of Wales, but I saw them at Lucknow, where I was on leave for Christmas. The fireworks and decorations arranged in their honour were worth going a long way to see, but otherwise the only difference from a procession at home was the absence of crowds, and the sight of a few natives standing around looking on. We are just at the beginning of the hot weather now (March) which I expect will not be much fun. I think I shall clear off to Kashmir on my leave, as I am told the scenery is rather fine. Please remember me to Dr Eppstein and all the other Masters who were at School in my time."

Before joining an Indian regiment a subaltern, newly out from Sandhurst would serve a year with a British regiment. He would study languages, learn the ways of India and be vetted by the regiment of his first and second choice. By joining the Lancers, N.F.C.Mulloy will have achieved a high standard and is likely to have passed out of Sandhurst amongst the top cadets in his class.

In the Lancers, to be good at Polo was considered to be the height of success. It did not much matter how competent you were as an officer. If you played Polo for your regiment you 'had it made!' Every officer in the Indian Army had his private charger which was fed free by the government as it was used for military purposes when necessary. It could also be used for sport. It was also possible to hire a pony at a cheap rate from the Army. Even so, it was usual that the more senior the officer the better he was at Polo for the simple reason he could afford to maintain a string of ponies.

Pig-sticking meetings were held in cold weather. The best country for them was in the flat alluvial plains of the Ganges near Meerut about 60 miles from Delhi. Each year the Ganges floods over a wide area and has created an extensive expanse of high grass broken by water courses and interspersed with patches of jungle...the perfect habitat for the fierce wild boar of India.

The 'hog-hunters', usually army or police officers, were armed with special spears called 'hog-spears'. They rode in groups of three or four. A Babu preceded the group on a camel so that he could see the boar in the long grass and direct the hunters to it. A file of beaters carrying six-foot poles for protection drove through the grass so as to flush the boar and send it towards the riders. If the boar passed near a beater he would leap up his long stick so as to avoid being savaged by the great tusks. A flagman carried a red flag so that he could warn the riders that a boar had been heard in the grass and direct the attention of the Babu on the camel who would then set up a 'hullabaloo' and point it out to the hunters.

Once a boar had been flushed, the horsemen would ride after him; the one nearest the boar when it was spotted was the 'First Spear' and had first stab at the animal. (The editor of the School Magazine had drawn the erroneous conclusion that this was an honour achieved by winning some sort of competition. In fact teams and individuals competed for the Kadir Cup, named after the best pig-sticking grounds.)

Fast and furious riding allowed a rider to catch up with a boar, which was a formidable quarry. The idea was to make it charge. The rider would then lean out of his saddle, lower his sharp spear and impale the animal. The boars had sharp tusks and could injure the horses and rider, if it escaped the spear. Pig-sticking was rated as the most dangerous sport of all. It required hard riding over long grass where it was difficult to see where one was going. Consequently horses sometimes put a hoof in a hole and riders were thrown...sometimes leaving themselves open to attack by the boar.

Once the hunt was over the riders would make camp and have a picnic. Often an old elephant would be used to carry supplies and cold beer. Sometimes this same animal would be used to flush out the boar from the undergrowth.

## 1906/07 - JASUL, THE PUNJAB, INDIA

### THE MIGHTY INDUS AND ITS TRIBUTARIES

### C.O. LOWSLEY AND F.A. FARQUHARSON

Between 1897 and 1904 four young men were encouraged by the staff at Reading School to prepare themselves for service in India. Two, Clinch and Sealy, became Indian Policemen and we follow the early part of their lives elsewhere. The other two, C.O. Lowsley and F.A. Farquharson, were able to make a real contribution to the future Pakistan by their work as civil engineers in the irrigation and water management projects in the Indus basin.

They had both entered the Royal Engineering College at Cooper's Hill, a college which was set up to train Civil Engineers with a future in India in mind. Whilst Lowsley, who had left the REC Cooper's Hill in 1904, was at work on the Fuleli Canals in the Sind, Farquharson was engaged upriver from him in the Punjab where it was becoming apparent that an integrated approach to river development was necessary. Between 1905 and 1915 the Triple Canal Project was undertaken. In the Punjab the tributaries of the Indus were important. The two western tributaries, the Jhelm and the Chenab had surplus water available. The three eastern tributaries, the Ravi, the Beas and the Sutlej had less and were obliged, as it were, to supply more water to irrigation systems down stream. The engineers, amongst whom we number Farquharson, decided upon transferring water from the two western tributaries to the three eastern ones.

Contributions from Lowsley and Farquarson follow. They are eyewitness accounts of young men working and playing under the most trying of circumstances. The sense of enjoyment and confidence is palpable, despite their complaints about heat, insects, servants, camels and dogs.

## 1905 - THE SIND

### IRRIGATION WORKS IN THE SIND

### C.O. LOWSLEY 1897-1901

C.O. Lowsley was an outstanding product of the Public School System. He was Vice Captain of School, Company Sergeant Major in the School Cadet Corps, School Prefect, House Prefect of his boarder's House (School House), Honorary Secretary of the Camera Club, a notably active and, in 1901, forward thinking club. He took a career path, which might, in the long run, have had a more beneficial and lasting effect than many of his contemporaries. He entered the Royal Indian Engineering College at Cooper's Hill in December 1901 from whence he joined the Indian Public Works Department in 1904 to work on the canals in the Indus Basin in what is now Pakistan.

The following letters appeared in the April 1905 and the July 1907 editions of the Reading School Magazine respectively:

*A letter of such interest has arrived from C.O. Lowsley, who is now engineering in India, near Karachi, that we are kindly allowed by the recipient to reproduce portions here:*

*April 1905,*
*The Sind.*
*No address given.*

"I am out in the districts till the hot weather, which I believe begins about the middle of May. Being out in the districts consists of travelling from one place to another checking canal banks and, later on, checking the measurements for canal clearance. I have nothing to do in this line until next year, when I shall have a sub-division to look after; at present I am supposed to be gaining experience and picking up the language, Sindhi. It is rather a dreadful language to learn, but the speaking it is nothing compared to writing and reading it, as they have a nasty way of leaving out vowels, and four different ways of writing letters, according to whether they come at the beginning, end or middle of a word. ...... At all the places we go to, or nearly all, there is a P.W.D Bungalow, where we stop for four days; it is always large enough for two, and sometimes three; when there are three of us one has a tent in the compound, and as I am junior, the tent falls to my lot. ... We employ a good many camels. I have six for my kit and a riding camel. The latter is a real good one (it is the third I have tried, the others being 'rotters'). Unless you get a good one they shake you up a lot. A riding camel goes about six miles an hour, the baggage camels 2 miles an hour. The districts are very nice until, the novelty wears off, when it begins to be rather monotonous continually packing up, and never seeing a white face, except, as in my case, you are out two together. Next year I shall be out by myself. It is a very healthy life .... As regards shooting, I have been out five times (we only go for about three hours in the early morning) and up to date we have killed 50 partridges, 47 duck and teal, six hares, one quail and two kunji. The kunji is a fine bird, larger than a goose; it is a crane of sorts, and excellent eating. I have two dogs, but have not invested in a horse yet, as I do not require one at present. ..... The place where we are now staying is very interesting, it contains the tombs of all the chief Mohammedans who died here years ago. I believe the place takes its name from a gentleman who died here 604 A.D. I have been to see his tomb, which is on the top of a hill with endless steps up to it. There are two fakirs in attendance; it is rather amusing to see them beat their drum and give their 'call to prayer' every night and early morning. We get

*plenty of jackals howling round the Bungalow at intervals during the night. ....*
*Please remember me to everyone I know at the School.*

*July 1907,*
*Begani Canals,*
*Jacobabak. (authors note: should be Jacobabab.)*

*I am just commencing my second hot weather in this district, so I know what I*
*have got to go through. The heat is bad enough, but the mosquitoes and sand*
*flies are the chief worry. I intend to take leave in August 1907, and hope that on*
*my return I shall get a transfer to a cooler station.*

*Being out in the districts most of the year my chief recreation is shooting, and*
*this season, which is just over, has been very good indeed, of course we only get*
*small game shooting in Sind. There has been plenty going on during the past few*
*months, the chief thing being a new Protection Bund. We are constructing four*
*miles this year, and hope to complete the 12 miles next. I have heard from*
*Clinch and Sealy; the former before he left England; the latter since he arrived.*

C.O. LOWSLEY

## LAYING OUT THE LINE FOR THE UPPER JHELUM CANAL

### F. A FARQUHARSON

1ˢᵗ XV.1903-4

Farquharson was at Reading School from 1900-04. He had been in the Army Class and was a House Prefect SH and a Sergeant in the Corps. He was in the Cricket XI (02-03) and the Rugby XV (03). He left in December 1904 to go to RIEC Cooper's Hill having passed the competitive examination in 17ᵗʰ Place.

## "I HAVE ONE KALAHASI DETAILED OFF TO CARRY MY REVOLVER AND KEEP AN EYE OUT FOR DOGS"

Published in the April 1907 Magazine

*"I sailed on December 13ᵗʰ, arriving in Bombay on January 8ᵗʰ where I met my father*
*and went on to Ceylon with him, next day on the P. and O. I had four days in*

*Ceylon, seeing my old home and friends, and then left for Lahore, via Tuticorin, Madras and Bombay. It is six days in the train from Tuticorin to Lahore, with a twelve hours' wait both at Madras and Bombay.*

*Never again will I go from Tuticorin to Bombay by train. I stayed a week in Lahore before going out to this "Jungley" hole. I arrived at Rasul, my headquarters, on January 29th, and went into camp on February 6th, where I have been since and shall be for the best part of another month. I am with another fellow, laying out the Final, or Pucca, (as they call it in Hindustani) centre line of the Upper Jhelum Canal. The line has been settled on from Jhelum, where the canal leaves the River Jhelum, to Rasul, and is being excavated. That is a distance of 25 miles and from there, 55 miles from Rasul to Khanki where it joins the River Chenab.*

*You will understand the difficulties to overcome when you have read the following red-tape stipulations from the Government: -*

- *No curves of less than 10,000 feet to be used.*
- *Depth of digging to be four feet.*
- *No graveyards or villages to be on the line.*

*Well, the villages round here average about one mile apart, and the graveyards are accordingly at similar distances. Then there are Fakirs' tombs about every mile or so, and if you were to destroy one of them the whole of the Punjab would be upon you. The Canal width is 400 feet, and it is that which makes it so awkward. I think the line is practically decided upon now, and there are only the Final levels to be done. I am getting four rupees a day extra for being on camp, but I don't think it is worth it, as you have to put up with the inevitable chicken in every form and for every meal. You cannot get beef to eat as to the Mohammedans cattle are sacred. I have not heard a word about Lowsley, Sealy or Clinch. Lee, I see from the papers, is making great scores for the Calcutta Cricket Club. Atkinson minor is somewhere out here, at Rawal Pindi, I fancy. I see he did pretty well at Sandhurst.*

*This is no white man's country in the hot weather.*

*In the winter from November to February, or even in the middle of March, it is very nice; but from April to September the temperature varies from 160 to 190 degrees in the sun and 90 to 100 degrees in the bungalows. This is an absolute fact though it may seem incredible. I have a disgraceful tent and there is a heavy storm coming. Some nights I wake up to find rain coming through to my bed. Servants are a far greater trouble here than at home, mine come and go every few days. I have eight khalasis (Government servants for survey or tent work), and six of my own, one camel man with seven camels. I am getting a pretty fair revolver shot now, thanks to good practice at the village pariah dogs. I have one Khalasi detailed off to carry my revolver and keep an eye out for dogs. There is nothing like putting Government Servants to good use. I have had some fair shooting on the River Jhelum at Rasul, getting about 30 or 40 duck or teal, and about ten snipe. Rasul is where the Lower Jhelum Canal – which has been finished about five years – leaves the River Jhelum. Well I must end, hoping to get the School Magazine some time, as I have not had one for a long time now.*

## A CHRISTMAS CAMP IN THE SIND – 1906

## C.O. LOWSLEY

The following article was published in the Reading School Magazine July 1907:

*On December 23rd after nearly a whole day in the train, I arrived at my destination, Larkama, (should be Larkana) which is the best rice district in Sind and renowned for its duck shooting.*

*I spent the night at my host's bungalow and in the morning we set out for Kambar some 12 miles distant, which was to be the Headquarters during the Christmas Holidays. In the afternoon three of us had a couple of hours after snipe which only yielded 9 couple, but on an adjunct "dhund" we saw plenty of duck and went home full of expectation of a good day on the morrow.*

*Christmas day arrived and the party being now complete (five guns and two ladies) we started at 10 o'clock for the "dhund" about two miles away. After taking up our positions, having previously drawn lots for places, the firing commenced. Duck and teal at first came fast and furious it being all one could do to load fast enough, but after a time, when they slacked down, we decided to beat round the edges for snipe, the bag for the day being 198 duck, 15 snipe and 3 various.*

*On the 26th we journeyed to Changro, there the "dhund" being deep and the reeds thick, we experienced a certain amount of difficulty keeping the duck, which were chiefly Mallard, on the wing, another pleasant day however provided 130 head.*

*The next day Lang was the appointed place, which yielded 117 duck and 51 snipe.*

*The 28th found us at a small "dhund" with plenty of cover, here the common Pochard were in abundance. After a general drive we started "carpet bagging" that is cruising about in boats and shooting them as they rise, not very good sport but it helped the bag considerably: the total for the day 221 head.*

*The wounded Pochard is very difficult to catch, he dives continually, the "mirbhas" or "mahanas" are however as a rule very good at collecting them and it is seldom one escapes after he has once been seen, the men I had in the boat bagged several by sticking them with a spear which they kept for catching fish.*

*Perhaps it would not be out of place to say a word or two on behalf of the "Mahanas," they are first rate fellows, gaining their livelihood catching fish, hence they spend most of their time in and out of water. They are usually excellent "Shikaris," imitating the "quack" of the Mallard with great success, and are generally very cheerful, they appreciate a good shot and will often make prayers for your success when trying to fetch a bird out of the "blue."*

*One fellow who was with me knew the English names of all the ducks and told me which was coming long before it came in shot.*

*On the 29ᵗʰ we went out in two parties; three guns going to Changro and another gun and myself to a small dhund called Drigh, our small dhund turned out to be "top-hole," the two of us getting about 220 in two hours, when we stopped shooting thinking it would be an excellent place for the whole party another day. The bag for the day was 297 duck.*

*The 30ᵗʰ was supposed to be a snipe shoot but it turned out to be a very mixed bag, 116 snipe, 12 partridges, 10 duck and 6 various, which included quail and hare.*

*The 31ˢᵗ we again parted company with very good results, 259 duck and 42 snipe.*

*The 1ˢᵗ of January, our last day, was the best and an excellent ending to our Christmas camp, we all went to Drigh where two of us had enjoyed such a good shoot three days before, everyone was determined to do his best and at 5 o'clock that evening we had 449 duck to our credit. This ended our holiday in the eight days we had killed 1,947 head, out of which 1,670 were duck.*

*What did we do with them? Well, we sent some to our friends in Karachi, Quetta and Sakkur, a good many were distributed to the Mahanas and men who had been beating for us, and we also sent several consignments to Station Masters on the line for distribution to Railway men.*

*Among the various kinds of duck killed were Pintail, Mallard, Shoveller, Pochard, Teal, Marble Teal, Widgeon, Gadwull and Smew.*

*The usual routine was "Chota Haziri" in your tent when you liked, breakfast about 9 o'clock, tea on returning from shooting, dinner at 8.30, and I think we were all ready for bed at 11 o'clock.*

*On Christmas Day we were invited to he Village School to see what was described as "Touching Scenes from Shakespeare." We went in force and I think we were thoroughly rewarded, Julius Caesar being too funny for words.*

*The second day of the New Year we returned to our usual daily duties, every one agreeing that we had had a very pleasant time.*

We know that by December 1914 C.O. Lowsley was Executive Engineer on the Fuleli Canals, because the birth of a son was announced in the magazine. The Fuleli Canals are an extensive irrigation system arising just upstream of Hydrabad and flowing into much of the Sind to the South of the Indus.

## 1906/08 - BENGAL

### BEING TWO LETTERS AND A TRAVEL ARTICLE BY AN INDIAN POLICEMAN

### GROOMED FOR THE RAJ

The two letters and the travel article by Wilfred Arthur Prince Sealy are published together because they help to give us a picture of a young man who could be the perfect product of an Imperial Education.

He was born on May 27th 1886 and was educated at Greenway House School Tiverton before entering Reading School in September 1897. He was a boarder at Reading School when Dr. Charles Eppstein, the Head Master, was at the height of his powers and his House Master, A.W. Gundry, at his most vigorous.

By the time Sealy sailed for India to join the Indian Police on November 11th 1905 he had been Captain of School and a House Prefect. He was captain of Rugby Football and Cricket, and a 2nd Lieutenant in the School Corps, then a part of the 1st London Royal Engineer Volunteers and commanded by his House Master. He had been Treasurer of the School Magazine Committee and served on the Games Committee for at least two years one of them as Secretary. In the absence of the groundsman in 1905 he had organised the maintenance of the games fields and he had take prominent roles in school plays.

He was a member of the Army Form and his House Master was also his Form Master. He won the Army Form prize in 1903 and was awarded a Foundation Scholarship in his last two years at School. He passed the Examination for the Royal Military College, Sandhurst in 1903 but declined a place, clearly having been advised to take the new examination for the Indian Police for which he would have to be 19 years of age. He passed the Indian Police Examination in 1905, 17th out of 21.

The Viceroy of India, Lord Curzon, found the police in India to be in a mess. He appointed a commission under Sir Andrew Frazer to report on the situation and recommend solutions.

The commission reported on  May 30th 1903:

*"Throughout India the police-force was in a most unsatisfactory condition and abuses were common everywhere. Radical reforms were urgently necessary and would be costly because the department had hitherto been starved".*

Frazer recommended that the pay of all ranks should be raised to reduce bribery and corruption, and that the structure of the Police be changed to include a British Officer Corps to fill the top posts.

On March 21st 1905 the Government of India decreed that in future the force should consist of an imperial branch recruited in Europe and a provincial branch recruited in India. The former would be known as the Indian Police Service. It was for supervision and should only contain enough officers to fill the superintendantships in the districts and a sufficient reserve for leave etc. The recruitment of the Indian Police Service would be by competitive exam in London open to British Subjects of European descent. At the time of recruitment the father of the candidate must be a British Subject, either natural born or naturalised in the United Kingdom. The Candidates had to be above 19 and under twenty-one. W.A.P. Sealy and his fellow Reading School Old Boy Clinch must have been amongst the first Indian Policemen of the "Imperial Branch" recruited in the new manner. Both of these men had passed the entrance examination for the RMC Sandhurst but had declined their places. Both had had similarly outstanding careers at School and it is reasonable to assume that the School must have had some foreknowledge of the new recruitment system for the Indian Police and, what is more, been fairly confident that these two would be successful in the selection procedure.

Sealy's form master, A.W. Gundry M.A, had a significant influence on him. He was a Scholar of Emmanuel College Cambridge, was first in the Second Class of the Classical Tripos, and first in the Ceylon Civil Service; though whether or not he had served in Ceylon is unclear. For several years he had been in charge of the Army Class at Bradfield College, Berks., before he joined Reading School, and was known to be a keen Volunteer (Territorial Army) officer and an excellent fencer. He was recruited by the Head Master to form and expand an Army Class and he and his wife opened East Wing House as a new Boarders' House in 1896. He was also the first Commanding Officer of the new Corps formed under the aegis of the 1st London Royal Engineer Volunteers. Mrs Gundry was an enthusiastic House Master's wife and raised money for improvements in the School Chapel. She organised a number of concert evenings which her husband's House put on for the whole School and found time to produce a son amongst all her other duties!

A.W. Gundry's health broke down in the summer term of 1904 and he was forced to take a long sea voyage to recuperate. Though what he was suffering from is unclear it is tempting to suggest that he was burnt out by the combined effort of starting a new Boarder's House, a School Corps and running the Army Form. He never recovered sufficiently to continue with his tasks and left in 1905 for a post at Eltham School.

## W.A.P. SEALY

### 1904-5 1st XV

The following is the first letter from W.A.P. Sealy and was published in the April 1906 edition of the Reading School Magazine. It was written just after he reached India.

*"We had a grand voyage. The ship was the biggest that has ever been to Calcutta, and as it was only half full we had a very good time on board, especially as from Port Said onwards the sea was absolutely calm. Bhagalpur is one of the principal Police Stations in Bengal. There is a training school here where the natives are educated in English Law and Criminal Investigation. There are about a dozen English families within a radius of a couple of miles. This week there is to be a big Police Meet and Conference here. About forty officers have come down, and there is to be an Inspection and Prize-giving. Sports have been going on; some of the natives are very fine athletes and I saw some very good wrestling. The Lieutenant-Governor is coming down, and so there is plenty going on. After it is all over, we, (i.e. the other Bengal Police Assistant and myself) shall settle down, I hope, to learn the language. At present we find a difficulty in making our servants understand our wants. I have a fine collection of nouns in my head but no verbs, consequently we speak in a mixture of English verbs and Hindustani nouns, and sometimes they understand but not often. The weather is of course at its best now, and is an exaggerated continuation of an English summer, but free from rain. The Mess is a large building made for a good many more than two; however I feel quite at home and am longing to start work. The last bit of work I did was in July, and it is getting rather monotonous. I often wonder how the School is getting on at Rugby. I am longing to see the magazine.*

The following was published in the July 1907 edition of the Reading School Magazine.

*W.A.P. Sealy has been removed from Bhagalpur to Darjiling. He writes:*

*At the end of last year, having finished my course at Bhagalpur, and passed all my examinations except Bengali, which is positively an awful language to learn, I was transferred to my first district – Patna. The headquarters of the district, Bankipur, is a large civil station, and I got on very well there both with my work and otherwise. The district work there is very heavy, and crime is abundant, from murder down to petty thefts, there being some four to five hundred cases a month. For a month I was in charge of the Police Office; my boss being out on tour – and during that month I learned a great deal, and am told did my work quite satisfactorily.*

*As regards the social part of life there, we get a fair amount of amusement, there being an excellent club there, and what with Polo, Hockey, Tennis and Dances, I had plenty to do. Just as the weather was beginning to get warm, i.e., about the middle of May, after I had been for my Bengali Examination, I got a wire to proceed immediately to Darjiling on special duty. I left the day after and I have been here ever since. I can tell you that I am very lucky to be here, and was very much envied. The work on which I was called here is in connection with the agitation, and is not at all heavy – at most I have only four or five hours a day the rest of the time being my own. There are hundreds of people here on pleasure and on duty, and I dropped in for the very best part of the Darjiling season, every day there is something to do. Now people are beginning to thin off, as the rains will soon be breaking, and then of course Darjiling is wrapped in clouds all day long. Even now for the last fortnight it has been somewhat depressing, the snows having been hid from view by mists and clouds. However, even when it pours there is something to do, as there is a fine Amusement Club here with half a dozen tennis courts, rink, dance room, a band playing every evening – or rather an orchestra. A band plays three times a week in the park, when it is fine the place is spread with tables and groups of people may be seen either taking tea or strolling about.*

*The air is wonderfully invigorating and I do a good deal of walking about, despising the 'rickshaws' and 'dandies', except when it rains too heavily. The first day I was up here I gasped for breath, as the air is very rarefied, and one takes a few days to get used to it.*

*The first week here I went to the Lieutenant-Governor's Ball. It was a grand affair, some 200 people being there. Of course I had hardly got to know many of the people at that time, but I also managed to enjoy myself.*

*Next Wednesday the Knights Errant, of which I am a member, are giving a Ball, and the Wednesday after is the Cooper's Hill Ball. So much for the social part of things.*

*Things have not been going as they should in the Province, and what with the row in the north-west and in Eastern Bengal, there is a great deal of unrest here. The only way to put a stop to it would be to deport one or two more of the leaders of the agitation. Bipni Chandra Pal for instance. The way the native presses abuse the Government, say things about the Lieutenant-Governor, and their treatment of the English generally in the street is unpardonable. There are of course a great deal of loyalists amongst the more educated; the chief offenders are a few men who have their following in the student class, men of 18 or 19 who do not know what they are doing and simply do what they are told. If only they could be well whipped they would come to their senses. As a matter of fact I believe something is going to be done in this province, and as a beginning three newspapers are being prosecuted for sedition.*

*Of course the Hindoos run down the Government, especially in Eastern Bengal, saying the officials invited the Mahomedans, who are their favourites, to annoy the Hindoos. But the bottom of the whole thing is the 'Partition of Bengal.' The anti-partition has never died out, and the Bengalis whose object is to boycott foreign goods, be rude to English, create disturbances, &c., think by these means they will harass the Government, and so get a modification of partition, but they are greatly mistaken! The deportation of Lajput Rai, and subsequently Ajib Singh, who was arrested the other day in Anuvistsar, has had a wonderful effect. Mr. Smendra Nath Banerjee, who as you know was crowned king of Bengal last year, has retired into private life for the present on account of his health apparently, but really because he was in mortal terror lest he should get suddenly planted in some unknown spot. The work here consists chiefly in reading the native newspapers, sending and receiving in cipher, telegrams to and from the Government of India, at Simla, and the heads of the districts of this province. My work is quiet, light and interesting.*

## THE PARTITION OF BENGAL

Towards the end of Lord Curzon's time as Viceroy it became clear that Bengal was in an administrative mess. East Bengal in particular was an unpopular place with Europeans as communications were bad, government buildings were poor and there were few police stations. There were no troops, no mounted police and civil servants drowned in a sea of paper, were tied to their desks and lost touch with reality. The population was becoming more litigious and better education had produced a number of young men who wanted only the law or the civil service as a career. There were not enough places or cases to go round and so discontent grew.

In 1905, Curzon partitioned Bengal into two provinces, Eastern Bengal where there was a majority of Muslims and Western Bengal where Hindus predominated. The partition of Bengal was administratively sensible but it came at a bad time in view of the discontent amongst the educated classes. In particular the Hindus resented the dominance of the Muslims in East Bengal.

In the years 1906 to 1909 no less than 557 disturbances came before the criminal courts in East Bengal and in most cases schoolboys or students were concerned. Young men belonging to the classes educated by the English had long been fomenting revolution and they were becoming armed with pistols and bombs. This was fertile ground for anti-partitionists and it gave ample opportunity for pitting Muslims against Hindus. A boycott of foreign goods was undertaken. Many anti-partitionist newspapers sprung up and the methods of the Russian revolutionaries and of Garibaldi were publicised all over Bengal. Terrorism spread fast. On December 6th 1907 Sir Andrew Frazer's train was bombed. A district magistrate was shot on the December 23rd 1907 and in April 1908, two English women were killed by a bomb thrown through their railway carriage window. The bomber had thought an unpopular judge occupied the carriage.

The Indian Newspaper Act was passed in June 1908 and the most inflammatory newspaper in Calcutta, the 'Jugantur', was suppressed. It had taken some time to get round to suppressing the revolutionary newspapers, some said that two women had to be killed before the Raj got up the courage to reduce the freedom of the press.

Curzon's unpopular partition of Bengal was set aside by his successor in 1911, the announcement being made at the Delhi Durbar on December 12th.

## 1907 - EASTERN HIMALAYAS

### A JOURNEY TO JELEP LA ON THE BORDER BETWEEN SIKKIM AND TIBET IN THE FOOTSTEPS OF THE YOUNGHUSBAND MISSION OF 1904

### W.A.P. SEALY

Published in the April 1908 issue of the Reading School Magazine.

*I left Kursoong by train for Ghum in the early morning of December 10th; a glorious crisp morning, frost on the ground. Arrived at Ghum 9 a.m., arranged for a coolie to carry my luggage, and duly started off walking to Peshoke, 13 miles off. A mile from Ghum, where a year or two ago a huge landslip had occurred, and here in consequence there was an entire absence of trees to shut out the scenery, I got a glorious view of the Kinchinjunga Range; the highest peak was just topped by a few light clouds, and from it could be seen what looked like smoke – in reality snow and ice being blown of the mountain, just as though the mountain was a large white volcano vomiting smoke. The whole was a fascinating scene; the glorious mountains, the finest in the world, sparkling in the sun, with here and there a patch to relieve the intense whiteness; patches which indicate precipitous rock where the snow cannot settle. Just below, and quite close, stretches the Darjiling Spur, ending in "Lebong," the military cantonments, and away to the right rugged hills varying from 15,000 to 24,000 feet, and down below a deep gorge of gorgeous green. The snow here was very high, only mountains above 20,000 feet showing snow on them, whereas in the Alps you get snow at the height of 6,000 feet or so. I took a good look at it all, as well as a photo, and then tramped on winding in and out of the spurs. After six miles I stopped to change my boots, as blisters were coming from the ones I was wearing; and after eight miles I began to descend, or rather the road did, and I also started to ask how much further Peshoke was. The answers I got were different. Some said 11 miles or more, some five, and one man told me it was only three quarters of a mile or more.*

*They have no idea of distance, these hill folk; not that the plains men have either. However, I eventually got to Peshoke at 3.30 p.m., having dropped from a height of 7,500 to 3,000 feet. Here at the bungalow I met W. and we introduced ourselves to each other, had some food and then rode on ponies three miles to Teesta, only 7,000 feet above sea level, the road taking us through heavy forest of the most luxurious tropical growth, most of the trees very tall and straight as an arrow. Teesta is a little village on the banks of the river Teesta, a glorious mountain stream of the deepest green water, rushing and surging over boulders between two mountain ranges which shut out most of the sky. In the rains the river is a roaring torrent 60 feet deep and 150 yards wide; even now it is at least 20 feet deep. There is a suspension bridge across it. We stayed the night at the Teesta bungalow. Woke up the next morning to find the sun stealing over the mountain tops, and doing its best to penetrate the deep gorge of the Teesta. After breakfast we started off on the ponies to Kalimpong, the new Scotch Missionary Settlement, on the other side of the river on top of a spur of some 4,000 feet.*

*The journey of seven miles took us some three hours, as the road was very steep, our luggage coming along on pack ponies. Kalimpong is supposed to be the most healthy spot in the hills and I believe is going to be made into the sub-divisional Head Quarters, instead of Kursoong. A railway is going to be built along the Teesta Valley. It is a favourite haunt of the Lieutenant Governors; and there is a fine Dak Bungalow here besides many other houses belonging to the Mission.*

*A good view of the snow is obtained, and as the sun set the scenery was weird and yet glorious. First of all the sky began to be fluked with light clouds, more especially circling around Kinchingjunga and Kebru. The latter is a peak climbed in October by the Norwegian party, forming the world's record in mountain climbing (24,000 feet). The clouds now begin to assume a light yellow colour as also did parts of the snows, changing to a deep orange, and finally to a deep pink, the blue sky behind setting it off. Ere long the sun's last ray had disappeared and almost immediately the snow clad mountain peaks turned a dull grey colour, then a ghostlike bluish white, the clouds still remaining pink; then by degrees the clouds also turned a grey colour and a mist ere long had hidden the whole panorama. The air at once turned chilly, and I was quite glad to get indoors.*

*Everything is different from the plains here, the people no less than the surroundings. Small men with cropped heads, and big men with long black hair plaited and coiled round their heads; all of them however ingrained in dirt. But for this they are far superior to the plains folk. They are truthful, straightforward, honest, care nothing if they get into a scrape, and never dream of telling a lie to get out of it, even though they have committed murder or any such heinous offence.*

*The little children are taken great care of, and dressed in neat and warm clothes – even the poorest. One trait of the children caused me some amusement. On seeing a European they run up for all they are worth, "salaam" most profoundly, and they ask for "Baksheesh" (or tip) as though the fact of having condescended to take notice of you were a deed that can only be requited by giving a coin; and what's more, some will run along with you beside your pony for ever so far, salaaming all the way.*

*The next morning I awoke to find it a dull cloudy day, and a bitterly cold wind blowing, rather dampening my spirits, as my trip would be a hopeless failure, if it were to continue like this for the next few days; however by the time we had started for our next halting place, it showed signs of clearing up, and ere we got to Pedong, it was a glorious sunny day. The journey was along a fairly level road, rising very gradually to a height of 7,500 feet, and then dropping to 6,500 feet. Pedong is on the borders of British India and Sikkim, which is a protectorate. Further than Pedong no white man is allowed to go without a pass from the Deputy Commissioner at Darjiling. From Pedong Dak Bungalow the whole view consists of three ranges of hill, all in Sikkim. Each range is a little higher than the one in front, and the higher ones devoid of vegetation, and generally in the clouds; away in the distance can be seen a rugged peak of red brown colour, some 18,000 feet high, and just below is a slight dip, known as the Jelep La Pass, wither I hope to go eventually. Below the bungalow is a valley in which a small stream flows, which is the actual border between Sikkim and Darjiling District. We stayed the night at Pedong and next morning started for Aritar on the opposite range. To get there we had to drop to the valley some 5,000 feet, then climb up again some 5,000 feet, all in the space of 8 miles, so you can imagine the road is pretty steep. I had no "Pass" but got through by explaining things to the Police at the frontier outpost. Halfway up the opposite hill is a little village called Rhenock. Here I got a new pony for the last stage of the journey, which is the stiffest part, viz.: from Aritar to Gnatong, of which more later.*

*At Rhenock I may mention one can get 500 oranges for the rupee, which works out at 360 for a shilling, and at that the loveliest juicy little oranges imaginable. I got through some 20 oranges a day.*

*The roads have now changed and are very steep and consist of slabs of irregular shaped rocks set into the ground, which are very tiring to the feet and ruinous to the ponies' feet; but Bhutia ponies are very strong, and my pony, which is only four feet high, carried me up the steepest bits without slipping.*

*Near Aritar the slabs of rock are all talc, which glistens like powdered isinglass, and can be crumpled by the hand.*

*We arrived at the Bungalow about 3.30 p.m. and soon had a fire lit as it was quite cold, owing to the thick fog which had come over the hills. However the next morning turned out glorious, and we descended some 4,000 feet to the Rangeli valley, down which the Rangeli flows, a steam very similar to, though smaller than, the Teesta in that it has a much more precipitous course, rushing over a continuous bed of boulders.*

*We cross the river by the bridge and the road now takes us along the Rangeli Valley for five miles, the river keeping some 50 feet below us the whole way, winding in and out of the prettiest valleys imaginable. On one side – the one on which we travel – bold bare rocks rising to a height of 6,000 feet; on the other side somewhat smaller hills covered with thick tropical growth. Above what little of the sky is visible is of the deepest, purest blue, reflected below in the sweetest rippling and seething stream; birds of gay plumage larking about in and out of the foliage, and scarcely any trace of man's handiwork; only here and there a hut, and now and then a mule caravan going down to Darjiling, its merchandise consisting of raw wool, which is* one of the chief exports of Tibet. Now and again also one sees a bare patch, where trees have been cleared. These mark the camping grounds of the last Expedition led by Col. Younghusband into Lhassa (1903-1905).

All along this road at intervals of five miles is a "mail runner's" hut. These runners carry the mail into Siliguri every day, changing at each hut, and handing the bags over to a new man. These men travel in pairs with the bags, and can be heard coming in the distance, as they carry a spear each, on which are hung half a dozen bells.

The natives up here are very polite and many of them, chiefly Bhutias, always took off their quaint hats on seeing us. This is not a trick learnt from others but is their natural form of showing respect. One old chap I met took off his cap in as polite and fashionable a way as one could expect to see in the best of London Society.

We halted at one of the villages on the way and stopped at the mail-runner's hut, where we partook of eggs boiled for us, and tea made by the runners who were off duty.

The halt was really more to let our luggage-laden mules get ahead of us, as arriving at one of these hill bungalows before one's luggage is a most unpleasant situation. However after some 40 minutes we proceeded and climbed a very steep ascent for three miles to Sedomchen, which is about 9,000 feet high. We arrived just at sunset.

Being somewhat higher than the neighbouring spurs and ranges we see over their tops; in fact the whole of the Darjiling hills are spread out in front of us – range after range of varying height, some sombre and dark green owing to the dense growth, others showing light patches where mankind has been at work and cleared the forests, to enable the cultivation of crops. Wheat, rice and oats are grown extensively on the hillsides, on terraces some five yards wide and each about a yard above the other. At Sedomchen there is none of this; the trade is wool; and one meets many caravans of 20 to 30 mules laden with wool – one bale on each side of the animal's back. The whole is in charge of say two men, and the consequence is that the mules just run along the roads as they please, and if one happens to meet such a caravan, it's no easy job getting by, for if one keeps to the inner side of the road, one gets wedged in between a mule and the rock, or if one keeps to the outer edge one is liable to get barged over the side altogether. One thing, each mule has either one large bell or a string of tiny ones round its neck, so they can be heard ever so far off, and there is no chance of being taken unawares, and the noise of the bells is very pleasing to the ear, quaint as it is.

But this is by the way. I was explaining the scenery.

Range upon range of hills, at all angles and in every direction for some 20 or 30 miles, ending up in the Kinchingjunga range, though the snow capped part of the *range is hidden by a spur to the right. Away in the distance, and only just discernible is the little spur (at least so it looked from here) on which Darjiling stands. The sun has just set, and the blue haze, which always forms about mid-day, begins to turn to a purplish hue in the valleys and yellow, turning orange, on the hills, ending in a lovely red about the ridges, with the pale blue of the sky above all, and perhaps a tiny, fleecy cloud floating about all by itself in the most unconcerned and aimless way.*

*Next day we marched to Guatong, our last halting place. I say MARCHED though most of the journey was done on a pony's back. From Sedomchen we ascended some 5,000 feet to the top of a mountain some 14,000 feet high from where we got our first real views of the snows as they appear from this side, the opposite to that which one sees from Darjiling. Here we have them spread out in full view, whereas at Darjiling they are seen at an angle, and hence are all foreshortened.*

*Now we were in reality going into the region of barren rocks. Scarcely a tree grows on these high peaks, but the whole is covered in rhododendron shrubs, which would be called trees in England. These rhododendrons grow to a height of 15 to 20 feet, and when they are in full bloom they must be a glorious sight as there are supposed to be at least ten different kinds and colours. Here also I saw more than one specimen of that rare bird, the golden eagle, though of course not at very close quarters. They have been seen up here up to 15 feet from wing to wing. Large mountain vultures also career about at a great height.*

*As I mentioned before, near the top of the peak we come suddenly into full view of the snows. The whole range spread out before us; and a more fascinating majestic sight is not obtainable anywhere in the world. We are no closer to them than Darjiling, and yet they look twice the size. Every detail is visible, precipices, glaciers, snowfields, and the peaks themselves, pinewhite, sparkling and scintillating in the sun. Below the snow line dark massive rocks, where no man – except the mad mountain climber – has ever set foot, and even he is a rarity here. Soon we turn a bend and get another view of the rocks of a fair height, including Jelep-La. The streams here are all frozen, and it is decidedly cold, and the snow lies on the ground in patches, so to get warm I walk a bit.*

*After winding around some half dozen spurs, all of a sudden only a few hundred yards in front of us we came upon a little collection of huts huddled together on a bare place, not a tree in sight, only bare rocks, and stumps of trees. It is Guatong, the last village before one crosses into Tibet, and the camp of the Expedition of 1903-1905. The stumps of trees were the only remains as every bit of wood was cut for kindling. There is also a graveyard of the eight or nine officers who fell during the mission. The village itself is at a height of 13,000 or more feet, quite a respectable height to live, in all conscience.*

*I get inside the bungalow as soon as I can to melt my frozen hands and feet. The sun soon sets and the moon and stars soon come out. One has no idea how brightly these heavenly luminants shine at this height. They seem – at least the stars do – twice as big as from the plains and far brighter, and one or two of the bigger ones seem to flash a purple light every now and then, and the moon shines on peacefully, serenely, and with an intensely white light, casting heavy shadows of all objects on the ground, and scarcely a sound is heard, but the occasional voice of man. No jackals or other animals to disturb one's slumber here; not a bird even; only man is here. Dinner over, I didn't waste time in getting into bed, or going to sleep. The temperature in my room even an hour after the fire had been lit was only a degree or two above zero.*

*Next day, December 13th, at about 10 a.m. we started out on our march to the pass and back. Up here there are no huts but those of the mail-runners between Guatong and a village in Thibet; and so our journey to Jelep and back had to be done on the same day.*

*We took a few hard-boiled eggs with us, and our guns, in case of any luck in meeting any mountain sheep, expecting to be back by sunset. The first two and a half miles uphill brought us to a pass called Deoraili No. 1 and a mile further to Deoraili No. 2. From the latter we look down into a valley in which is a small lake, surrounded by the most bleak and barren rocks of red, purplish black colour. At the end of the lake are two or three huts, the mail-runners' lonely quarters. From here a three mile bridge along another valley at right angles to the lake brings one to the pass – the Jelep La Pass, 14,997 feet, according to the best observation.*

*A strong wind was blowing and one could scarcely breathe on account of the coldness of the blast combined with the rarity of the atmosphere. Aping half-frozen and only kept warm by continual motion, we climbed a little hillock a few hundred feet higher and surveyed the landscape. Straight in front a series of flat-looking red-coloured hills, stretching to right and left, somewhat barren-looking, though in reality covered with forests. Just below was a Thibetan monastery, and away behind all rose up in awesome splendour and loneliness one snow-clad peak, Chumulari (24,000 feet).*

*At the foot of this peak is Phari, a big Thibetan city. Beyond the peak is the real Thibetan plateau, invisible as there is a haze on it. To our left could be seen Kinchinjunga – showing between two large peaks close to us- which it was our intention to climb, but the wind was so strong it prevented us. However, 15,000 feet is a pretty respectable height for any one to have got to.*

*After we had got down we scanned the rocks to our left for some mountain sheep which we were told had been seen there in the morning. At last we saw them across the other side, but they had evidently long ago spotted us, for they stood on a prominent rock and sniffed the air, and sort of defied us to chase them. We stalked them from both sides, and when our two parties met there was no sign of them. These sheep are as big as a small pony, and their horns measure 18 inches in diameter at the base. They can leap from rock to rock with the greatest ease; "Krag the Kootenay Ram" gives an exact idea of these animals in Seton Thompson's "Lives of the Hunted." At any rate we wasted three hours over them and all to no purpose; and now the sun was nearly set I proposed making straight tracks home; and suiting the action for the word started off for the pass where we had left our ponies, &c. It seemed only a few yards off, but took over half an hour to get to it, and by that time the light was gone.*

*I shouted for the ponies, but got no reply, so I sat down and waited. W. seemed a long time in coming, and I began to think he had got by in front of me owing to the cloud which had rolled up and closed upon us. I yelled and shouted but got no reply. At last I saw three of our men, from whom I learned he was coming on behind, so I waited and waited and whistled and called, but only heard my own voice re-echoed. At last I saw him coming over the edge and I at once noticed something very peculiar about his gait. On coming up I learned that he had had a seizure of mountain sickness; his limbs had gone paralysed all of a sudden and everything swam before him. These seizures are the result of the atmospheric action on the heart and often end in heart failure.*

*Naturally I got alarmed at the state of affairs, as here was I in a lone and barren spot with a couple of natives and an invalid; almost dark; four miles to go to the nearest mail-runner's huts, wither our ponies had gone and everything else. I gave him my arm, and so we trudged slowly for half a mile, when we sat down I started rubbing his hands to bring back the circulation, gave him gloves to put under his own, and then proceeded.*

*The scene was to say the least terrifying. Big rugged rocks of weird appearance in the moonlight, booming of ice-breaking heard at intervals, the whole bringing to mind at once those weird telescope photos of the craters of the moon one so often sees in magazines. The rugged bareness and ghostlike appearance are almost identical. It is no place to be stranded in I assure you, and I was jolly glad when we at last arrived at the huts.*

*We went inside and nearly got suffocated on the spot by the smoke of the wood fire. It was now about 7 p.m. The men, all Nepalese, soon made us comfortable. Some started preparing tea, and others chupatties, while I looked on, and W. recovered himself soon with the eggs we had brought and the chupatties and tea. We had satisfied our hunger and thirst, and really shuddered at the idea of getting out in the open again and riding five more miles home. However, we did not hurry, and stayed in the huts for an hour or so.*

*These Nepalese were awfully good-natured men, and really it was a pleasure to be entertained by them, uncivilised barbarians though they were. What struck me was their rare geniality, always ready to help one another, no beastly prejudice, no cringing before Europeans, no pestering for tips; full of fun and often very witty. They live in these desolate spots and carry mails their share of the journey day in and day out, sometimes having to cross the pass with 18 feet of snow on it at four in the morning. Of course they are well paid; they get food and clothes free and £1 a month cash, which they club together and keep for brandy and cigarettes, of both of which they are very fond, though seldom get drunk, using the brandy more as a stimulant than anything else.*

*Well, we left their abode very much refreshed at 8 p.m. and W. was feeling better and got home at 9.30 p.m. I can tell you I was glad to get home to Guatong without any mishap, thanks chiefly to the moon. No one knows where the ponies might have taken us, over the first precipice, more likely than not.*

*This ended my journey to the Jelep La Pass.*

*W.A.P. SEALY*

This is a marvellous piece of travel writing. It may be difficult for tourists to repeat the journey as Sikkim, which Sealy entered with such cavalier disregard for the necessary permit after he left Pedong, has some military significance in the eyes of the Indian government

Though Sealy says that Sikkim was a 'protectorate in his day it had been an independent Buddhist kingdom until the war between China and India in 1966 and the Indian Government saw it as a crucial corridor between Bangladesh and Tibet. It was annexed by India in 1975 and is now a fully-fledged Indian state but with special status. It is a small state measuring 65km by 115km and lies between Nepal to the west and Bhutan to the east. Tibet surrounds its north eastern and northern borders.

## ONE LAST IMPERIAL EFFORT

Notes on the Younghusband expeditions to Tibet 1903 and 1904.

Throughout the Victorian era Russia was playing a strategic game and expanding her empire. She realised that Britain had command of the seas but that if she threatened British India through the mountainous states on its Northern frontiers she could keep Britain off guard and tie up a great number of British Troops guarding India against insubstantial threats. The 'Great Game', immortalised by Rudyard Kipling in his book 'Kim', was the result. Russia, at little cost, kept the British in India on a knife-edge by sending missions to threaten the neutrality of the Northwest frontier states. The British kept up a spy operation by sending 'Pundits' into the mountainous area, which separated India from the southern reaches of the Russian Empire. The 'Pundits' were specially picked and trained agents who mapped the forbidding and often forbidden countries of the buffer states and listened to bazaar rumours about Russian activities. Their intelligence reports together with rumours of Russian missions and reports on the feasibility of Russian military attack were fed back to eager people like Roberts, Kitchener and Curzon. The Russians could achieve a lot for little outlay.

In essence, the Russian Empire was expanding southwards towards British India. The British had set up buffer states between India and Russia's southwards march. Afghanistan, Nepal and the like. Tibet was an exception. It was mysterious, unknown as far as Britain was concerned and its borders joined with both Russia and China. It was effectively part of the Chinese Empire though officially ruled by the Dalai Lama.

There were constant rumours that Russia had gained control over Tibet. Curzon, the Viceroy, was alarmed. He wrote to the Dalai Lama on several occasions during 1901 and 1902 to explore the idea of Anglo-Tibetan friendship but his letters were always returned unopened. In the end he flimflammed the Government in Britain and set up a punitive expedition to Tibet under an unusual army officer, Colonel Francis Younghusband of the King's Dragoon Guards. He was a loner who had once made a solitary journey overland from China to Kashmir and had been the British Political Agent in Chitral. He had in fact been the Raj's Russian Watcher up in the wild country between the two Empires. He was a bit of a mystic, who had been to school at Clifton with Henry Newbolt. He was married to an MP's daughter, and had said of himself that he was 'not really suited to my wife'. He had been a correspondent for the Times and was said to have witnessed the Jameson Raid.

On his first mission in May 1903 Younghusband crossed Sikkim to the north and met the Tibetans at Khamba Dzong. They refused to discuss anything. He retreated back through Sikkim and reported to Curzon in Simla again. In effect this mission was undertaken to justify further action by Curzon.

The Viceroy suggested that Younghusband should return to Tibet with a substantial military mission. He was to occupy a Tibetan valley, the Chumbi, and penetrate the country 150 miles deeper to the town of Gyantse. Balfour's government in England sanctioned the incursion with reluctance. Kitchener, then commanding the Indian Army, allowed Younghusband 'a section of a British mountain battery and two Maxim gun detachments, all British soldiers'. He gave orders that 'not a single man is to be under six feet'. In all there were to be 1,200 combatants supporting Colonel Younghusband on his 'Mission to Tibet' in the winter of 1903.

The Second Younghusband Mission to Tibet followed a route similar to that which W.A.P. Sealy and his friend W. took on their pony trek to the Jelep La Pass and it accounts for the remarks about the damage done by the soldiers. The Jelep La, the main pass from Sikkim into Tibet, was rough and narrow, and no wheeled vehicle could cross it. Therefore the Mission had to carry all its food, tentage, arms and ammunition on the backs of animals or humans. Some 10,000 porters, men and women, were recruited. Nearly 20,000 animals - mules, bullocks, buffaloes, ponies, Nepalese Yaks, Tibetan Yaks, six camels and 2 "zebrules' (half zebra/half donkey). Zebrules were bad news. At least 99.2 % of the buffaloes, 98.9 % of the Nepalese Yaks, and all six camels perished on the campaign.
*(Ref. Farewell the Trumpets - James Morris - Faber & Faber 1978. p131/132)*

Younghusband and his Invasion Force entered Tibet and penetrated as far as Phari where they provoked a moment of hostility from a rag-tag army of Tibetans on whom they opened fire with their Maxim guns killing hundreds in the process. He persuaded Curzon that he had been provoked into an unwanted battle and gained permission to attack the capital, Lhasha.

He trekked on to Lhasa with his force but much to his surprise found no signs of Russian influence there. He signed a trade treaty with the Dalai Lama. Curzon may have thought of bringing Tibet under British influence by taking over effective power and leaving a Military Mission in Tibet. The British Government had no stomach for the affair and reneged on Curzon. The Mission slunk back to India and Younghusband, its leader, was dammed with faint praise and given a 'lesser Knighthood' for his efforts.
*(Ref. From Farewell the Trumpets p128 etc)*

## 1905 - ADAM'S PEAK, CEYLON

### H.H. BANKS
### OR 1904

This article appeared in the School Magazine, December 1907.

*I left Drayton Estate, Kotagalla, on Wednesday the 21st of February 1905, with the intention of climbing Adam's Peak. January and February are good months for the purpose, as one can then look forward to seeing the Shadow of the Peak.*

*I sent off my baggage by coolie and then rode to Kotagalla Station and trained to Hattan. Here I got out and began my ride. Going at good pace I soon reached the point where I left the road. The path led through Tea and was rather too steep for easy riding. It soon improved and I rode on till it once more became steep and winding. It continued so up to the Glentilt Gap, where I left Dickoya and entered Maskelyia. It is quite hopeless to get up without pushing one's cycle, and the coolies are always on the look out to take it up for you, for the huge sum of 25 cents. I was glad when I arrived at the Gap, as it was pretty hot walking up and the zigzag paths seemed endless. The roads were in good condition and all downhill, so I had a fine spell of free-wheeling. I could of course see the Peak quite clearly now.*

*It was a pleasant change to spin along as I was doing after the toil up to Glentilt. I soon reached the Laxapana rest-house, and before long my box-coolie turned up and I was able to change and have tea. Afer dinner I turned in till about one o'clock, when a start was to be made. It is well to dress warmly, as it is very cold on top of the Peak. My guide had a lantern and we set off. The way through the Estate was pretty easy to follow, although there was no moon, but when we entered the jungle I soon found the difference. The path was only wide enough for one man, and there were plenty of slippery stones and sharp roots to fall over, I soon found that climbing the Peak was not unattended with difficulties. At several different points the path comes to an end at the face of the rock, and steps have been cut out if the face of the cliff and chains fixed to enable one to ascend. These steps I found to be far easier of ascent than I had supposed from descriptions. The chains are very old, but they are strong enough, and there are plenty of them. At one point of the journey I passed through quite a number of native pilgrims sleeping or squatting round small fires. Here and there along the route were small images of Buddha with boxes for offerings in front of them. I hardly met a single pilgrim on the way up; the majority of them had already ascended and I could hear them chanting on the summit. I had a rest and drink when about a mile from the top, and was precious glad of both; then up we went again, and at last we reached the last stone step and had completed the ascent.*

*The top of the peak was crowded with pilgrims sitting round tiny fires and chanting. How could they stand the cold I can't make out, as there is no shelter whatever for* them. As it began to get light I went up to the shrine and watched the pilgrims marching and chanting, 'Sadoo! Sadoo!' and striking a huge bell which is hung by the stone parapet. I believe a pilgrim gives the bell a toll for every time he has been up the Peak; several of them rang it seven or eight times. As the mist cleared I began to understand what a height up I was, more than seven thousand feet above sea level. All round I could see dense jungle stretching away; on clear mornings one can look right away into the low country. As the sun rose the colours of the sky became glorious, patches of yellow and flaming red and pink and purple. The sight is one to remember for a lifetime, but it is impossible to do it justice in a description. As the sun rose and the colours grew brighter the chanting increased in volume and the procession ceased; everyone looked towards the sun and raised their arms to it. It was a magnificent sight, worth all the climb times over. I then moved over to the other side of the shrine to watch for the shadow of the Peak. It was there all right, showing up splendidly on the clouds; slowly it came nearer and nearer and then vanished. The pilgrims were now leaving the Peak; the shadow did not appeal to them in the least. They had seen the sunrise and that was enough for them; the shadow was no part of their religion. I had a look at the shrine, saw the footprint of Buddha (or Adam!), which is not a bit like a footprint, tolled the bell once and started down the steps. The pilgrims kept up their chanting all the way down; they were quite civil and made room readily for us. Going down one gets a good look at the jungle, which is very pretty. The worst feature of the descent is the number of cripples who line the path and beg. Some of the pilgrims paid up a good deal, but I noticed that most of the coins were half-cents.

I got back to the rest-house in about 2.5 hours and, having changed and sent off my box-coolie, had breakfast and rested. About ten o'clock I started back to Kotagalla. From Glentilt Gap I had a capital run down the cart-road. I stopped at Hattan for tea, intending to take the train thence to Kotagalla; to avoid delay, however, I ended by cycling the extra miles and arrived at Drayton rather tired but well pleased with my trip. It is well worh doing and need not cost much, even if one takes the coach to Hattan, as many visitors to Ceylon do, besides having guides up the Peak, carrying chairs etc. Guides, coolies and all accessories can be obtained at the rest-house in Laxapana.

H.H. Banks

(See also page 102)

# 1908 - JAFFNA, CEYLON

## C. HARRISON-JONES

In the December 1902 edition C.H. Jones wins the Palmer Prize for mathematics and the Giles Ayres Cup for shooting. He is also on the Valete as Captain of School 1902, a School prefect and a House prefect in Town House. He was a Corporation Scholar in 1902. He was treasurer of the Prefect's Common Room and was made a 2nd Lieutenant in the School Corps one year after its formation. Harrison-Jones won a White Scholarship, St John's College Oxford (£100 for 4 years).

In the December 1904 edition of the School Magazine the following appears:

*'In his first year at St John's he played Rugger for the "A" team and rowed in the winning junior four. Harrison-Jones (St. John's), has our very heartiest congratulations on his place in the Trial Eights, amongst what are admittedly the best recruits produced for some years, and for some of whom it is thought Old Blues will have to stand down. He is also Captain of Boats at St. John's'.*

In December 1906 he is reported as gaining a 3rd Class Honours, History Finals.

*Jaffna, Ceylon*
*June 23rd, 1908*

*Dear Mr. Editor,*

*I read with great interest in your last December number a letter from H.H.Banks, describing his ascent of Adam's Peak in the hill-country of central Ceylon. When I came out in November last, it was not my good fortune to be sent to that part of the island among the planting districts. Bye-the-bye, I am very interested to know whether there are any other ORs in Ceylon besides Banks (if he is still here) and myself. I have not so far heard of any.*

*I am afraid the district to which I have been sent is very different from that described by Banks. It is in nearly every way more like the greater part of the Madras Presidency of India, which I believe my contemporaries Buchanan and Clinch patrol the land as policemen. The natives up here are the same race, Tamil, but I believe the Jaffna Tamil excels his Indian brother in that shrewdness and industry which causes him to be termed the "Scotsman of the East." But I am afraid that those are almost the only qualities in which the Tamil resembles the Scotsman, for in many ways he is not a pleasant character.*

*It is a wonderful sight on riding or bicycling through the Jaffna Peninsular, which is attached as it were, to the northern extremity of Ceylon, to mark the industry of the people. The country is dry and flat, and uninteresting and the soil is inferior to the rest of Ceylon. Yet the population to the square mile is enormous, with the smallness of the lots, into which the land is divided up, makes the peasant proprietors of France appear large in comparison. They cannot cultivate enough paddy-rice to support themselves on, owing to the drought through more than half the year; but instead they cultivate tobacco (which, however, it is advisable to leave to the natives to smoke) and various grains. They work the whole day, watering or digging their fields, to the astonishment of all those who are acquainted with the majority of Eastern peoples. The fishermen along the coast are equally as energetic, and the congestion of the population makes it sometimes not altogether pleasant in the towns and larger villages.*

*But to the industry of the people there are compensating drawbacks. They are so interested in their own occupations and concerns that they are entirely without the courtesy that one expects to meet in the East; and in this they form a contrast to the neighbouring Singhalese, who, though extremely indolent, are the better gentlemen. The Tamil coolie with a basket on his head will not think of getting out of your way as you pass, and in fact, bicycling through the roads is a dangerous proceeding. Still, perhaps, on the whole it is better to have the people like this. They have less time to devote to litigation and writing false petitions, though even here the amount of these is distressing to the young Western Civil Servant. Unfortunately, now for some years the Jaffna Tamil, who receives on the average a better education than the Bengali Baboo, always desires to leave the land and become a Government servant or lawyer. Consequently we have the same political cries out here of "Back to the Land" and "Educational Reform" as at home.*

*It will be seen from all this how difficult it is to write of any interesting personal experiences. Everything is very quiet and humdrum. While the rest of Ceylon is one of the finest places in the world for big-game shooting, it is hard enough to get a few partridges, which are soon found to be distinctly tough, Luckily, we have plenty of tennis and fair golf. For cricket it is impossible to get enough together, though the native boys at school play both this and football with great vigour.*

*When I think of the interesting letters I have read in the School Magazine from various ORs in India, South Africa, Canada, &c., I am afraid this will appear very dry, but I must ask the reader to consider it is due to the uninteresting nature of the country.*

*I am looking forward now, as always, to the next number of the School Magazine, and I hope to read of a successful cricket season and a good performance at Bisley.*

*I am, Mr. Editor, Yours, &c.*
*C. HARRISON-JONES.*

## A PREMATURE OBITUARY

## H.G. CLINCH

Indian Policeman, 1909.

1st XV 1903-04

In the December 1909 issue of the Reading School Magazine this obituary appeared on the front page:

*"It is with deepest regret that we announce the death of H.G. Clinch, who got into the Indian Police only last year. At present, only the bare fact of his death has reached us.*

*Henry Gordon Clinch won an Entrance Scholarship here in May, 1899, from Mr Rowley's, Clifton. He was the Captain of the XI. from 1902 to 1904, Captain of the School for the same period, played for the 1st XV. in 1902 and 1903, and passed the examination for the R.M.C. Sandhurst, in 1903 though he did not go into the Army. A good cricketer and boy of strong sterling character, we had hoped that with the ability that was his, he had a career before him. Indomitable and persevering, he was the stuff of which our best Empire–builders are made. The shock of his death to his old School-fellows and Masters is great, and difficult to realise. But our sympathies go out especially to his relations in their grief at a loss as tragically sudden".*

It is worth adding that Henry Gordon Clinch also served his School as a House Prefect, a member of the Games Committee, the School Magazine Committee, the Tuck Shop Committee and the Debating Society Committee. He was Secretary of the Shakespeare Society and of the Tennyson Society. He appears to have found time to be the Treasurer of the Prefect's Common Room and a 2nd Lieutenant in the School Cadet Corps.

There is an interesting sequel to the obituary in the April 1907 issue of the School Magazine, which opens with this paragraph.

*"We very greatly regret that we announced the death of H.G. Clinch in our last number, thereby causing a good deal of pain to his relations. We can only plead in extenuation that the information came from a contemporary who is also in India, and the announcement of the death in one of the London Dailies seemed convincing. Happily the report turns out to be false; Clinch had been very ill, but the last reports are eminently satisfactory. It only remains for us to wish him an extra long life, and the fulfilment of the hopes, referred to in his obituary notice".*

## 1909 - SRINAGAR, KASHMIR

### F.E. LUCEY 1894–1896

F.E. Lucey was a prefect at School and won an open mathematical Scholarship to Worcester College, Oxford. He rowed at Stroke for his college and had the distinction of being in the boat which made five bumps in Torpids. In December 1897 he is reported in the 'Oxford Letter' as; '....taking change from last term's labour in the galleys, by wandering in country lanes and going out to tea. He is becoming a wit at our little social parties when we go to take tea and make hay in each other's rooms'.

In 1898 he gained a First in Mathematical Moderations and won the Goldsmiths' Exhibition.

The following appeared in the Reading School Magazine in July 1909:

*The Head Master has received a very interesting letter from F.E. Lucey (OR) who is at the CMS College in Srinagar, Kashmir. We are allowed to print the following selections:*

*"I am sending you one of our school reports. You will see that the school is not run on exactly orthodox missionary lines, but I think most people who have had much to do with the Kashmiris would know that we are on the right lines.*

*The in-school work falls chiefly to me. We have one period a day for all classes for scripture. I am sure that many of the boys are interested, but to be baptised means being turned out of doors by their own people, probably having false charges proved by false witnesses who can be hired at 4d. a head, and running a very real risk of life. One boy has had the courage to face it since I have been out. We had rather an exciting rescue of him in the bazaar, a tug-of-war to get him into a boat, and finally had to send him down country. He is turning out splendidly and we hope that some day he will return as a master to witness to his people.*

*During my first two years I was wrestling with Urdu, now I am struggling with Kashmiri; it seems as though I am never to get out of schooling, and I am sure I hate my grinding as much as any school-boy hates his lessons. I find Kashmiri an appalling language, the verbs seem to inflect for the subject, direct object and indirect object, so that for each person of each tense you get about half-a-dozen different forms.*

*The Kashmiri, I think, could give the Cretans points and still win.*

*It is impossible to take a boy's word, and there is a very real risk of losing faith out here and becoming suspicious of all men.*

*The idea the average Kashmiri master has of keeping order is strange, as quietness does not seem to have anything to do with it.*

*Some time ago we had a football match against a State School. In the second half our boys scored a deciding goal. SA Punjabi was referee. The State School Master rushed onto the field to say it was no goal. The poor referee tore his hair, not having the courage to decide, while all the State School boys crowded round him. Pandemonium reigned for about half an hour, then a happy thought occurred to the referee, and he sent for the Inspector of Education, who was playing cricket a few fields away, to decide. He however could not throw much light on the subject and by that time darkness intervened and we moved off.*

*I am writing this in a kind of houseboat, travelling up to Islamabad. Kashmir is looking almost at its best – there are fields of brilliantly yellow mustard, the willows are fast showing their fresh green, the fruit trees are coming out in masses of blossom, and behind, the snow covered mountains. It is a lovely country – if only the people had some idea of cleanliness.*

*If any boys want to have a good fight against a most irreligious religious ceremonial religiousness and a most uncleanly ceremonial cleanliness, let them come out here.*

*Yours very sincerely,*
*F.E. LUCEY*
*April 10th, 1909*

## 1909 - PERAK, FEDERATION OF MALAYA STATES

### A SLADANG HUNT IN PERAK

#### H.H. BANKS

*Taking advantage of the holiday time during the Christmas week, 1909, I determined to give myself the pleasure of a few days hunting after Sladang (the Malayan Bison, or Gaur, of India) and, having previously received information from the Peng-hulu (Headman of Bidor) that a small herd of these animals had come down from the mountain haunts to the Ulu Sungkai, a forest-covered hilly region to the south-east of Perak, started from Gopeng for Bidor to make final arrangements. Here, I was joined by Mat Jassin, a Malay hunter, who had accompanied me on former similar occasions.*

*The first day I took two Malays and two Sakais, (The Sakai are an aboriginal race dwelling in dense forests of the interior), and set out to explore some likely spots near the Dusun Pisangkap (Dusun, an Orchard, or Plantation of Fruit Trees) where we hope to find Sladang. We came on lot of old "spoor," so worked round Chungkat Baviritz where I knew there was a fair chance of finding our game; we struck nothing, however, so decided that the Sladang were moving towards the Ulu, and accordingly bent our steps in the direction of a place called Melor where we had camped on a previous visit. We soon struck tracks of a single bull and followed him to Melor; he was travelling fast, however, and had not stopped to feed, only eating a few mouthfuls of grass here and there, on the way; in one place we found where he had devastated a patch of bush and wild pisangs; evidently he was annoyed, but what had "put him out" we of course could not tell. As it was late we decided to abandon the chase for the day. We knew that the Sladang had moved to the Minerang Valley, between Pahang and the Ulu Sungkai side; we accordingly returned to the Dusun Pisangkap, where our hut had been made ready for us, and made preparations for the next day's fray.*

*Next morning I awoke at four, and saw that my followers were already astir getting our breakfast ready. On these mountains it is pretty cold in the early mornings, and I confess that I did not much relish turning out. "What did I want with a Sladang"? "Why couldn't I leave the poor brutes alone?" were the thoughts that occurred to me; but then I remembered those big tracks of yesterday, and thought of what might be waiting near the warm spring of Pukat, so rapidly dressed for the hunt, swallowed some hot cocoa and as much rice and dried fish as I could manage, And then waited until it was light enough to see our way through the jungle. As soon as possible we started, our intention being to make a rapid march to Melor and then take up the old tracks of yesterday and follow them up to the end. We picked up the tracks*

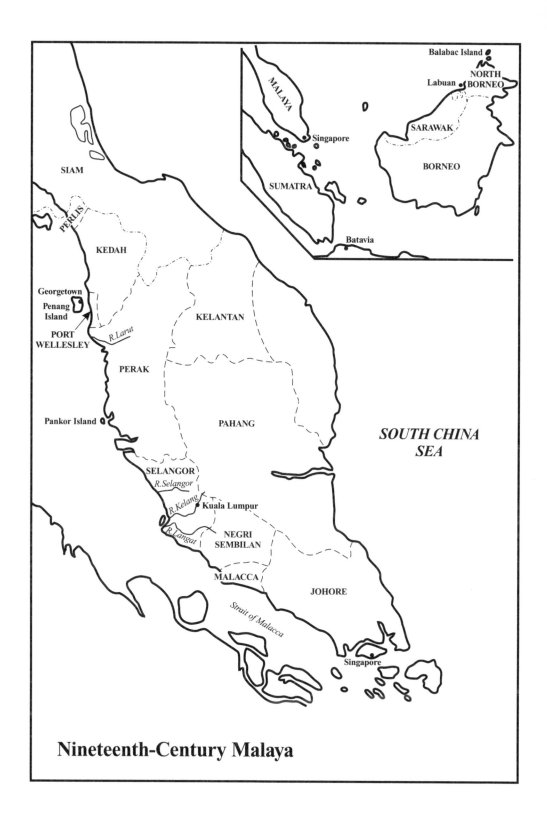

**Nineteenth-Century Malaya**

*without difficulty, and following hard along the hills in the direction of Ulu Sungkai; at length the tracks freshened and we went more carefully as it was not unlikely that we would come on the animal feeding – a very great advantage to us. However, luck was against us as we found the animal standing in thick Bertrams (a sort of bush growing in clumps and armed with long and sharp thorns; its leaves are used for roofing huts). He was evidently thinking about settling down for his mid-day siesta, and I think I should have had a shot, but just then the Sakai behind me spoke, and the Sladang was off before I could get a sight of him, but my tracker had a glimpse before he sprang away. We followed, as he was leading us in the direction of the warm spring where I had no doubt he would halt; even if he did not do so we would find other Sladang in the vicinity. The "going" on the hills was pretty good – nice open jungle and not too much thorn, except for the Bertram and its long brittle spikes; it was difficult, however, to see very far as the amount of "leaf" was very great; in fact this is the great difficulty I have encountered in the FMS., the quarry sees enough of you to make him bolt, whilst the hunter does not see enough of his intended victim to warrant shooting. Proceeding carefully we descended into the valley and soon came on more Sladang tracks, while near the warm spring there was ample evidence of their presence. Creeping carefully along the tracks of a single bull we suddenly heard the sharp bark of a Kijang, (the barking deer; the Muntjac of India), and my tracker whispered that no doubt the deer had come to drink and had seen the Sladang; the "bark" had come from about fifty yards on our right. We crept softly in the direction of the sound, sitting down at intervals and doing our best to make out the forms of the bison. Every now and then we could hear them quite near us: luckily the wind was steady. After about half an hour of this sort of thing we arrived at the edge of a small trickle of water, crossing which were the tracks of three bison; we followed them and as we crossed the water I got a sudden glimpse of a tail swishing to and fro about eight yards in front. Instantly I ceased Mat Jassin by the shoulder and we sank under cover in a sitting position. I could only see one Sladang, and that dimly, but from its size I was sure that it was a bull, and raised my .500 (HV Cordite). Mat Jassin had a .375 (a Magazine Rifle, Cordite) and was seated along side me with it held ready. What happened was that the Sakai behind us had not crouched down as we had done, and some very slight movement on his part had attracted the Sladang's notice. I don't think he saw Mat Jassin and myself as we were seated, and our greenish clothes matched the jungle. As I was afraid that he had spotted us and might be off I got the foresight "on" to his chest and fired. The roar of the heavy charge of cordite in the thick jungle was almost deafening, but thanks to the anti-recoil pad on the rifle-butt I never felt the recoil. I got a glimpse of the Sladang as he made a great plunge and stagger; then he was gone, and two others which we had not seen, along with him. We could hear the jungle crashing as they made off. We went forward to see the effect of my shot, and sure enough the place where the Sladang was standing was smothered in blood. We followed up the watercourse in great glee, finding a heavy blood trail all the way. The wounded animal had turned up the hill, and, as we followed, our hands, clothes and rifles were covered in blood from the leaves and branches which were heavily splashed with it, while all along the track it lay in pools. On reaching the top of the hill we decided to halt and give the animal half an hour to stiffen; we felt sure of getting him as it was evident he had been shot through the lungs.*

*After waiting the time agreed we again took up the trail, and as the jungle here was fairly open went on as hard as we could, the blood tracks never stopping for a moment; yet we saw no sign of our victim, though his stride was getting shorter. My tracker expressed surprise at this; he said the animal should have lain down, and remembering what I had read and been told about these brutes, I too thought it odd. But neither of us guessed what was urging our wounded Sladang forward. The chase had now lasted from 12.15, when I got the shot, till 3 p.m. and we had not even got a glimpse of the Sladang since the start. At last we came into a broad belt of blukar, which was so thick that one could not see a gun's length ahead and as this was a likely place for the animal to turn "nasty" we proceeded warily. Presently we heard him staggering about in the blukar, everything of course going down before him like grass. By the noise it sounded as if he was lame – no clean leaps or steps, but crash after crash. Wounded though he was he could of course get through the stuff quicker than we could. At last we emerged into open forest again, and I had barely got clear with Mat Jassin when the snarling cough of a tiger sounded from the blukar we had just passed through; I must have walked within a few paces of the brute! The other Malay and the two Sakais hastily got behind Mat Jassin and me, and we waited, facing the thick bush which was only about four or five yards away. The snarls grew louder and fiercer and we could hear the tiger rushing hither and thither in the dense mass of leaves. Personally I quite expected to hear what the Malays call the "charge song" and see the brute charge out at us; several times he rushed up to the edge of the blukar but "funked" the last few yards; no doubt he saw us with rifles raised waiting to receive him. Then we heard a creeping rustle and one of the tigers (for there were two of them) made off up the ridge – needless to say we did not see him – the other remained "swearing" at us. I could now see why the Sladang had gone on so steadily; the two great cats had smelt the blood and had been hunting our game one on each side while we had been following behind them! In a case like this the wounded beast would of course go on till he dropped, or came up with others of his kind. On coming to the blukar belt the tigers had drawn in on the stricken animal, and it was then we had caught them up. Although the tiger was in a great rage he refused to show himself. Finally, Mat Jassin spoke addressing himself to the tiger, and asked him "why he interfered in other peoples affairs," reminding him the Sladang "belonged to us, and not to him" and finished by inviting him to "come out and have his head blown in". During this harangue the tiger kept quiet except for an occasional growl, and then, instead of accepting Mat Jassin's cordial invitation, he too cleared out in another direction, leaving us free to take up afresh the tracks of the wounded Sladang. Well, we followed him until nightfall although the blood trail was not so heavy at first, as in the heavy forest there is not so much leaf for the blood to be smeared on.*

*That night we camped at Minerang, and next day took up the trail anew. We found that the Sladang had come up with two or three others and, tried to mix with them, which they did not appear to want, as these wild animals dislike the smell of blood. They had walked round and round on a hill, the wounded one after them, and it was enough to make ones head spin following the tracks; every now and again we found blood and could see where the wounded one had slipped, the right foot swinging inwards. Then after many hours we came upon the spot where the Sladang (the uninjured ones) had fled madly but the wounded one was not with them. We searched for ever so long as we felt sure that the Sladag had fallen which would account for the flight of his friends; but although we made every effort, and although both my trackers were certain the carcass was not far off, to my great disappointment, and that of my men, we did not find it. The tracks were so mixed that tracking was very difficult; on thing was certain and that was that we found no more blood after leaving the hill. The trackers were very sore about it; even if we had not been in time to cut the beast's throat and so render the meat fit for the "True Believer" we should have had the head, which judging by the glimpse we got at the time I fired was a pretty good one.*

*During the remainder of my leave we found no more Sladang, and a wait for a Bear at the Dusun Pisangkap also proved unsuccessful. Here I made the near acquaintance of that vile-smelling fruit, the Durien. I have never been able to eat it before, but consumed quite a lot when in the jungle; when consuming the creamy pulp the smell is not so noticeable. The bears had a fine time in the various Dusuns, which they visit for the fallen fruit, and signs of their feasts were very much in evidence. I met many of the Mai Darat (Sakai) and told them about the lost Sladang, and have every hope that they will recover the skull and horns for me, for which I have offered a reward, for as decomposition sets in, their noses will be attracted and will guide them to the right spot. At this time, luckily, the Sakai are daily on the move visiting the clumps of Durien trees. A Sladang, shot some years ago and lost in the same place, was discovered by them a few weeks later, so I hope that mine has not wholly disappeared. We should certainly have bagged him but for those tigers having kept him "on the move" (and also delayed the pursuit) for he evidently wanted to lie down, as he leant against trees in one or two places. The quantity of blood he lost must have considerably weakened him; from the first to last I must have seen about two gallons of it along the trail.*

*H.H. Banks.*
*Gopeng, Perak,*
*5th January 1910*

POSTSCRIPT. – *Since writing the above I have been absent at Taiping on duty, but on my return to Gopeng a day or two ago I had the satisfaction of receiving from the Peng-hulu of Bidor a telegram containing the welcome news that the carcass of the Sladang had been found, though, as was to be expected, in a state of decay, only the skull and horns being fit to be kept. These were brought in and I sent for them; I am very glad to have them, and they are now being cleaned and prepared for mounting. The Sakai who found the carcass described it as a "good big bull." I have measured the horns and find them to be 36 inches from tip to tip, across the forehead; they are not long but thick, being 12 inches around the base, and I should judge the animal to have been about five years old. I am hoping for better luck next time and to be able to secure a good head for preservation whole, which I fell pretty sure I should have succeeded in doing on this occasion but for the hindrance to which I have referred.*

*H.H. BANKS,*
*18th January, 1910*


## PERAK

Perak is the second largest state on the Malay Peninsular in Malaysia. It is hot and the humidity usually exceeds 80% and therefore somewhat testing for hunters. 10,713 sq. km, that is almost half of the total area of the state, is covered with forest. It began as a state under Sultans descended from Sultan Shah of Malacca in 1528. In 1848 tin was found in Larut and the state became rich and interesting. Natural rubber was, and still is, an important product.

British interest in Malaya commenced in the early 19th century when the British East India Company established settlements in Penang and Singapore and bought the trading port of Malacca from the Dutch. The three settlements were grouped together as "The Straits Settlements", a colony with its Governor in Singapore.

In the 1870s and 80s 'internal strife' in some of the neighbouring states caused their rulers to seek British help and protection, although to some it may appear that the British were not loathe to be asked. In this period treaties were signed with the states of Perak, Selagor, Negri Sembilan and Pehang which became protectorates and were each given an advisor or 'Resident'. In Perak the British intervened through the Pangkor Treaty in 1874 after a riot in Larut. James W. Birch was appointed as the first Resident but was assassinated in 1875 in an uprising under the leadership of Datuk Maharaja Lela. However the Residential system continued until the arrival of the Japanese in 1941.

In 1900 the four states formed the "Federation of Malay States" under a Resident General in Kuala Lumpur. The other states in the Malay Peninsular remained outside British influence until 1909, at the time that Banks was hunting his Sladang in Perak, when Siam signed the Treaty of Bangkok relinquishing some of the Northern Sates to Britain. The process was complete when all the States had come under the British Residential System in 1930. Malaya had not, therefore, been a unified Colony for long before the Japanese Invasion. It was to undergo the further upheavals caused by Communist terrorists from 1948 until the end of the 'Emergency' in 1954. Malaya was 'granted' independence in 1957.

## THE SLADANG OR GAUR - AN ENDANGERED SPECIES

This species of large oxlike animals is now very rare in their homelands of India, Indochina and South East Asia. The Gaur, or as Banks says Sladang, has been hunted for sport for generations and its habitat of forest, bamboo jungle and grassland has been diminished severely by man. The combination of habitat loss and hunting has reduced the world population to roughly 36,000, according to the World Conservation Union–IUCN Red Book. It is listed as an endangered species and the Convention of International Trade in Endangered Species has banned the trade in live Gaur or Gaur products.

According to the magazine "Cloning", Advanced Cell Technology of Worcester Mass. USA has recently made an attempt to reproduce a Gaur by cloning. It is possible that Biotechnology, much dreaded as it is in some quarters, may prove the only way of redressing the errors of mankind and preserving endangered species. It remains to add that the current cloning techniques (nuclear transfer) are open to scientific criticism in that they are unable, apparently, to deal with the problem of passing on mitochondrial DNA.

## 1910 - ASSAM

## OUT TO A TEA ESTATE

## HARRY COX

*Kuturi Tea Estate, Assam.*
*15th November 1910*

*Dear Dr. Eppstein,*

*I am now quite settled down. I reached Calcutta on November 1st, and left there for Kuturi on the 2nd. Whilst in Calcutta I saw the Eden Gardens where the band plays every day at this time of the year, and also the Red Road. In the cool of the evening everyone goes for a drive. I had, on leaving Calcutta, a five days trip up the Brahmputra. There I saw alligators; most of the alligators stretched out on the sand banks, looked exactly like pieces of rock. I also saw many kinds of birds, such as paddy birds, vultures, innumerable crows, cranes and pelicans with their peculiar hatchet-shaped bills. The steamer's calling stations are called 'ghats' here. Our first call of importance was Duhbri Ghat. It looked very nice with its bungalows belonging to the padre, doctor and commissioner of police. It has also a very fine though of course small, English Church. Our next important stop was Gauhati, where the government of Assam is carried on. Gauhati is a fine example of the up-country stations. Whilst there I saw the volunteers at work; practically every planter is attached to a volunteer corps. The next stop after Gauhati was a place called Mangeldai. Here are many tigers and leopards in the jungle. After leaving we came to Tezpur, meaning City of Blood; here it was that the Burmese beat in a very decisive fashion the Assamese. During the war with the Burmese, who have lately taken to cocaine, so many Assamese were killed as to leave Assam with scarcely any population. Assam is now getting populated by coolies coming over to help the tea planters, and staying here. The Assamese are far too lazy to work. The Assamese are distinguished from the rest by the fact of their being so light in comparison with the other natives. At last we reached the tea estate which consists of 1,200 acres, 350 of which are under grant. The tea-house here is fitted up in a very modern way. From one part of the garden the snowy peaks of the Himalayas can be seen. It is awfully interesting to trace the seed to the germinating bed, from the germinating bed to the nursery, from the nursery to the garden, until finally, after about five years, the leaf is plucked. The leaf after withering is carried to the tea-house. Pruning commences in another month. I hope the House succeeded in retaining their grasp of the Rugger Cup, and that the School XV has had a successful season. Please remember me to Mrs Eppstein and Miss Fenn. There is a very fine orchard here. Bananas, pineapples, guavas and mangos are very plentiful, whilst in the kitchen garden there are plenty of cauliflowers, cabbages, turnips, carrots, mustard and radishes. The home domestic fowl runs wild here. In the Kuturi villages there are the coolly houses, hospital and native shop. Every Monday there is a market for the natives. Shop keepers bring their things miles to attend. Hill men often walk miles with three bamboo mats which they sell for 2 annas (2d) each. The hill men are practically savages, going about when in the hills nude, but on entry into Assam the law compels them to enter a certain place and there receive clothes , which on their return they have give up. Please remember me to Mr Newport and Mr Belcher and the other Masters. Hoping you will have a Merry Christmas and a Properous New Year.*

*Yours very sincerely*
*Harry Cox.*

*There is any amount and any sort of shooting and fishing to be obtained here, and also a very good deal of tennis and polo.*

## ASSAM AND THE TEA BUSINESS AND THE CITY OF BLOOD

Assam was ceded to the British by Burma in 1827 and was taken over by India at independence despite the vigorous opposition of Pakistan, which wished to claim it for what was then East Pakistan. There had been a great influx of labour from Bengal to work the tea plantations and related trades. It was divided into the seven Northeastern Hill States in 1960. It is surrounded by China, in particular the Tibet Autonomous Republic, and Bhutan on the west, Myanmar, once Burma, on the east and Bangladesh to the south. A "Chicken Neck" of land, 20 kms wide between Bhutan and Bangladesh, joins it to India. The Indian Military keep a nervous eye on matters and it is now difficult to visit. Assam itself now consists of the low-lying valley of the Brahmaputra while the other six states occupy the surrounding hills.

The mighty Bhramaputra, one of the great rivers of Asia, dominates Assam. It rises on the slopes of Kalesh, a sacred mountain in western Tibet and wends its way via Assam to the Bay of Bengal via Bangladesh.

Tea was first discovered growing wild in Manipur, a princely state in Harry's time, in the east of Assam bordering on Burma. From that state considerable quantities of seeds were exported. Nowadays Assam produces over half of India's tea from its 800 estates. They were mostly laid down by the British during the Raj and are well served by roads, and golf courses! When Harry Cox was starting in the Tea planting business, India was said to be producing about 370 million pounds of the stuff. Assam contained, according to best reports, about 900 tea "gardens" and an 'out-turn' of 230 million pounds. of manufactured tea. The average 'out-turn' of manufactured tea per acre was about 600 pounds and there was 0.77 acre under tea for each unit of labour. Harry makes the point, though with colonial overtones, that the labour question was one of great importance in Assam where the area was large and the population sparse.

Harry was not quite correct when he stated that Tezpur means City of Blood. In fact Tezpur stands on the site of Sonyipur, the City of Blood, which, according to legend was the site of a battle between Krishna and the local ruler, King Asura. The latter had imprisoned Krishna's grandson because he had married his daughter secretly. Krisna is said to have released his grandson from prison and the lovers lived happily ever after.

## 1911 - LAHORE, THE PUNJAB

### WORKING FOR THE CIVIL AND MILITARY GAZETTE. KIPLING'S OLD NEWSPAPER.

### EDWIN HAWARD

Edwin Haward left Reading School in 1902 having been a School Prefect and on the School Magazine Committee under the editorship of the Rev. A.D.H. Allan. He was also Hon. Sec. of the Debating Society. It is interesting to note that in the debate reported in the December 1902 issue of the School Magazine, E. Haward moved the motion "That the pen is mightier than the Sword". At the end of the debate "the mover made a reply which probably harmed his own cause more effectively than any of those of his opponents and the motion being put was lost." Even so Haward eventually became the Manager of the Civil and Military Gazette and used his pen to some effect.

The following appeared in the April 1911 issue of the Reading School Magazine.

*Mr. M.S. Waller, OR., has sent us the following letter from E. Haward, which will doubtless interest contemporaries of his:*

> *Lahore,*
> *9th February 1911.*
>
> *My Dear Waller,*
>
> *I was very pleased to get your letter, which was forwarded to me from London. I thought I wrote telling you I had "chucked up" the L.C.C. for journalism, and I am here on the staff (managerial) of the Civil and Military Gazette, Kipling's old paper. I have now been here a little over a year and I like the life – although the work is hard – immensely.*

*I am afraid we shall not be able to meet and have that little talk you mentioned for some time as I do not expect – if things go well – to be round your way again for some years.*

*By-the-bye, is there any news of the Allans? I have written to Mr. Allan twice, but had no reply.*

*The climate in Lahore is one of great extremes, varying from 120 degrees in the shade in July to 19 degrees in December. We get very little rain, but the cold is very trying to one after having gone through the then hot weather months. I had a fortnight in the Himalayas in August (Mussoorie) on leave and in November I had a business tour – combined with pleasure! ! – which took me to Karachi, thence by sea to Bombay, thence to Calcutta and back again to Lahore, after having travelled nearly 5,000 miles in twenty-six days. You get plenty of varied sport here. This week for instance, I was riding and playing golf on Sunday, playing "rugger" on Monday, cricket on Tuesday and tennis yesterday. Hockey and "soccer" also form part of my sporting repertoire with dancing four nights in the week. Next Tuesday, the "Ten of Clubs" – ten bachelors – give the dance of the season – fancy dress.*

*I have joined the Punjab Light Horse and we go into camp in a week's time. It is more a social affair than anything else.*

*I get very slack with my correspondence: it is such an effort to take up a pen after writing all day.*

*Yours sincerely,*

*EDWIN HAWARD.*

*P.S. – Do you remember Farquarson? He is often in Lahore. How is School?*

In the April 1916 edition of the Reading School Magazine the following notice appeared:

*'EDWIN HAWARD (1900-1902 VI.M.). 2ⁿᵈ Lieut. 1ˢᵗ Punjab Volunteer Rifles, has been promoted to the managership of the Civil and Military Gazette, Lahore (Kipling's old paper)'.*

## THE CIVIL AND MILITARY GAZETTE

In 1882 Rudyard Kipling returned to India after completing his schooling at the United Services College, Westward Ho. He joined his parents as Lahore, in the Punjab, where his father was the principal of the Mayo School of Art and Curator of the Lahore Museum.

Lahore was the capital of the Punjab and the British Military maintained an infantry battalion and a battery of artillery in the military town of Mian Mir just across the canal from Lahore proper.

Lahore is indelibly marked on the minds of all who read 'Kim'. It is the place where the great and ancient bronze cannon, Zam-Zammah was found on which the urchin Kim 'sat, in defiance of municipal orders'.

Kipling went to work for the Civil and Military Gazette as Assistant Editor. He was still 16 years of age when he commenced his job and within weeks his editor went sick and he found himself in charge of the paper.

The Civil and Military Gazette had been founded some ten years before Kipling arrived by James Walker and William Rattigan, both of whom were the sons of soldiers who had remained in India after their service. When Kipling was there the Civil and Military was the newspaper arm of a large printing house housed in two sheds. The printing house had the contract for the provincial authorities of the Punjab and was thus thought to reflect the views of the Punjab Government. Its readership was mainly Army Officers and Government Servants who frequented the Punjab Club when off duty. It will also have included the Civil Engineers working for the Indian Public Works Department.

The editor was Stephen Wheeler, a tough man, in poor health. Wheeler drove Kipling hard but he stuck it out and went on, in 1887 to join the 'Pioneer' in Allhalabad, the other paper owned by Walker and Rattigan.

Kipling's first book of poems, "Departmental Ditties", was a collection of those which first appeared in the Civil and Military Gazette under the heading of "Bungalow Ballads". He also wrote about them in his book "Something of Myself" in a way which illuminates tension between the Editor and Manager of a newspaper.

*"They were made to ease the perpetual strife between the manager extending his advertising and my chief (the editor) fighting for his reading matter. They were born to be sacrificed. Rhukh Din the foreman would say; "Your poetry was good, sir, just coming proper length today. One third column, just proper."*

*(Ref: Charles Carrington 'Rudyard Kipling. His Life and Works. Penguin. p116)*

Kipling also wrote a number of "Page Turners" for the paper, which were collected together as "Plain Tales from the Hills".

# Chapter 4

## THE WEST

### THE USA

The one contribution from the USA, an account of prospecting in Colorado in 1894, is included because it is interesting. The USA had long ago fought for and achieved its independence from Britain. Reading School has little record of contributions made by its old boys to the establishment and government of the 13 British colonies, which existed at the time of the American Revolution. However, it shares with Eton the doubtful honour of hastening the defeat of the British Army by the revolutionary army in Carolina in 1781 through the incompetence of one of its notorious Old Boys, Colonel George Hanger, 4th Baron Coleraine.

On the September 25th, 1780 George Hangar was a Major in the British Army fighting against the Americans. He was leading the British Legion, the most dreaded of all the British units in the war, and was sent with them to attack the town of Charlotte, then occupied by a small force of Americans. He made a spectacular mess of it all. So badly did he fail that the retreat to Yorktown and the eventual surrender of the British by Cornwallis was hastened significantly.

George was the third son of Gabriel, Lord Coleraine, and grew up sampling the country women and avoiding study. His father eventually packed him off to Reading School as a pupil of Spicer. He interrupted the academic routine of the school so much that he was regularly beaten with a rattan cane. In the end Spicer was forced to expel him and he eventually ended up at Eton where he was said to have learned more about the local women than about Latin Grammar. After his spectacular failure at Charlotte he reached the rank of Colonel and succeeded to his title. He went on to become the friend of the Prince of Wales though he was too rude and reckless even for that connoisseur of human eccentricity.

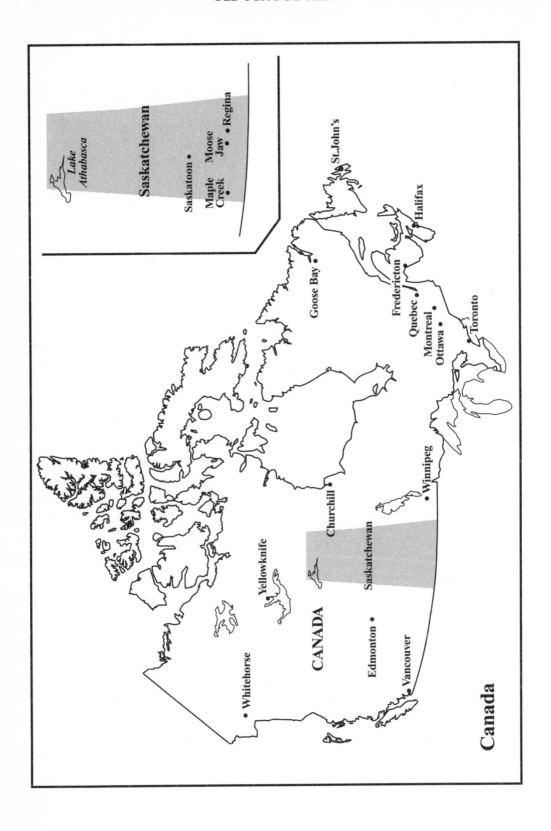

## CANADA

The contributors from Canada write at a time when the West was won by hardy pioneers and enterprising farmers. The problem with Canadian History, like the problem with Canada, is that it differs between its French and its British versions. The problem is alive today, as it was when our contributors were writing, in that the Quebecois are still restive and seek independence.

There are three contributions from Seskatchewan and one from Ontario, but they present a picture of a Canada in the process of becoming a nation. It has always been part of a frontier and men have always struggled against the odds to tame it. It now comprises 3,845,000 square miles and extends from the Pacific to the Atlantic. The geographical boundaries run along north south lines and the inhabited regions appear to be continuous with those of the USA. The "pull of the South" is thus not only economic but also geographic.

To build a nation called Canada, the politicians in Ottawa had to think in terms of East-West communications and thus they gave a huge amount of their energies to building the railways, which would eventually connect Vancouver in the west to the Maritime provinces in the East.

In order to build the railways, without going to the south of the Great Lakes and hence into the USA, the engineers had to overcome the formidable obstacle presented by the Canadian Shield, the massive sheet of granite which extends from Hudson's Bay in the north right down to the Great Lakes in the south. It makes for a land of forest, sphagnum bog, lakes, rivers in deep gorges to bridge and high mountains to tunnel through. The major achievement of the civil engineers and surveyors in driving railways across it are illustrated in the letter from D.H.Wells in 1913.

Three of the contributors wrote from the province of Saskatchewan. Together with Manitoba, Saskatchewan comprises a region commonly called the prairies. These are flat treeless plains confined to southern Canada. The prairies are divided into two regions. The semi-arid short grasslands, which border the USA, and the crescent shaped wheat-growing belt to the north.

The temperatures in the winter in these regions are fierce, as there is little shelter between them and the arctic north. Our contributors write about that hazard vividly and they must have been hardy souls to live through the winters in their wooden houses. The one story about the nail, which protruded through the cabin wall and became encrusted in ice on the inside, is an excellent example of what extreme climatic conditions they had to put up with.

That they achieved so much is a great tribute to their hardiness and enterprise but there was a cost and the debt will be hard to repay. As result of the white influx the nomadic culture of the Plains Indians, the Blackfoot Federation and the Cree, was destroyed. The survivors, disease ravaged and half-starved, who had lost their livelihood with the near demise of the bison, were herded into reservations. Though the Canadian treatment of the Indans was marginally better than the Americans to the south, it left much to be desired and is only now receiving some attention.

The Métis, descendants of French fur traders and their Indian wives, who for more than two centuries had acted as intermediaries between the two cultures, found themselves overwhelmed. In an attempt to save their nation they raised two futile rebellions under the leadership of Louis Riel. The last of these took place in Saskatchewan in 1885.

The end of the Riel rebellion opened a new phase in the conquest of the west. The first train from Montreal to Vancouver ran in 1886. Settlers rushed into the prairies and the population rose from 250,000 in 1890 to 1,300,000 in 1911. These immigrants from Europe, including a great number from Eastern Europe, turned central Canada into a vast granary.

Old boys of Reading School were encouraged to go to Saskatchewan because Myles Cooper Bolton, the brother in law of the Head Master, The Reverend Charles Eppstein, owned a ranch near Maple Creek. He readily accepted boys as hands on the ranch and one of the Masters, Percy Newton, worked there as a cook during his long vacation. It is the story of the Prairie Fire which ties the history of the school and Saskatchewan together.

Unfortunately Myles Bolton was killed in a railway accident in 1909.

> 'We deeply regret to announce the sad death of Mr Myles Cooper Bolton, Mrs Eppstein's brother, in a railway accident near Moosejaw, Saskatchewan on November 23rd 1909. The circumstance was the more pathetic in that Mr Bolton was intending to come to England for Christmas after an absence of 11 years. By a curious coincidence an article appears in this number by a Schoolmaster, Percy Newton, who had for the nonce been serving as a cook on Mr Bolton's ranch. Several Old Boys who have gone to Canada have owed their start to the help given by Mr. Bolton; Temple is now in charge at the ranch.'

*Magazine December 1909.*

## NORTH AMERICA

### USA, COLORADO: MINERS IN WINTER QUARTERS.

### SKURRAY (MAJOR)

This story about prospectors in the Colorado Mountains must have been written with some insight. However before reading it we might note the following report which is said to have appeared in Harper's Magazine some years ago. "The students of the University of Colorado have named their Student Union dining room the Alfred E. Packer Grill – after the only American ever convicted of cannibalism. Packer, a gold prospector, killed and ate his five companions when snowbound throughout the winter in the Colorado mountains. Sentencing him to death, the judge, a Democrat, is supposed to have said: "There were only seven Democrats in Hinsdale County, and you, Alfred E. Packer, you greedy son of a bitch, have eaten five of them".
Letter to the Times. 1894

This article appeared in the December 1894 edition of the Reading School Magazine.

*Today some 50,000 Colorado Miners are actively preparing to go into winter quarters. For while the warm October sun is flooding the valleys and plains with summer-like heat, thirteen and fourteen hundred feet above the sea, above the timber line, away up where not even moss can be coaxed to grow upon the barren rock, the snow is already lying six inches deep, and the reign of King Winter is nearly set in. It is there that the adventurous who, in pairs or by threes, cut into some outcropping vein which the storms of ages have laid bare in the eternal rock. It is there that they have their little cabin of mud-chinked pine; there they have a darksome tunnel running into the side of the precipitous peak, which rises yet a thousand more feet into the sky. To these aerial retreats the miners are now by toilsome efforts packing upon their own backs and the back of the faithful burro or donkey the fuel and food which will supply them with the means of sustaining life through the long months of isolation which they will follow. The Colorado miners who are working upon these lofty claims make almost as deliberate preparations for the cold season as would explorers in the Arctic regions. Experience has taught them the winter, once fairly begun, they have little or no hope of communication with the world below until the sun of early summer has unlocked the icy gates of the walls which are closed around them. And it is none too early now that the bacon and corn, meal and potatoes, and indispensable tea, together with tobacco and simple condiments are stored away in the low roofed cabin. Fuel in liberal quantities too must be piled up within arm's reach of the door of the hut, or the mouth of the tunnel. The miner's cabin at these dizzy heights is not built with a view to the sightliness of the location; rather, if such a place can be obtained, it is constructed under the protection of a rocky ledge: and if no such natural formation is found, an artificial quarry is blasted out from the mountain side, and the little abode is placed there. The terrible snow slide is the ever-menacing dread of the lonely seekers after fortune. Last year over a hundred, and a few years ago three hundred miners were swept away to their deaths by the avalanche. Already this fall two victims have been found in the serried region of the Silver San Juan. To guard against these catastrophes the cabins are hidden from view from above, and if the slide does come, at the worst it can only bury beneath its glacial mass the little abode within which the prospectors find refuge.*

*There are in Colorado very high mines, which are in constant operation during the winter, when the men are able to obtain fresh supplies and their mail by tramways, on which one is carried to the railroad tracks or the wagon roads which are kept open. But the men who are labouring in twos and threes to develop new properties which they fondly dream will make their fortunes, find when the days of November arrive, that, alive or well, sick or dead, they are banished from all intercourse with the rest of mankind unless it be by the hazardous method of snow shoe travel upon the treacherous crust of deep piled snow. One of the most highly developed and operated properties is the Sheridan mine, 14,000 feet above the sea. It is in the red mountain district of the San Juan. And yet all around this mine are the prospects as high or higher, where men of brave hearts and brawny arms are now industriously preparing to endure at least seven months of voluntary exile.*

*But it must not be supposed that this isolated existence is in any sense hibernating. It is rather a season of most industrious and unremitting labour. The tunnel which may have been pushed into the mountain side but a few yards is driven on and on, until the grey streak of shining metal, which is found cropping out hundreds of feet above, is reached, and it is demonstrated that from that point up to the surface a true fissure vein exists, and that it goes downward for an unknown depth below. Then the two or three men, who have toiled with the pick and drill through all the weary months and perhaps years, grasp each other by the hand while they laugh and cry alternately, and send up cheer after cheer to echo along the rocky heights and be heard by the silent crags alone. The reward for the exile, for the labour, for the isolation, for the sustenance of the poorest fare has come. The "Bonanza King" or the "Mary Jane" or the "Golden Queen," is no longer a hope; it is a fact. The ore is in sight, and the men who are looking at it know that only their own folly can take it from them now. It was this way that the Colonel Seller's mine at Leadville was struck. It is now a well- known mine producing property with an annual output of over $1,000,000. The discoverers of this property worked ceaselessly for three years. They were exposed to great dangers and encountered untold privations. Not the least of the problems of the lives of these peculiarly intrepid and determined men is how to procure their winter supplies. It is this which is now causing many a shaggy-bearded fellow in this State to scratch his head. About 100 pounds of bacon,*

*500 pounds of flour, 100 pounds of potatoes, 10 pounds of tea, 25 pounds of sugar, and a quantity of salt and other small items are needed to carry a man who labours through this period of exile. Comparatively small as is the amount of money required to purchase this, the not over provident prospector is by no mean sure to have it. It is here that the "grub-stake" plan becomes a feature of the mining industry. The keeper of a store in the most accessible camp is solicited to part with the necessary provisions, and in return receives a contract that an interest in the property to be worked is his. Not a few very wealthy mine owners in Colorado owe to their ventures in this way all they now possess. It cannot be said that the prospector is naturally a thief, but in emergencies of this kind his code of morals does not recognise the appropriation of the necessities of life as theft. Thus it happens that oftimes a good many sacks of corn-meal and many a side of bacon disappear in a most mysterious manner from the occasionally unprotected confines of the mine-camp stores. There may be nothing heard of the matter afterwards, but the instances are not infrequent of a decidedly surprised store-keeper finding in his mail a registered letter containing the money for articles of an edible nature which he had missed, and had never been able satisfactorily to account for.*

*The rigours of the winters at these elevated prospects and in the higher mining camps among the mountains of Colorado are but faintly appreciated; and perhaps less by the people who live even within sight of the great peaks of the back-bone of the Continent than by others. For in the valleys where the elevation is not more than 7,000 feet and upon the eastern slope of the range, no more delightful winter climate can be imagined. Comparatively light falls of snow, many cloudless and bright warm days, and a freedom from cutting winds are all characteristics of a Colorado winter in the more populous cities and towns. But up in the mountains the snow even now is two feet in depth. It is not unusual for it to fall and lie at a depth of eight or ten feet on a level. Ruby Camp is populated by 300 miners. It is in the Elk mountain region, and surrounded by some of the loftiest peaks on the Continent. Last winter the camp was snowed under, and the cabins were all covered. Efforts to keep the thoroughfare clear were futile almost from the beginning of the snow-fall. The imprisoned inhabitants gave up the idea of open communication and ran tunnels. It became in a few days literally a town of tunnels, every man had his tunnel to the saloon he chiefly favoured and the store he patronised. It was light enough by day, and withal, not uncomfortable. No more curious condition of affairs ever existed; the people lived through three months of this kind of existence. The fuel, fortunately, held out, and there were large stores of provisions to draw from. The curious fact, also, is recorded that not a death from natural causes occurred during the whole time these buried-up miners were thus shut out, except for some circular openings, from the light of day.*

*In the mountains, where the great altitude of 12,000 and 14,000 feet is reached by the prospectors, the cold is intense. The temperature experienced by Greeley and his party at Lady Franklyn Bay was no more severe than that braved by many hundreds and even thousands of prospectors, who toil to reach the mineral wealth of the State. It is not uncommon, consequently for the cabin to be abandoned and existence to be continued for weeks at a time within the mining tunnels. With proper guards at the mouth of the tunnel it is comfortable enough, and only the darkness is objectionable. But these bluff, tough, rough, honest and infrequently cultured men toil through their working hours, fry the bacon and cook the "dodger" and the flap-jack, smoke their pipes with philosophical contentment as they rest after their meal on the rough skin covered bunks, playing poker and "seven up" with as much zest as if they were gambling in earnest, and go to sleep with the same soundness that they would enjoy amid a city's comforts.*

*The isolation possesses its peculiar charms as well as other unusual modes of life. Old prospectors who have "struck it" and feel perforce, that they should live where the world does, often sigh for the long days of absolute separation from all the world but some one or two faithful "pards" It makes these men, too, particularly tender and generous of heart. They know that exiled as they are from the world it will not do to quarrel. If one is sick the other waits upon him and nurses him like a woman. They have no need for money, and it gradually loses for them its standard value. Their thoughts are upon thousands not units; and for the single dollar they acquire a pleasing contempt. Still it is not strange that when, released by the rays of the May's sun which melt the icy prison gates, they reach civilisation's domains again, they are carried away by the excitement the unusual contact causes and proceed to "paint her red."*

*The conceits of the men who are thus "cooped up" are sometimes ludicrous. Last winter in the Red Mountain district three prospectors were smoking their pipes and talking, after the day's work was done, of what they would do when they reached the "bonanza" they were after. One said, "Well, I'll tell you what boys, I'm going back to Michigan to get mother, and then I'm going to New York, an' the first place I strike'll be Delmonico's, an' I'm going to get something to eat." "What would you eat now, if you should go there?" asked one of his "pards." He studied for a long while, and finally he said, "Well, I'll tell you. I'd just take two orders of ham and eggs."*

*Another class of people who are not infrequently made prisoners by winter in Colorado are the mountain ranchmen. Their experiences, however, during these months are by no means as severe. They suffer far less hardships than fall to the lot of the ranchmen of the plains. In comfortable cabins, usually blessed by wives and children, and content in the consciousness that their cattle are sheltered in friendly "draws" and canyons from very cold winds, and sure to obtain abundant food. The lot of a mountain stock-raiser is not an unhappy one. He can generally, too, keep the larder well supplied with game, and though the canyons are deep, there is plenty of resinous pine and dry quaking-asp for his cheerful fireplace. Through his enforced rest he becomes invigorated and has time for reading, which does not come to the constant worker in the town. In the spring his work begins, and through the warmer months his faithful ponies carry him over and around the range, gathering, branding, and disposing of the saleable members of his herd.*

*But his is the business of slow and steady growth. The prospector is the one who hunts during the short summer of the mountain peaks that he may toil through the winter. If he "strikes it" he is "fixed." If he doesn't he tries it again the following year.*

## 1903 - CANADA, NORTH WEST TERRITORIES

### F. BARROBY

Football XI. 1900

(Note: Part of the North West Territories became Saskatchewan in 1905)

Magazine April 1901
'F.Barroby, *who went out to Canada a year ago to learn ranching, seems to be enjoying the life immensely and finds riding buck-jumpers a most elevating pursuit; also, it would seem, intellectually stimulating, furnishing occasionally practical illustrations of the accuracy of Sir Isaac Newton's reasoning. He intends shortly starting a ranch of his own and would be glad of any old school-fellows, who would care to join him'.*

The following appeared in the December 1903 edition of the School Magazine:

*Letters from F. Barroby have been kindly handed to the Editor for perusal. With the owner's permission we print his account of his life:*

*I have been having a pretty easy time since haying; lately I have been fixing the buildings up for winter, i.e. mudding and stopping up any little cracks in the mud. You see, buildings here are made with logs, pieces of wood being made to fix in between them and then mud is put inside and out. After which a wash is made of white mud to fill up any little cracks in the mud when dry. I shot a coyote today quite near the shack.... I had a week's holiday a little while ago and went to Maple Creek for the fair, which consists of a show of live-stock and horse races. The latter were good; in the half mile there was a little girl of about fourteen riding, and one of the half breeds, in for the race as well, tried to crowd her horse off the course, so she slammed his horse over the fence and had him quit the race. I thought it was awfully plucky of her. Those half-breeds are a low down lot. If they get a chance to roll a fellow off anything they will. The Indian race was good as well; they paint themselves up for the occasion and scorch round the track on their ponies to beat the band. All the squaws troop up from the camp in blankets of all colours to watch and sit on their haunches in the most solemn way. The one wrong impression one gets in the old country about the Indian is that he is thought to be a sort of worrier flying about the place with a tomahawk, &c. He is very different in reality. A whole heap of them are kept on preservations down east, and those up here would not touch a fly. Their ferociousness ended in '85-'86 in Riel's rebellion (I expect you have heard of it) when the half-breeds and Indians revolted, Riel, the leader was hanged in the end. Then in the fair there was a cowboy race in which there was a lot of tearing about to show the best cowhorses. ... I hope to get a small bunch of cattle next Spring. ... I can give them to somebody to run for me until I start up for myself. The cost of putting them out is three dollars per head per year; the cost comes in the hay they eat in the long winter; for after a very bad blizzard sometimes the whole bunch has to be fed on hay which is no light thing when there are two hundred or so of them. Of course young stock if they come from the east are fed on hay straight through the winter, these are called "dogies" and if I get any I think I would get these. An animal is worth about forty-five to fifty dollars here when it is ready to be sent to England for beef, and one can buy yearlings about eighteen or twenty dollars. They go when they are three years old, of course some of the "dogies" only fetch forty dollars, they are not as good as cattle bred up. ..... Come out here, it is not half such a bad life and not half so rough as people in England make out. ...*

Magazine December 1904
*F. Barroby paid a flying visit to the School in November. He spoke of meeting with some old school-fellow (was it J.H. Temple?) and singing lustily on the prairie 'Floreat Redingensis' though not a soul could hear them.*

## 1907 - CANADA

### FRENCHMAN'S CREEK SASKATCHEWAN

### F. BARROBY

The following appeared in the July 1907 issue of the School Magazine:

*F.D. Corry, has just gone out to Canada to join F. Barroby, who is ranching at Frenchman's Creek Sask.: and has received two letters from the latter, from which, with Corrie's leave, we cull the following: -*

*In sizing up the country I might say it is the absolute essence of free and easiness, it is rather (some people would say VERY) lonely, it is very healthy, there is practically no sport except shooting, the people are very hospitable, mosquitoes are very bad, but they say this is mild compared to other parts of Canada. The winters are long and sometimes severe ... It went down to 36 degrees below zero last week. Work is pretty hard in summer and very easy in winter. The riding part is not so wild and woody as people think in England.... A fellow in this country wants three things; a bed, bought here preferably, or if bought in England blankets must be grey (or red) no sheets. ... A horse and saddle. ... There are four OR's in this district. Temple, Whitworth, Howland and self. Seaward was here 1905-6 and I believe is in Winnipeg now. Temple is with Bolton, Whitworth at Crane Lake, 35 miles from here ... I have only Howland with me now.... there is always a lots of work on a ranch: ploughing, riding, fixing fences and corrals, &c. ...This is more or less of an open country, and people drop in when they want ... Maple Creek is a fairly prosperous town.... it has three churches, four saloons and two banks ... I would advise you to bring out some good pipes if you smoke; camera if you go in for it, any musical instrument and shotgun if you have one.*

F. Barroby had carved out a life for himself in the prairies. The two contributions he makes to the magazine show that he had established himself as a rancher between 1903 and 1907. The letters straddle the time when Saskatchewan became a province rather than a part of the North West Territories, an event that occurred in 1905. His attitude to the "Indians" and the "half-breeds" is not unusual for the time and deserves some further thought.

## THE PLAINS INDIANS, THE MÉTIS AND RIEL'S REBELLIONS

### The Plains Indians

The original inhabitants of Saskatchewan were the Cree, whose territory was mainly to the north of the Saskatchewan River and the Blackfoot Federation who kept mainly to the south. They were buffalo hunters and their livelihood diminished as the herds were wiped out by white hunters who were ruthless and indiscriminate killers.

There was great battle in 1869-70 between the Blackfoot and the Cree at Cyprus Hills, a few miles west of the Barroby ranch. Both tribes were exhausted by their rivalry and further demoralized by the adulterated whisky that the American traders sold them. In fact the country area around the Barroby ranch was often called 'Whoop-up Country' because of the activities of the whiskey traders.

The Métis were the descendents of the early French fir traders and their Cree wives though some of the Scots who worked for the Hudson's Bay Company sired some children in like manner.

### Louis Riel

In 1869-70 Louis Riel led a rebellion of the Métis in the Red River district of Manitoba. He won many concessions for his people but was unable to protect the Métis way of life against the flood of white settlers. He went to the USA and many Métis moved to the west. They made homesteads on the banks of the South Saskatchewan River and worked as intermediaries between the Indians and the whites. They were horse traders, horse breeders, translators and small farmers.

In 1871 government surveyors arrived ahead of the railways and commenced to divide up the Métis country into lots for white immigrants. The Métis felt that they were back in the same situation as they were in 1878 and became discontented.

This sense of unease spread to the Plains Indians. The white settlers were also agitated by the high freight charges levied on their produce by the railways though they did not join the Metis and the Indians in the subsequent armed rebellion.

The Métis leadership sent for Louis Riel who was in Montana, south of the Canadian border. Riel had become carried away by religious fervor and he thought that the Mètis were god's chosen people and that he was their Messiah. Consequently, he was easily persuaded to travel to South Saskatchewan and lead a rebellion. He declared a provisional government based at Batoche and required the nearest Royal Canadian Mounted Police at Fort Carlton to surrender. The Mounties would do no such thing.

The Mètis attacked a small force of Mounties at Duck Lake. The Cree joined the uprising and attacked the Hudson's Bay Company store at Frog Lake. All this brought the Government Militia down on the rebels. The Militia, Louis Riel's Mètis and Big Bear's Cree met at Batouche. The rebels were beaten and Louis Riel taken to Regina for trial. He was found guilty of rebelling against the Crown, despite his obvious insanity, and executed on November 16th 1885. That was the end of the rebellion. The French Canadians in Quebec were extremely annoyed about the whole incident, which served to further divide the English and the French speaking Canadians.

## INDIAN RESERVATIONS

F. Barroby points out the Indians are placed on "preservations". The British North American Act made sweeping laws on behalf of the Indians and had the effect of replacing tribal government, confiscating valuable resources, changing the way in which land was "owned" and imposing western concepts of marriage and parenting on the tribes. The idea was to "Encourage the gradual civilization of the Indian tribes" and Indians of "good character" could be declared "non-Indian" by a panel of whites. There are records of only one Indian who was made into a "whiteman" in this way. The Sun Dance, a ceremony that was at the core of the culture of the prairie Indians, was outlawed.

Reservations were created and supervised by government Indian Agents. No outsider could come into a reservation without permission from the government and sometimes Indians were forbidden to leave. Indian communities were, at one time, moved from place to place by the government "for their own protection". Perhaps the most draconian thing was the creation of residential schools for Indian children. The government had decided that they could cure Indian savagery by taking children away from their families and putting them into residential schools where they could be westernized. The tribal languages and customs were suppressed and the family relationships between hundreds of Indian children and their families were jeopardized.

## 1912 - CANADA

### ELFROS - SASKATCHEWAN

### F. BLACK

The following appeared in the School Magazine December 1912:

*Dear Mr Williams*

*A letter received a short time ago from Costin has brought home to me that I must write at once to the School Magazine as I am rather keen to know how the Sports team gets on this winter. You can't imagine how I missed the games this fall. Nobody here is very keen on exercise of any sort.*

*There's an Irish chap in the office, and we are both considered pretty 'bughouse' (Canadian slang word for 'mad') because we bathed in the Creek, when it began to get cold and because we went for long walks. Now, however, we go out whenever we can for ducks and chicken (prairie chicken are like partridges).*

*We can get out sometimes at 4 or 4.15, if the work has been light that day, as we close doors at 3.o'clock, and then we take our guns and go about an hour or two. That sounds nice doesn't it? If you don't feel inclined to carry a gun you can take a .22 repeater and shoot them as they sit on the piles of oats or wheat in the fields. Of course you don't get as many that way, and it isn't as satisfactory as a gun, as the birds get pretty wild near town and don't give you so many chances to shoot them sitting. As for ducks you have to go to the sloughs about 7 o'clock in the morning and earlier in the evening. The evenings are the best time, because you can get them during their evening flights before they settle down for the night. I expect I shall go out goose shooting next Sunday. They are a lot harder to shoot than the ducks, as you have just to get under cover and wait for them to come along. Sunday is the day for shooting in the West. There are usually four or five parties out in rigs on Sunday. They get a rig to hold four and then cram another person in as well. The hotel-keeper here won the championship shoot of Canada this year, and he and his friends, making a party of three or four, go out sometimes, Friday night or Sunday morning early and come back Monday with 200 to 300 ducks.*

*The town, that is the name given to it by the inhabitants, consists of a population of 103, according to the Canadian Pacific Railway time-table, with a tributary population of 2,500 consisting of farmers, as all the farmers for five or six miles around come in here for stores. There are three general stores, two hardware shops and two butchers. In the general stores you see* *preserves, clothing, tobacco, china, jewellery and fruit on the same counter. A good many store-keepers get most of their income from the interest on notes they hold. A man will buy a plow, not plough, and give the store-keeper a note for it. The other day I came across a note made out three years ago for about 23 dollars, (£5). It was due about three months or so after the date, but the man has only paid about $7 on it so far.*

*I've already heard tales of the winter, which sound pretty bad. You cannot, for instance, catch hold of a door-knob on the outside door in mid-winter with bare hands or they would freeze to it. If a nail projects into a room from outside, all the houses are made of wood here, the cold travels along the nail and you get a piece of nail inside the room white with frozen moisture.*

*After Xmas they get prairie wolves, the coyotes, round the town, and I've heard you can hear them howling just a hundred yards or so out of the place. If it is quiet, they come in and prowl around to see if they can pick up scraps. They are smaller than the timber wolf and are cowardly. In the North the hunters ride on horseback, and, when they see a wolf, surround him and drive him off the beaten track into softer snow, where the horse with its longer legs has the advantage, and then they can shoot it when they come up close.*

*Cattle (oxen) are used for farm purposes all over the West.....In all cases they guide the oxen by attaching ropes to their nose. This must be rather painful at first, I guess, but they all seem indifferent to it after.*

*Yours sincerely*

*F.Black.*

(Black was killed in action on the Western Front in 1915, see page 195).

## FINANCING THE PIONEERS

Between 1895 and 1914, the part of Saskatchewan, from whence F. Black writes, turned into the one of the most productive wheat growing areas of the world. It was converted from Prairie and Aspen parkland by hardy emigrants from Europe brought in by the opening up of the Canadian Pacific Railway.

Black draws attention to the second factor, which underpinned this remarkable achievement in agriculture. Of course the railway was essential to bring in goods and people. However, without money, the pioneers could not have survived. Credit extended by the storekeepers financed the farms and in turn the banks made their profits by lending to the stores.

## 1913 - CANADA, UNIONVILLE, ONTARIO

### RAILWAY CONSTRUCTION IN NORTHERN CANADA

### 'TYING IN THE RIGHT-OF-WAY'

### D.H. WELLS

*Unionville, Ontario,*
*24th September 1913.*

*Dear Dr. Eppstein,*

*I thought perhaps you might like to hear of the doings and whereabouts of your sometime scholar – hence this letter. I have just returned from a two months' trip in the North of Ontario and have enjoyed it immensely. I was one of a party of four engaged in what is known as "tying in the right-of-way," and we were working for the CNO Railway. This railway is completing a trans-Continental line and, of course, a great deal of surveying has to be done in connection with its construction, as well as in accordance with government regulations. We had about 170 miles of line to "tie in" and the last 100 miles was still in the hands of the contractors.*

*We moved camp about once a week and we were alongside the steel all the way. We had a handcar to enable us to move quickly and also to save packing our dunnage. I was for some unknown reason chosen as cook and my first meal was a trial to the other three, but a source of much amusement to myself. After a while I got along better and am now able to act as a rough kind of cook. I have had rabbits, partridges and fish to clean and cook; have made soups, the name of which I have decided on after tasting; have fried bacon, ham and eggs; and have made puddings of all kinds; but as we had no flour I couldn't venture into the realms of pastry. We had no fresh meat except the game we shot, and existed principally on pork and beans, and tinned salmon.*

*The hunting was good though, unfortunately, we had nothing but a .22 rifle, which was, of course, no good for big game. If we only had a heavier gun we would have got plenty of moose and deer, as they are plentiful in the North.*

*The construction trains are brutes to travel on. As an example, I may give you our last journey back. We started from Ballast Pit 5 at midnight Friday, and the 60 miles to Ruel took us 7 hours to do. We were in an old coach filled with garlic smelling Mohawks, seats with no backs and no springs and two miserable lamps for illumination. It is no surprise for the train to be half a day late and it often runs off the rails.*

*The scenery would be tiresome in the extreme were it not for the lakes, of which there are a large number. The fishing in most of them is good; we were trolling on lake Minniesinaqua and caught six pickerel and a pike in twenty minutes, just by going backwards and forwards in front of a clump of weeds; we had a strike every time and only missed two. It is these lakes which give the most wonderful sunset effects and to paddle on them as the sun is setting below the pines makes one quiet and thoughtful at the beauty of it all. And the moonlight effect is just wonderful, only one feels a little eerie and the minutest sounds magnified a hundred-fold.*

*The bush is very thick and travelling in it is hard and slow. When chaining you never know what is coming up next, a swamp up to your waist or hard rock steep and slippery. Fallen timber and soft yielding mushey make the going hard, and a mile through good thick bush is as bad as five in the open. I found the flies and mosquitoes very trying in the bush; if you once loose your temper and begin swearing you inevitably become demoralised by their attacks, but if you can treat them with patience, you can just manage to exist for an hour or two.*

*Men of every nationality are met up in the construction camps. "Mohawks," which include Scandinavians and, I believe, Austrians and the Slav races, "polahs" particularly applied to the Russians, and "dajoes" are Italians, while "hobos" are English-speaking tramps. The terms apparently are used indiscriminately and the exact classification is impossible. I haven't had any real adventure but my experiences have been novel. I have been hurled off the handcar when we were going about fifteen miles an hour and the wheels left the track; have been taken for a tramp and refused admittance to a boarding shack; have worked a "speeder" (a sort of tricycle running on the track) until my hands were so blistered I couldn't move the machine any longer; have slept in all manner of places, principally on the bare floor of some deserted shack; have been without shaving for six weeks; and done a lot of things I wouldn't dream of doing in the Old Country.*

*Most of the men I have met have been hard drinkers, strong swearers, and heavy smokers; missionary work amongst engineering contractor's camps wouldn't be a bad thing, but it would want some nerve on the part of the missionary.*

*I like the open air life very much and these trips have made me more able to do things for myself than before.*

*I am sorry to see that the amalgamation of the School with Kendrick is again threatened. I was a scholar at the Kendrick and so write with no ill will, but I always felt the difference between the two Schools is more a matter of the loyalty of the scholars than anything else. The Kendrick School has men to be proud of, but at the Old School I always felt a pride in and a sense of loyalty to the famous men of old which I never felt at Kendrick. I hardly see how any heart can fail to be stirred on Speech Day, with its special service for the praise of famous scholars of old, and with the constant allusions made to the grand tradition which is behind the School.*

*If I ever get on the honours board I shall be prouder of that than anything else, and even if I don't succeed in attaining that ambition, still I can act up to the traditions which were made part of my school life. Floreat Redingensis!*

*With kind regards to Mrs. Eppstein,*
*I remain,*
*Your sometime scholar,*
*D.H. WELLS.*

(Douglas Wells was killed in action on the Western Front on May 3rd 1917, see page 271).

## CANADA

### FIGHTING A PRAIRIE FIRE

### PERCY M. NEWTON

*'O Lord, we do not ask thee for shipwrecks, but if there is a shipwreck, let it be at Templemore Bay.' Such was the prayer of some ingenuous youths, full of faith, who were at school on the south coast of England. Much akin to this was the wish of my heart. I didn't want a prairie fire to happen for my benefit, but if there was one, I longed to see it, and to help fight it.*

*I had spent the summer on Myles Bolton's ranch, thirty-seven miles south-east of Maple Creek, Saskatchewan. Several times at night I had seen the glow of conflagrations and sniffed the smoky air of fires far away. Once in a heavy thunderstorm the lightning struck in five different places around the ranch. But I was within doors and quite unconscious of it. In a few minutes the rain descended in torrents and all was over. One hot August day I thought I really was to have the experience I longed for. Columns of smoke were seen rising just in line with where our outfit was lying on the bench. I saddled up, took four wet sacks, and rode out only to find that the fire was miles further on. So I had dinner with my friends and rode back again.*

*Not until the fall was my wish gratified. On the first of October I was riding on the bench with two friends, when we saw smoke of a fire to the north. The sight is not unusual, and as the fires had usually proved to be far out of our range, it made no particular impression upon us. But as we were sitting down to supper at seven o'clock, Bettington, a neighbouring rancher, arrived with the news that he was hunting up men to go and fight the fire. As Bolton and Bettington are both fire guardians, and can by law commandeer the services of all males over sixteen, we were in for it, though not unwillingly. One man being left behind to look after the ranch, a party of six proceeded to the stables to saddle up.*

*It was rather a weird sight, the catching of our horses in the corral, fitful rays of a single lantern occasionally being required to distinguish Ginger from Dick. Everybody was busy with bridles and bits, blankets and saddles, and the sacks were being served out and strapped behind the cantles; at length we were ready, and off we went into the night. Whither, I knew not! All was in the dark to me. Trails, familiar enough in daytime, had absolutely vanished. The derrick, even, as we swept past it, showed only for a moment against the sky line. But the responsibility of direction did not rest with me. I simply kept with the crowd, secretly grabbing the horn of my saddle during those first few moments, with an uncomfortable feeling of insecurity, and not knowing what was going to happen next.*

*A night ride of this description was altogether a new experience for me. But the feeling passed off, as gradually the outlines of my companions and their horses became more clear, and the ground proved not to be full of bottomless chasms, as was my first impression. The timidity of uncertainty passed away, and I became callous to hidden dangers. "Up the creek! Up the creek!" was the cry, and up the creek we went. Though if we had gone down the creek I shouldn't have known any difference. Crossing it near the old, and now deserted Police Department, I got left behind a bit. My horse took me somewhere through the bush, and eventually emerged into the open. Here I dashed straight ahead to find that I was alone. My comrades had missed me, and a few reciprocating shouts enabled me to find them again. They had turned sharp to the right outside the bush. In relating my experiences afterwards I declared that my horse had shied at a haystack, which had suddenly loomed up before me; but it appears that there was no haystack there! I hope, however, that my readers will not distrust this account of my adventures. "Things that are seen by candlelight are not the same by day."*

*Our horses began to enjoy the fun. Bolton was on a fine animal, Latigo, and set the pace. All our horses were good. I was riding Banjo, endeared to me by occasional acquaintance of his good qualities, though I once or twice in the early part of the ride gloomily reflected that he had, a few days previously, tried to buck an experienced rider off. He is, perhaps, a little inclined to be lazy, but once he took the bit between his teeth and dashed on beyond the rest, quite distastefully to me. When I managed to rein him in and wait for the others, Bolton's remark to me that I had better not try to race, as the ground was very uncertain, was a little wide of the mark if he had but known it.*

*About four miles on we left the creek and wended out way through a coulee up on to the bench. There we could see that the fire was a big one. Its glow lighted up the sky for miles. I confidentally expected to see the actual flames after surmounting the next rise. But many rises were to pass beneath our horse's feet before we reached our destination. We were travelling fast, galloping or quick trotting over the prairie, walking only when we came to unexpected coulees, making straight for the western point of the line of the fire. I, a novice in the art of riding, began to feel pretty sore. Occasionally I lagged behind, but Howland and Barry were very good, and falling behind too, would urge my horse at a quick lope until we caught up with the others.*

*When we started it was generally supposed that the fire was about ten miles distant. But it proved to be fifteen. As we neared it the darkness was dispelled and the night grew light except in the deep shadows of the coulees. My trouser legs and undergarments had crawled up to my knees, and the calves of my legs got a fine scratching in the bush just before we crossed the creek.*

*Half a mile beyond we got our first sight of the fire. It was a magnificent spectacle. The first impression I received was that of an extravagantly well-lighted city in a smoky fog. For the edges of the fire were running in long lines in every possible direction, and at different heights according to the rise and fall of the ground. Smoke tempered all and at one place we seemed to pass under a huge verandah of it.*

*We rode along the line for about a couple of miles seeking for the fighters. Suddenly Bolton's horse put its foot into a badger hole, stumbled to its knees and then rose again like a camel. I didn't like the look of that much. The prairie was full of badger holes, but in my daylight rides I had never yet had a mishap. A prairie horse can be trusted for that. But at night it is different. At any rate my turn came next, for I suddenly found myself looking through Banjo's two front legs, with a complete view of my left stirrup. Banjo righted himself quickly, and so did I, though I got a bit of a strain.*

*At length we found a group of men, nearly all unknown to me, who had been fighting the fire since daylight. At first, I thought they were Indians, so black were their faces with the smoke. I could see, too, that their eyes were bloodshot. A wagon containing a water barrel was being driven slowly along the line, and at intervals the fighters retired to it to wet their sacks, and then returned to beat the flames. These are astonishingly easy to put out, though they are sometimes fanned into life again by the breeze. This necessitates at least one man following behind about half-a-mile or so. His work is easy, but responsible, and must be thorough or the fire will get away again. Most sacks were tied at the end of a stick, and some were lightly stuffed with willow boughs. This seemed, so far as I could gather, a new idea. It is certainly as excellent one, for the sacks thus stuffed did notably good service.*

*I gained a peculiar impression of the vastness and landmarklessness of the prairie by the fact that nobody present could tell exactly where we were. A trail nearby led nobody knew whither. Armstrong's ranch was known to be somewhere about four miles distant, but in what direction nobody could point out. The majority of men we found there were just about to depart, for there was no food or drinking water left, and by the following line of burnt ground back they expected to strike some shack within the course of few hours. So, besides our own party, there were only two men left and the water wagon.*

*Our task seemed hopeless. The line of fire from the west to east extended about twelve miles, and it was travelling southwards at an enormous rate under a strong north wind. Of course we knew that other groups of workers must be operating at other points but we seemed to have miles of it under our own special charge. We worked along steadily and it was some satisfaction to leave a black, charred, flameless waste behind us.*

*Part of the time I held the horses. First, with all their lines in one hand, and then later with each horse's line attached to the saddle horn of another. I let them graze a bit as we worked slowly along. On returning to the fire line with my sack, I came up behind Bolton just as he was remarking to Bettington, 'Well, I hope Newton is satisfied, I doubt if he'll pray for any more prairie fires.'*

*He was right. I had had quite enough of it. Thirsty and nothing to drink; hungry and no prospect of food; shivering in a biting blast; sore from my hard ride; a bit crippled with my stumble; sleepy and nowhere to sleep; and with the chance of the fire lasting for days. I almost felt that life offered no further attractions. It was but two o'clock. More than three weary hours before the dawn. 'Oh, that morning, or Armstrong would come!'*

*Now we came to a mile or so of extinguished grass put out earlier in the evening. Some mounted and rode back to see all safe behind, while the rest of us went forward. Shall I ever forget my joy when we saw silhouetted against the sky the outline of a log shack! There, at any rate, was water, and perhaps food.*

*Our hopes were more than realised. A nice supper with hot tea was soon ready for us, accompanied by a genial prairie welcome. The shack was that of a new settler, Ingram, who had come in during the summer, and had a few hours before he lost three haystacks, after he had considered that all was safe. Poor Mrs Ingram had been up for two nights and days, yet catered cheerfully for our wants. We learned that the fire had nearly reached the head of Frenchman Creek, and was fast travelling down Farewell Creek, on which Bolton's, and Gibson's ranches were situated. So it did not take long to decide that we must go back and protect our own houses.*

*But it was useless to ride before the dawn. Coming up with the fire to guide us was one thing. Riding from it into the gloom was another. So, after a soothing pipe we stretched ourselves on the floor to sleep. I don't see what prisoners have to complain about in a plank bed. I'm sure I found mine comfortable enough. I pillowed my head on my coat, and stretched out my legs beneath the stove. Bettington's head lay on my stomach, and his long legs reached far towards the centre of the room. Howland, I believe, constructed a pillow out of the coal scuttle. All of us slept the sleep of the just.*

*A little before five, Barrow opened the door leading outside to prospect. He started us with the exclamation: 'It's snowing hard!' We were all awake in an instant. The news seemed too good to be true. We went out to verify the statement and found not indeed snow but a heavy Scotch mist, the ground perfectly wet and no glow of fire visible. It was all over. What would probably have been the biggest and most destructive fire for years, and would have taken many men many days to extinguish, had been swamped in an hour. 'Heaviness may endure for a night, but joy cometh in the morning.' Our spirits rose to summer heat.*

*At Armstrong's ranch we were cordially invited to breakfast, and spent a couple of hours in discussing the events of the fire. The six men there had had their work cut out to save the place in addition to fighting the flames in general.*

*Hot soup goes well after a long ride, and the ladies at the ranch had prepared an excellent one to commence our meal. But it had a soporific effect and most of us retired immediately afterwards to the bunk house, there to spend the afternoon in deep slumbers. Something prompted us to wake at supper time, and a musical evening followed.*

*The expedition will ever remain a memorable one for me. The midnight ride, the glowing sky, the illuminated city, are imprinted on my mind; and above all two of the pleasantest surprises of my life...the welcome shack and the heaven sent mist.*

## 1910 - SOUTH AMERICA

### LETTER FROM BRAZIL

### JOHN AVERAL WICKHAM

John Averal Wickham was born on May 22$^{nd}$ 1881. He entered Reading School in April 1890 and left from the Army Class in July 1894 when it seems he continued his education at the Upper School in Cirencester. He was awarded the Humane Society's Medal for saving a man's life on October 17$^{th}$ 1904 when working as one of the chief engineers on the harbour in Malta.

He wrote the following letter to the school magazine in November 1910 via Mr. Newport who was acting Headmaster at the time.

*c/o Messrs. S.Pearson & Son Ltd.*
*Caixa 448*
*Para,*
*North Brazil*
*15$^{th}$ November 1910*

*Dear Mr. Newport,*

*Just a line to let you know where I am, and to wish you the compliments of the season. We are building a Harbour Works here for the benefit of the robbers who make their fortunes in rubber. The place has a very evil reputation as a health resort and it is very difficult to get men to stay out here for any length of time. Our great enemy is yellow fever. The port is the main outlet of the Amazon, so is very busy, every ship going up the river being compelled to come in here. Ships of 6,000 tons can navigate the Amazon for upwards of 1000 miles, while smaller craft run right into Peru, a fact which very few people at home realise. The country round about here is absolutely virgin forest, no attempt has been made to clear the place. The price of labour and living is impossible, and our personal expenses would give one fits at home; the washing bill alone is never much under 20s. per week and the luxury of a whisky and soda means 2s.*

*We are quartered in a camp, laid out in a forest clearing on the banks of the river. The houses are all built up on piles about four feet from the ground, to keep out the ants and other insects, a precaution which is very necessary. I hadn't been here a month before two vests were eaten by ants; and now, after*

*14 months, my wardrobe is a sight. We generally reckon to have leave after 18 months, I am hoping to be home about March or April when I hope to be able to look you up.*

*With kind regards to Dr and Mrs Eppstein.*
*Yours sincerely,*
*J.A.Wickham.*

## 1913 - CHILE, VALPARISO

### CONSTRUCTING THE PORT WORKS AND HARBOUR

### J.A. WICKHAM

*Vaplariso, Chile,*
*South America*
*13th June, 1913.*

*Dear Dr. Eppstein,*

*We are commencing the construction of Port Works and Harbour improvements here which is estimated to take 7 years to complete – at present there are no facilities for dealing with the rapidly increasing movement of the port; the general obstacle in the way of engineering works is the great depth of water – quite near the shore we have as much as 60 mtrs., or about 200 feet, and as the official scheme includes a projecting breakwater arm founded in this depth we are up against something tough. Divers cannot work safely and continuously in water exceeding 60 to 70 feet in depth, we have therefore to tip an artificial mound of granite to bring the level of the sea base up within these limits. The obtaining of so large a quantity of granite entails quarrying operations on an immense scale, our installation includes the most modern pneumatic tools, &c., and these, with the help of gelignite for blasting, are to do the work. The scheme also provides for about 5 kilometres of quay walls, reclamation of foreshore and construction of sheds, coaling jetties and railway connections.*

*We travelled out here in March via Rio-de-Janeiro, Buenos-Aires, and the Trans-Andine Railway – the latter part of the journey avoids the long sea trip around the south through the Straits of Magellan. The Trans-Andine route is open for about eight months in the year; the remaining four months of winter, when heavy snow falls, the railway gets blocked and there is no through connection. This period generally commences early in June but this year we are lucky and are still receiving our mail once a week. The highest point reached on the line is just under 12,000 feet above sea level; when we came through on a beautiful day it was not too cold although we were at times in the snow region. The most troublesome part of the trip to most people is the mountain-sickness which this altitude brings on.*

*The terrible earthquake which occurred here in 1906 has left its mark on all the old buildings in the town; a few have been built in reinforced concrete but it still remains to be seen how they will last. The majority of houses are of wood in two layers, the intervening space being filled with mud, the roof of corrugated sheeting – no houses have fireplaces, the only means of keeping warm on these cold nights is to sit huddled round an oil stove which is carried from room to room.*

*We have had an average of one earthquake per week since our arrival, some people say they do not mind them much but I confess they scare me badly; although the shock lasts not more than 15 to 30 seconds it seems very much longer and is usually accompanied by a general downpour of pictures and ornaments, rather like the noise crockery makes on board a ship in rough sea.*

*I hope you are having a good summer for cricket at home; we are of course in mid-winter now but nevertheless take just as keen an interest in the scores as if we could buy our "Evening News" daily.*

*With kind regards to Mrs. Eppstien and Mr. Newport.*
*Yours sincerely,*
*J.A. WICKHAM*

# Chapter 5

## CHINA

### PATROLLING THE YANGTSE RIVER IN A BRITISH GUNBOAT

### E.C. HOLTOM

By the 1890s Britain had a stranglehold on China's foreign trade. Opium was the primary import into China with an average value of £10m per year and Lancashire cotton came second with around £3m.

Of the other great powers Russia took a controlling stake in the Chinese Eastern Railway, France grabbed some lucrative mineral rights and Germany had Hankow for its commercial gain and turned Kiachow into a naval base. An Anglo-Japanese alliance, struck in 1902, allowed Britain to reduce her naval presence 'on the China Station'. Even so, with such powerful rivalry for the dominance of China, it is not surprising that HMS Thistle was visiting China when Holtom wrote to the school.

*HMS THISTLE*
*China*
*February 1913*

*Dear Dr. Eppstein*

*I have never yet sent any communications to the School Magazine, and it has just struck me that possibly a letter from the Far East might be of interest to you.*

*The 'Thistle' is a gunboat which spends most of her time on the Yangtze, with short coasting trips in the summer; this year we hope to get down to Hong Kong. The Yangtze is a remarkable river in many ways; for instance, it is always muddy, and varies from a dark brown in summer to an olive brown in winter; the amount of mud and silt carried out to sea every year must be enormous. The river floods every summer from the melting snows in the interior near Tibet, the difference in the water level in winter and summer averaging 40 feet, though much greater in some places even than this. Then*

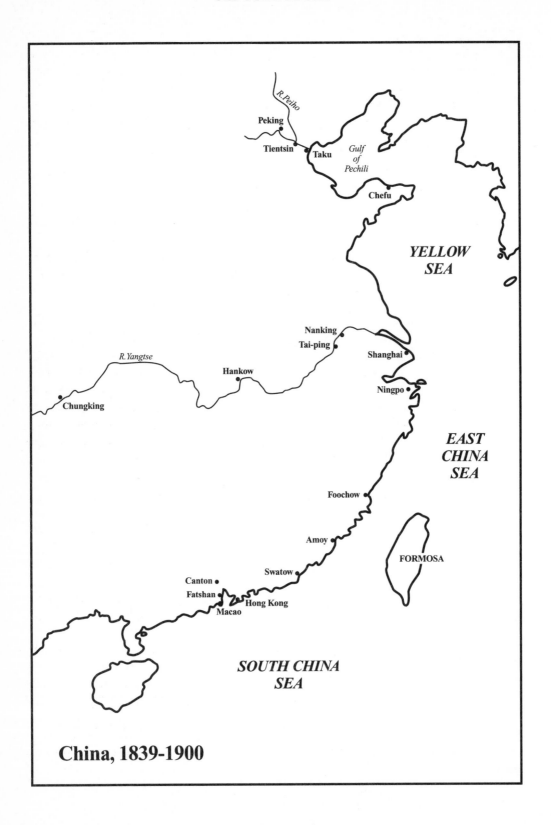

**China, 1839-1900**

*again it is very broad; after the Yangtze one is inclined to look upon the Kennet as a creek; at Hankow, about 600 miles from the sea, it is considerably over a mile wide. Shanghai and Hankow are now the two chief ports on the Yangtze, though Wuhu is still the centre for rice export trade, and Kinkiang for tea, but all the tea nowadays simply passes through Kinkiang and goes up to Hankow, where the tea-tasters and merchants assemble in strong force during June and July, and where it is exported direct to all parts of the world, ocean going steamers being able to get right up to Hankow during the summer floods.*

*I arrived out here in March 1912, just too late for the revolution[1], but needless to say no one could talk of anything else, especially at Hankow which was in the thick of the fighting; Wuchang, the revolutionary centre, being just opposite across the river. The 'Thistle' was at Hankow at the time and my predecessor had plenty of surgical work on Chinese patients in the Mission Hospitals, which were filled to overflowing.*

*The native city of Hankow was burnt in November, 1911, and it is only beginning to arise from the ashes, the chief difficulty being the want of funds. The New China Party have planned to lay it out in wide streets and rectangular blocks of buildings like New York, but I fancy it will be but an idle dream; already the owners of land, tired of waiting for Road Councils and Surveys, are running up their houses and shops where and how they please. The Chinaman does not believe in wasting valuable ground space making wide roads especially as in this part of China there is no vehicular traffic as all merchandise is carried by coolies or on wheelbarrows. The streets of a Chinese city are narrow and winding, the main streets unevenly paved with rough stones, the side streets merely mud, which becomes ankle deep in wet weather. The eaves of the houses all project in varying degrees over the roadway, and when it rains shoot streams of water on to the passers-by below. Added to which there is no system of sanitation such as we take as a matter of course in Western lands, so consequently cholera, dysentery and fevers are always frequent in summer, at which time also the various smells are, to say the least, unique and not to be met with elsewhere, and always prove overpowering to anyone with a sensitive nose.*

---

1   There had been ten attempts to have a revolution in the Chinese provinces, mostly in the south-west. The revolution of 1911 began in Szechwan on August 24th where students took to the street in protest about the nationalisation of the railways. The leaders were arrested and fighting broke out between the demonstrators and soldiers during which 32 people were killed. This led to widespread fighting in the province. To begin with the movement was led by the wealthy, who wanted their financial concerns met, but the refusal of the government to listen to their demands meant that they shifted their support to the revolutionaries. By the end of November 66% of China had broken away from the Ch'ing Empire. In December, China was declared a republic and elected Sun Yat-sen, leader of the Kuomintang, as the provisional President.)

*One fact which struck me particularly on my first coming out, was the almost entire absence of queues which markedly changes the appearance of the Chinaman from the typical picture book idea.*

*E.C.Holtom*

(Holtom was taken as a POW in German East Africa in 1915, see page 205).

# Chapter 6

## EUROPE

There are two curious, and anonymous, contributions from German universities about duelling and one from an engineer working on the Danube in Romania. It is said that Europe was more exotic than India to English schoolboys during the period of the Empire and these letters support that hypothesis.

The streotypical 'Unspeakable Hun' is implied, perhaps conciously, in the duelling letters. (The 'Unspeakable Hun' is also refered to by A.G. Wilken, see page 299). In the Romanian contribution, traces of the Ottoman and the Austrian-Hungarian Empire are seen, before the cataclysm of the First World War.

The letter and articles are included to to give a picture of the Europe available to young Englishmen who would find their greatest challenge there in 1914 and the subsequent years.

## 1895 - GERMANY

### DUELLING IN THE GERMAN UNIVERSITIES

*'The town of Gottingen, which is famous for its sausages and its University, belongs to the King of Hanover and contains 999 kitchened houses, an observatory, a student's prison, a library, and a town-hall cellar where the beer is very good'. Thus Heine commences his most curious and interesting Harzreise and, if we neglect the changed political conditions, Gottingen is today much as it was in his time: a quiet University town surrounded by a raised earth-wall and a ditch, where learning reposes undisturbed by all which agitates and moves the great world beyond.*

*It was my good fortune some years ago to visit Gottingen, and to pass a few weeks there, which I shall always look back upon with pleasure. I remember well the old German doctor who though nearly seventy years of age still carried the marks of his early duelling days; his pretty niece, who seemed to think a man could lay small claim to the possession of physical beauty unless his face was furrowed by scars; and his little boy, who might indeed have been the identical boy mentioned by Heine as refusing to associate with the comrade because the latter did not know the genitive of Mensa.*

*A German is very different from an English University town; at Gottingen there are no Colleges, and the students live in rooms in the town. The teaching is by means of lectures, and the numerous beer cellars are made use of as meeting places by students for the purposes of social intercourse. Those who compose what may be termed the physical aristocracy among the students belong to clubs whose main object of existence is the promotion of the exercise of rapier fencing and its accompanying duelling.*

*Each of these clubs has its special colours, while the members always wear caps differing in hue according to the particular club to which they belong. The members of the Hannoveraner Corps wear red caps, and there are some seven or eight Vereins for duelling in all. I had the free run of the Hannoveraner Corps while in Gottingen; of this club Prince Bismarck was, while at Gottingen, a member. In the club room of the society I often passed five or six hours of an evening engaged in talking German and drinking beer. The club possesses a special cup, and any member who can drain its contents in one swallow has the right to have his name engraved upon the lid.*

*On Sunday afternoons all the various Duelling Clubs used to meet in the Beer Garden a little outside Gottingen, and here with the members of each seated around their own table healths were drunk, prosits were interchanged, and a general feeling of conviviality and friendly good fellowship prevailed. On one occasion I was invited to witness a duel on the Monday at the little inn some two miles out of Gottingen, I believe at Boyden, where these encounters take place. Every Corps-student must be prepared to fight a certain number of duels every term unless physically disabled, the men of different clubs being pitted against each other in pairs by lots being drawn; if any legitimate reason for a fight exists it does away with the necessity of drawing in the case of any particular individuals; but speaking generally, rapier duelling is indulged in between the clubs as much as cricket or football is here by devotees of those games. My friend on the Monday, called for me with a carriage and we started early for the spot where the duels were to take place. When we arrived we found many students there before us. My friend, who was on this occasion a personage of some importance, was profuse in his apologies for having to leave me somewhat to myself while he attended to the business of the day. I mention this because it is not easy for us to understand the importance which the German student attaches to these meetings. There were on this occasion three duels to be contested. The men fought with pointed swords or rapiers and the face was the only part of the body attacked, and here the eyes were protected by iron Brillen, the neck was swathed in linen so as to protect the large vessels, the nose seemed to be the favourite point of attack, and the cheeks suffered somewhat too. A doctor was present, and as soon as blood was drawn he examined the combatant to see if he was suffering from a 'gefahrliche Wunde'; if the wound was dangerous the duel was declared to be at an end. Two of the duels I witnessed were harmless enough, merely left cheek scars, but in the third the vanquished very nearly lost his nose, the tip of it hanging from his upper lip by the merest vestige of skin; the missing member was stuck on again, and I trust its owner recovered.*

*I do not wish my readers to leave me with a false impression with regard to the practice of duelling in the German Universities; it has its uses, it encourages a spirit of manly athleticism among a large body of young men who are phlegmatic by nature and in need of some stimulus towards the development of physical activity. It is not really dangerous by reason of the precautions taken against its being so, and in all probability the worst of the duels I witnessed was a exceptionally severe one. We must in passing judgement on this custom remember that it is much to the German Universities what boating is for Oxford and Cambridge, and to rightly apprise its value we must examine it from the German and not the English standpoint; it promotes the use of the rapier and may be instrumental in the future as it has been in the past in saving the Fatherland.'*

J.C.T.

Magazine April 1895

Another OR witnessed more bloodletting scenes in German Universities in 1912:

*'The particular University of which we were members, numbers about two thousand students, and rather more than half of these belong to one or other of the colour-bearing corps. Each corps has its own clubhouse, in which communal meals are served, meetings conducted and kneipe or 'drinks' take place. The members of a corps are detailed by their president to fight duels, and in such cases the general procedure is for the student to pay a trivial insult to a member of another corps, when a duel necessarily follows. Such duels are looked upon as of minor importance, and are fought with rapiers. These Schlager duels vary from five to sixty rounds in length, according to the nature of their excuse. In the case of a serious insult the sabre is used, a much more formidable weapon.*

*After some time the throng of students increased, and the chief figures in the drama made their appearance. The latter were dressed in what would have been very suitable attire for a cricket match, but wore ordinary boots, since, although the floor was slippery, no footwork worth mentioning played a part in the encounter. A leather strap passed from the belt behind, between the legs, and was fastened to the belt in the front. The left arm was kept out of the sphere of hostilities by grasping this strap from behind at its lowest point. The rapier-bearing arm was thickly swathed by tight black bandages except at the elbow joint, where free play was necessary. A heavy bandage protected the neck, and a narrow mask was held in position over the* eyes by an elastic passing behind the head. The combatants saluted each other, not by shaking hands, but by raising their corps' caps, which resemble in shape the English field-service cap, but which are vivid blue, pink, and so forth, according to the colours of the corps. The seconds had bandaged right arms, and were provided with ordinary fencing head-guards. Each second in turn briefly stated the conditions of the duel, and then took up their positions. The duellers were only some two paces apart, with rapiers crossed high in the air. The seconds crouched close off the left of their men, with rapiers ready to intervene between those of the latter. Hats were removed, the word was given, the seconds lowered their rapiers, a rapid interchange of blows took place, and the seconds intervened. The round was over, each round consisting of only five strokes on either side. The strokes were difficult to follow, appearing more wild than scientific, and confined in possibilities to two overcuts and two undercuts. The two most suggestive figures in the scene now each approached his man. They were medical students, in complete white surgical attire, and provided with bandages, plaster and other surgical appliances. One man had just been touched on the scalp, we had seen the hair fly. His attendant fingered the wound, and covered it by a strip of plaster. Four more bouts followed, and the contest was over, without serious damage to either party. We then proceeded to a second public house…..Here we found the same environment and witnessed two Schlager duels. The second of these was one of sixty rounds and showed us why every corps' student bears one or more conspicuous scar. One of the duellers was considerably taller than the other, and the latter wore a guard over an unhealed wound near his mouth. The size of the guard was objected to by the opposer's second, and a smaller one substituted. The procedure was as before, but in the third round a long red line appeared on the tall man's cheek, while his opponent was also touched. The wounds were in this case left unstaunched. Two rounds later the forehead of the taller was streaked from top to bottom and in the next round he again mutilated the cheek of his opponent. In the fifteenth round, however, the latter inflicted a wound on his adversary which crossed the previous one, and was thus considered dangerous enough to bring the conflict to an end.

We descended to the bar …….where we learned that a sabre Mensur was fixed for three o'clock in a village two miles further on:

The proceedings bore the marks of a more serious affair than a Schlager duel. The combatants were stripped to the waist with the exception of the guard over the heart and another on the side of the neck. Heavy cavalry sabres were the weapons. Four doctors were in attendance, moving about with uplifted arms dripped with antiseptic. It was an Inter-University affair, both men being renowned fighters. Broad chalk lines were marked on the floor six feet apart, behind which the foot of neither combatant must slip. Whereas in the Schlager duels an erect attitude at close quarters was adopted, in this case the left leg was stretched out rigidly behind, and the right knee bent to the front. The duel was one of sixty rounds. It was easier to *follow the strokes, and it seemed altogether a more scientific affair. The atmosphere was terrible, heavy with cigar and beer fumes which could find no outlet through the closed windows. The details of this fight were gruesome in the extreme. It is best not to attempt to convey a true idea of the attending circumstances, as the whole environment is foreign to the English sporting imagination. It is sufficient to mention that a red veil soon obscured the face of one participant, while the other received three separate serious wounds. Of the latter, the first cut deep into his forehead along a line of some three inches, the second slashed his chest for six inches, and the third completely traversed his face in a horizontal direction severing the bridge of his nose. As his nose had to be held on, this wound terminated the duel which lasted for thirty-five rounds and twenty minutes. It was impossible to distinguish the injuries inflicted on his opponent from the gory mess which represented his face......'*

## 1908 - ROUMANIA

### E.T. WARD

*Commission Europeenne du Danube*
*Soulina,*
*Roumania*
*16th June 1908.*

*My dear Broad,*

*Please note my change of address to the above. I came out here last week via Berlin, Breslau and Lemberg, a most tedious journey, but I was told, the quickest route. This I now find is open to doubt. Arriving at Galatz on Thursday night, I spent Friday paying duty calls on the British and some of the other delegates to the C.E.D., continuing down the Danube by steamer to Soulina on Saturday.*

*Galatz is the headquarters of the C.E.D., which it may be interesting to note was formed by Art. 16 of the Treaty of Paris in 1856 after the Crimean War, for the control and improvement of the Danube navigation for the first 80 miles or so up from the Black Sea.*

*It is an interesting place and has a strong element of the orient about it, but has some fine Boulevards lined with lime trees, the Strada Domemeasca being the principal one, and some handsome buildings. One sees a great number of springless carts, commonly used by the Roumanian peasant folk, each drawn by a pair of white bullocks. Then there are the droschkis with their Russian ponies and drivers in peaked caps and long blue velvet cloaks with red or yellow sashes. These are said to share with those of Bucharest the reputation of being the best in Europe. The brilliant uniforms of the officers of the Roumanian Army add a very picturesque touch of colour in the street.*

*On the way down to Soulina in the steamer via Touchla one has in view for the first part of the journey the blue hills of the Dobrudja on the south side, not unlike the Devonshire or Yorkshire moors. A little below Touchla one enters the delta by the Soulina arm of the Danube, which is about 35 miles long. Soulina is a quaint straggling town with squalid back streets, the backdoors of the houses opening almost on to the dense overgrowth of reeds which completely covers the delta. It has fine broad quays, and as far as the Commission Quarters are concerned is quite habitable. We have a sort of Compound planted with fine trees and with nice gardens enclosed by a green fence. The houses and offices of the Commission are well built; in fact it is a veritable oasis in the desert, with fine views out on to the Black Sea, the islands at the Kilia mouths of the Danube being just visible to the northwards.*

*There is a pretty little English Church, the only one in Roumania, which was built by Sir Charles Hartley, the first engineer to the Commission. There are about five English families all told, but generally speaking it is a most cosmopolitan town, and I am told it is not uncommon to have seven different languages in the same room at afternoon tea-parties, which are great institutions here. It is a good spot for the study of natural history. Coming down on Saturday, I saw storks and herons on the banks and caught a glimpse of an old brown eagle with hooked beak, sunning himself on one of the groyne posts. Then there are myriads of insects including mosquitoes, but these are effectually kept out of the houses by wire gauze in frames fitted outside the windows, and one can sit with the latter wide open in the summer evenings with perfect impunity, although it is not wise to go out of doors too much after dark during July and August, the hottest months. The air is sometimes perfectly thick with dragon flies about 3 inches long, beautiful creatures with blue and green heads and gauze wings. They are quite harmless, and do good by eating the mosquitoes and, incidentally, each other as well.*

*The place is not unhealthy. There are people who have lived here 35 years without a touch of fever, which is, however, still fairly prevalent among the peasants, who live in miserable mud huts in the swamp.*

*There is plenty to interest one, our surveying work on the shoals, which are constantly forming on the bar and in the river, requiring constant attention as well as dredging to remove them. We have four powerful dredgers constantly at work and there will be shortly be another, which has just been launched.*

*There is a great deal of shipping of all flags, but by far the greatest proportion is British. This morning I saw a picturesque Turkish sailing vessel in the river, not unlike the Viking ships of which one sees in pictures.*

*As you know, the climate of Roumania is one of extremes and they generally get about six weeks skating on the numerous fresh water lakes.*

*I remain*
*Yours etc.*
*E.T.Ward.*

# Chapter 7

## EDUCATED FOR LEADERSHIP

*'When scholars of Reading School come into this chapel
in the future you, and those who come after you will see this
memorial, and when you go out into the greater world and
are faced, as you will be faced, with all the troubles and
difficulties that are ever increasing in these days, when you
join in the great battle of life, do everything in your power to
prove yourselves worthy of these young men who in the pride
of their youth gave everything they could; remember the great
sacrifice they made, and do what you can to prove yourselves
worthy of that sacrifice by giving yourselves to the service of
your country and your empire'.*

Lt-Col Wilson, DSO, MP at the unveiling of the Chapel War Memorial, February 1922.

While their forebears and early contemporaries were writing about their experiences on the North West Frontier, pig sticking on the plains of the Ganges or Tea planting in Assam, the 'Valete' of 1914 were about to embark on what for them was probably the greatest 'imposed' adventure of their lives, the Great War of 1914-1918.

By December 14th 1918 the magazine was reporting 418 ORs who had served in all branches of the forces of whom 77 had been killed in action, or as a result of wounds received. This latter figure was amended and the War Memorial in the school chapel lists 82. Although, it is now apparent that this should be 84 as two ORs are not commemorated.

Cyril Bisdee Major, who was reported 'Missing' in the Magazine of April 1917, had in fact been killed in action on Sunday November 5th, 1916 while serving as a 2nd Lieutenant in the 7th Battalion East Yorks Regiment. He is however, commemorated on the Thiepval Memorial on the Somme (Pier and Face 2C).

Private Harold Louth, 4th Battalion. Seaforth Highlanders, who was killed on May 9th 1915. He is commemorated on Le Touret Memorial, Pas de Calais. Panels 38/39.

Casualty figures of almost 20% was a high price to pay and it is remarkable that the 'boys' of this generation, for that is all that some of them were, were prepared not only to lay down their life for their beliefs, but exhort other members of the school, not yet at call-up age, to follow them. Why did they do it?

Perhaps the answer can be found in three statements. Two made at the 1914 Speech Day on 17th October.

The first by the Recorder of Worcester, F.W. Sherwood O.R, in his address, to replies of 'Hear Hear', when remarking on impending changes:

*No change he had heard of would affect the continuity of the School or make any difference in the affection of the Old Boys for that ancient institution, which had sent out so many gallant men on land and sea to fight for the honour of the nation'.*

And the second, from the then new Headmaster in his reply:

*'Public-school spirit and tradition helped them to turn out honourable gentlemen and citizens to take their place in moulding the destinies of the Empire. (Applause). Never had there been a time when the Empire more required the qualities which were associated most closely with the public school spirit and which depended upon a regard for truth, for honour and for duty'.*

And the third from the address by W.M.Childs, Principal of University College (now the University of Reading) entitled 'Spirit of the Empire' given on Empire Day 1916. Having explained the chief points in which lay the strength of Germany, notably the habit of passive obedience, wonderful civil and military organisation and government by a military despotism independent of popular control, he went on to describe the virtues of the British Empire which rested on liberty, justice and goodwill. He concluded by saying;

'.....Such an Empire (the British) the Germans could not understand. They failed to see the spirit underlying it and they thought that it would collapse at the first pressure from without. It was now being put to the test, and the results had astonished not only the Germans but ourselves. The response from all classes in the great daughter nations and in India had been wonderful. Like those to whom the summons of the fiery cross came in Scott's 'Lady of the Lake', every man dropped his work there where he stood and hastened to obey the call of duty. So in this most wonderful moment of our history every boy now growing up would have to fit himself for his great task; and 'he will have to remember that the snares of death and destruction lie about the feet of those who, possessing great dominions, cease to be humble of heart'.[1]

Boys at the school at this time were unable to escape the implications of such statements. There was an expectation that they would do their duty and few, if any, were to rebel against such ideals. The fact that they adhered to this philosophy, despite all the hardships and deprivation at the front, was testament to their education, their belief in team spirit and peer-group pressure. It is not insignificant that, as we shall see, many of those who served had been members of the school's sports teams. In hindsight, one can see them simply 'swapping' their roles on the rugby/cricket field for those on the battlefield! Many obituaries list the sporting achievements of those named and it is not unusual to read of their deaths as 'following the glorious path' as if to reinforce both the school's and society's expectation that they had died for a cause worth fighting for. For some it was simply a game played out on a bigger field. Under these circumstances such sacrifice would not have been considered so surprising. In fact it would be more surprising if any mention of Conscientious Objection were found in the magazine, or even among the topics discussed in the Debating Society. We would suggest that it would have taken a very courageous boy to 'buck the trend', not to heed the exhortations and expectations, and refuse to fight!

1   This type of oration was not limited to Reading School and was replicated in one way or another in similar establishments across the country. In 'Testament of Youth', Vera Brittain, a guest of her brothers at the Uppingham School speech day on July 11th 1914, recalled 'the breathless silence which followed the Headmaster's slow, religious emphasis on the words "If a man cannot be useful to his country, he is better dead".'

This theme of self-sacrifice and heroic examples of previous ORs was one which was returned to on a number of 'School' occasions throughout the war. On Speech Day, November 1st 1916, the Rev. Dr. H.R. Cooper-Smith, drawing on the fact that this was 'All Saints Day', spoke of the 'clouds of witnesses' who have 'fought their fight' and are now 'anxiously and sympathetically watching us in our conflict'. Members of such a great and historic school ought to have an especially vivid sense of comradeship. For 'we have before us not only the example of our immediate predecessors, the tale of whose gallant deeds or, it may be, noble deaths, stirs our hearts with pride, but we also have the memory of a long Roll of Honour of the past'.

However, those sitting in the audience at speech day in 1914 were yet to be aware of what awaited them on leaving school because, in 1914, they were still more interested in another, altogether more peaceful, 'feud':

*'On the outbreak of war abroad and on our own participation, the nation showed a united front to the world by laying aside all internal struggles. Some of these feuds will doubtless be resumed on the termination of the war, but it is a great satisfaction to be able to record a peaceful and honourable ending of a feud in which we ourselves were involved, and we believe and hope that it is ended. We refer, of course, to the so-called 'War of Amalgamation'. The school is to be fused with the Kendrick School, and it is a matter of congratulation that those who opposed the scheme of amalgamation should not merely abide by the decision, but offer their services to help to work the scheme successfully'.*

It seems remarkable today that this Reading/Kendrick issue should have been the main thrust of the Editorial in the December 1914 magazine when some fellow pupils of just a term before had already been killed or wounded on the Western Front. It is not until 32 pages later, in the pen-portraits of the 1914 1st XV, many of whom were to see action within a year, that we get to any mention of the War. In the intervening pages we read reports that the Debating Society had voted 11-3 against the motion that 'In the opinion of this House the German Emperor is insane', 6-6 (with 3 abstentions) on 'In the opinion of this House Conscription neither has been, nor is necessary for this country', 7-6 in favour of the motion, 'Though the Government had every legal right to place the Home Rule and Welsh Church Bills on the Statute Book, from a moral standpoint their action is to be commended', and 10-5 against 'This House believes in the existence of Ghosts'.

Four members of that 1914 team, W.M. Cooper (outside half), C.J. Fuller, (Forward. 2nd Lt.), D.J. Davies (Forward. 2nd Lt. ) and L.C. Shore (Full-Back. Pte) would be killed in the war and of the others, A.P. Aveline MC., (Captain. Forward. Lieutenant) and W.L. Pauer DCM Bar. MM. (Forward. Sgt.), were wounded. The others were; A.H. Bull (Forward. 2nd Lt.), H.B. Preece (Forward. RN. ), R.F. McIlroy (Wing Three-quarter. Sapper), B.H. Churchill. MC. Croix de Guerre.

(Centre. 2$^{nd}$ Lt), G. Devos (Wing Three-quarter. Gunner), W.G. Mattingley (Scrum-half. 2$^{nd}$ Lt.), L. Wright (Forward. Pte), Dymore-Brown (Forward). There are four Dymore-Browns listed in the final Roll of Honour. Two were Lieutenants and two Privates, all saw action. D.E. Pope (Centre) is not in the Roll of Honour, except there is an E.D. Pope listed as a Midshipman in the RNVR. Bearing in mind that some mistakes were made on the spellings on the final Memorial, this might be the same person.

Seven members of the 1911 Rugby XV also lost their lives and others were wounded. It is only when one views the impact of the war on these individuals and the school, that one gets a true picture of the devastating effect it had on that generation. Some of these characters already had their places at University, and although we know, from reading the 'Letters from Oxford' and 'Letters from Cambridge' in post-war magazines that many resumed their places, there were those who were not able to.

*Back Row (l to r):*     *Dymore-Brown, Clarke, Davies, McIlroy, Wright, Preece, Devos, Churchill*
*Middle Row (l to r):*  *Bull, Pope, Aveline, Cooper, Pauer*
*Front Row (l to r):*    *Shore, Mattingley*

# Chapter 8

## THE GREAT WAR

*'It will either be good or bad by the time you receive this letter and I expect it means that I shall either be on my way home wounded or I shall remain here for ever....the first I hope. I do so want to see you all again. I am going over the parapet with a shout of 'School' on my lips and then pray God's will be done!*

*If the worst comes to the worst, tell any young fellows in Reading (School) who can, and there are many, that they must come out and take our places'.*

Giles Frederick Ayres, OR 1897-1901.

### Background

During the early 1910s the vast majority of people in the United Kingdom, except for those 'in the know' or with specific interest, paid little attention to the seemingly unending string of newspaper headlines featuring various alternatives to 'Trouble in the Balkans'. However, it took more than the average daily reader to understand the complexities of the issues which had their foundation many years before.

Serbia, seemed always to be at the centre of things. First between Turkey and Bulgaria, then Turkey and Russia and then between Russia and the Austro-Hungarian Empire, which covered a vast area from Eastern Europe to Asia.

Although the Serbs had been forced to hand over territories in Bosnia and Herzegovina to the Austrians, creating a great deal of ill-will, they did hold on to their independence, although somewhat tenuously. Russia was also not happy about the Austrians now holding Serb territory as Serbia had at one time been under Russian protection and she felt that the area should belong to the Russian Empire.

However, by 1913 Serbia's star was in the ascendant. After the Balkan War that saw the defeat of Turkey and her 'removal' from Europe, Serbia benefited from the allocation of conquered territories to the Balkan states. There was a great deal of

**Austria - Hungary, 1914**

nationalism and pride within Serbia, Bosnia and Herzegovina that culminated in a series of terrorist and guerrilla attacks against the Austrians.

Members of the Austrian secret service, based in Belgrade, sent back information to Vienna that the Serbs were supporting and financially underwriting the activities of the terrorists and the country was seen by many guerrillas as a safe-haven should they need one. By 1914 Austria was looking for an excuse to give Serbia a 'bloody-nose' and their excuse came on June 28th in the town of Sarajevo, a known 'hot-bed' of Slav nationalism. The area had been deliberately chosen for military manoeuvres by the 15th and 16th Corps of the Austrian Army in order to demonstrate their military power to the Slavs. In addition, the 'combatants' were also to be inspected by the Inspector-General of the Austrian Army who also happened to be the heir to the Austro-Hungarian throne, Archduke Ferdinand.

Archduke Ferdinand and his wife arriving in Sarajevo
*(Ref. Robert Hunt Library)*

Although the inspection was meant to be a formality, it became anything but! On the journey from the train station to the parade ground a bomb was thrown into the Archduke's car and although unhurt he and his wife were shaken and a member of their staff was hit by shrapnel.

The Archduke remarked 'So you welcome your guests here with bombs!'
*(Ref. 1st World War. Martin Gilbert. Harper Collins. P16)*

Princip in Austrian custody

*(Ref. Fotoarchiv Pamatniku Terezin)*

The terrorist, Nedeljko Cabrinovic, was caught and identified as a Serb but fatefully, as it turned out, the local police never considered that he could have been working with someone else (there were in fact six others, Danilo Ilic, Vijetko Popovic, Mohamed Mehmedbasic, Vaso Cubrilovic, Trifko Grabez) and therefore never extended their search or take further precautions to protect their guests. Within half an hour of the first arrest the Archduke and his wife had been shot dead by the seventh conspirator, Gavrilo Princip.

The Archduke had asked to be driven to the hospital to visit the officers injured in bomb attack. During the journey his driver had taken a wrong route down a street where he was unable to turn around and as a result he had to slow down to reverse. By coincidence, Princip was standing just eight metres away. He stepped forward and fired two shots into the car, killing both passengers. This was the excuse Austria needed to go to war with Serbia and quell Slav nationalism for good.

By July the confessions, so-called, of the two assassins were reported in the newspapers and as new details emerged, such as the men acting on orders from Belgrade and Cabrinovic being given the bomb by an anti-Austrian member of the Serb army, and the bomb and pistols having come from the Serb armoury at Kragujevac, they were released to the world's press in order to maintain a semblance that Austria was the injured party and therefore had the right to take action.

Later reports indicated that gold had been found in Princip's lodgings and that the whole incident had been planned by very senior officials in the administration in Belgrade. According to Lyn MacDonald in '1914' the most important endictment came with the reported statement made by Princip and printed verbatim: 'I hope that the fatal revolver shots will open the way to the Serbian Army to march and occupy Bosnia, for this land is destined by its inclinations and traditions to belong to Greater Serbia'. *(Ref. Lyn Macdonald. 1914. p23)*

Having convinced herself that Serbia was to blame, Austria issued an ultimatum on July 23rd, allowing only 48 hours for a reply. Not only did the message make serious accusations it also included a series of demands which Serbia had to comply with. These included:

- A publication by the Serbian government formally condemning all Anti-Austrian propaganda and interference in the lives and affairs of all inhabitants of the Austro-Hungarian Empire.

- Special laws to be introduced to deal with those inciting hatred against Austria.

- The revision of history teaching in Serbian schools.

- The suppression of Serbian newspapers.

- The willingness to dismiss any officers in the administration or in the armed services considered guilty of any propaganda against the Austro-Hungarian monarchy.

- The arrest of border personnel who let the assassins travel across the frontier.

- The arrest of all high-ranking officers implicated in the plot.

- The arrest of all Accessories to the plot of June 28th.

- Finally, Austria demanded the right to enter Serbia to conduct her own investigations and to suppress any subversive elements.

Serbia agreed to seven of the ten demands and suggested that the others could be discussed within the context of international arbitration. The following day Sir Edward Grey, the British Foreign Secretary, received the following note from the Austrian Ambassador in London:

> *'In order to bring to an end the subversive intrigues originating from Belgrade and aimed at the territorial integrity of the Austro-Hungarian Monarchy, the Imperial and Royal Government has delivered to the Royal Serbian Government a Note in which a series of demands were formulated. The Royal Serbian Government not having answered this Note in a satisfactory manner, the Imperial and Royal Government are themselves compelled to see to the safeguarding of their rights and interests and, with this object, have to recourse to force of arms....'* (ref. 1914 op cit p24)

Austria declared war on Serbia on 29th July.[1]

The protagonists rattled their sabres. Tsar Nicholas asked the Kaiser to restrain Austria, the Kaiser asked his Ambassador in London to sound out British intentions, the French President, Poincaré and Prime Minister Viviani returned

---

1    It was not apparent until after the war that the Kaiser, having read the full text of the ultimatum and Serbia's reply, could see no reason at all for Austria to declare war. He wrote the following in the margin of the Serbian reply:

'A great moral victory for Vienna; but with it every reason for war is removed and Giesl (the Austrian Ambassador) ought to remain quietly in Belgrade. On the strength of this I should never had ordered mobilisation'. (Ref. 1st World War. Martin Gilbert. Op cit. p24)

from a visit to Russia to be welcomed by a huge crowd at the Gare du Nord singing the 'Marseillaise'. All, except Serbia, felt they had something to gain by entering the conflict. However, it was to be a simple case of newspaper misunderstanding that led to the final downhill slide. On July 30th the Berlin Lokalanzeiger had been informed that the German army had mobilised. This was in fact untrue, but by the time a retraction was forthcoming the damage had been done. The international press had got hold of the story and in true journalistic tradition were quicker to pass on this news than the denial. Before the latter reached Moscow the Russian army had already been mobilised. By August 1st rumour was so rife across Europe that it was difficult to tell fact from fiction. Among the tangible events, the Royal Navy was mobilised and Germany had formally asked Russia to cease mobilisation. This was refused and Germany had mobilised her own forces and declared war on Russia. The French also ordered mobilisation, but no French troops were to move within 10 kilometres of the German border.

The German plan, drawn up in 1892 by Field Marshall Count von Schlieffen, depended on the quick movement of troops through Belgium to France. On July 29th the Germans warned Belgium that the French were about to break through their borders and march on the Meuse through Namur. As a result of this Germany demanded unrestricted access to Belgium in order to repel this attack. This demand was not handed to the Belgian government until 7pm on Sunday August 2nd. They were given twelve hours to reply. At 9pm King Albert and his Government decided on their answer and at precisely 7 am the answer of 'No!' was delivered to the German Embassy.

On August 3rd, Bank Holiday Monday, the British Government sent a message to Germany asking for assurances that Belgium's neutrality would not be violated. It took a long time for an answer to be forthcoming and only then was it the same 'story' which had been used to try to persuade the Belgians to open her borders.

At 8.30am on Tuesday, August 4th 1914 the German army crossed into Belgium. The Belgians appealed for international help. The British ambassador in Berlin gave the German government an ultimatum that unless they withdrew its troops from Belgium by midnight she could consider herself to be at war with Great Britain and her Empire.

Within four days British troops were on French soil.

The war did see a rise in interest in the OTC and the magazine of December 1914 reports 'a rush of recruits at the beginning of term'. But there are poignant reminders of what was to come. 'Its training has become a more living reality, it does not seem to be a mere playing at soldiers as it might have appeared to the casual observer in peace time. We hope, however, that they will never have to fight. Our school grounds have been used for a purpose never dreamt of'.

Other exercises, influenced to some extent by the war, had taken place off-site. One tactical scheme took place on the South Oxford Golf Course. The idea had been that 'the British Empire is at war with Germany and has been invaded'. The scenario was that a group of the enemy, made up chiefly of irregulars and aliens with a knowledge of the local area, had established a camp in the area of Sonning Common, five miles north of Caversham Bridge, with the assumed intention of destroying the bridge. There was a report that the 'enemy's' mounted patrols were in the Emmer Green area on the 26th-27th October and they had an outpost line one mile north of Emmer Green village. The school contingent, the Main Body, moved from Earley at 11am on October 27th and marched in the direction of Sonning Common covered by an advance guard of the OTC, whose role was to ascertain the strength and position of the enemy's forces.

This advanced guard proceeded to Emmer Green on bicycles and the Scouts immediately made contact with the enemy. An attack developed slowly and after warding off several flank attacks the object of the advance was accomplished.

However, this did not meet with the approval of the Commanding Officer who criticised the days work pointing out where there was room for improvement, especially in the area of 'providing covering fire when advancing, the use of cover, the passing of messages , adjustment to sights and the economy of ammunition'.

It would seem from the magazines at the time that the Golf course and the Emmer Green area were popular 'targets' in the OTC's war games throughout this period.

There are also a number of references to visits of serving ORs to the school throughout the war. How many of them played upon the question of hero-worship to get their message across isn't known but it would be easy to imagine the opening scenes of the film 'Aces High' (based on the play 'Journey's End' by R.C.Sherriff) replicated in the school ethos at the time.

One could quite easily see the hero standing in 'Big School' in full uniform persuading those in the audience to take his place in the line, and later on sympathising with the 'hero and the worshipper' when they perhaps met under different circumstances...

*Stanhope:.....That boy's a hero worshipper. I'm three years older than he is. You know what that means at school. I was skipper of Rugger and all that sort of thing. It doesn't sound much to a man out here, but it does at school with a kid of fourteen ('Journey's End' p27).*

*Osborne: He's awfully pleased to get into your company.*

*Stanhope: Yes. I'm his hero.*

*Osborne: It's quite natural.*

*Stanhope: You think so?*

*Osborne: Small boys at school generally have their heroes.*

*Stanhope: Yes. Small boys at school do.*

*Osborne: Often it goes on as long as –*

*Stanhope: ....as long as the hero's a hero. ('Journey's End' p26)*

In the Lent term 1916 one of these 'heroes', Capt. C.St. Q. Fullbrook-Leggatt DSO inspected the OTC and afterwards gave a short address in which he emphasised the importance of discipline and that it was only by them learning discipline themselves that they could hope to become good officers when they left school. (It is interesting that he made no mention of 'other ranks'. An assumption that all boys leaving the school would gain commissions!)

On June 30th 1916 another, 2nd Lt. H.P. Dymore-Brown (left) acted as range officer during the competition for the Imperial Challenge Shield.

For those about to leave in 1914 and others who followed in subsequent years there was really no escape from 'expectation' and 'the example' of many ORs who had gone before them.

This is perfectly summed up in a letter written to the school magazine in December 1908 by H. Smith-Masters (below). The tone and sentiment is certainly a product of its time.

1st XV 1908

Left School in 1910. School Prefect. Shooting Team 08-09, Football 08, Cricket 09, Hockey 09; Champion of Sports 09. He became the Lt. Rev. Smith-Masters, Chaplain to the Forces and spent sometime as a prisoner of war. After the war he was appointed to the living at Hagbourne and took part in the service to dedicate the Chapel War Memorial.

We are not sure what gave Smith-Masters the credibility to make these statements, only that he introduced the original motion to the Debating Society on February 13th 1908. However he did seem rather concerned about British defence...In a debate on 'This House is in Favour of Old

Age Pensions' he spoke against the motion because 'the expense of working the (1908) Act would mean yet further dangerous economy in our Navy and Army'.

*'Dear Sir,*

*I must confess that it came as a very startling surprise to me to learn that the motion proposed by the Debating Society that 'in Universal Military Training lay the only hope of safety for the British Empire' was only carried by such a small margin 11-7. It seems to show, either that the members of the above society are lacking in patriotism, or else that they have not fully comprehended the seriousness of the question; indeed, some members, who opposed the motion, seemed to treat the whole matter as a joke, which I think is little short of disgraceful.*

*I will, therefore, endeavour to lay before the readers of this magazine, more especially those who are members of the Officer's Training Corps, some of the chief reasons which show that some form of Univerisal Military Training has at length become a vital necessity for the Empire.*

*Let us first glance at the so-called Voluntary System, and see the utter injustice of it, for it is high time that we should see this matter in its true light. Putting aside preconceived notions on the subject, is it not juster, fairer, more honourable, that a nation should take the burden of its defence upon its own shoulders, rather than shift it on to the backs of those who are compelled by circumstances to bear it? For the so-called voluntary system really means that the people who have sufficient money, instead of having to pay their just debt to their country in their own persons, are allowed to hire others to fight for them, who have little choice but to accept. This, it seems, is the only system that will satisfy the highly developed consciences of those so-called Britons who cry out against Compulsory Military Training, and say that it is an infringement of the liberty of the subject.*

*The right of the State to demand the service of every able-bodied man in the defence of the country is founded on nature and reason. It is obviously the first duty of a citizen to defend his country, and moreover the law as it actually stands, at the present moment, is that the universal personal service for Home Defence. The voluntary principle overlooks the great moral value of the idea of a general patriotic obligation. As every citizen in this country has a right to have a choice in the control of its destiny, so he is bound on the same principle to be prepared to serve for its protection.*

*History shows that man naturally passes through three stages in his attitude towards military life:*

*There is the early stage of society in which every man is a warrior, partly from dire necessity, partly from the mere love of strife and bloodshed. In the next stage, when wealth has been accumulated and security obtained, men turn to agriculture and commerce in order to obtain from them the means of enjoyment, leaving the military life to the more adventurous spirits. Finally, the last phase is reached in which nations are compelled to revert to the original conditions of universal military service. Just as necessity made every man a warrior to defend the community in the early struggle for existence, so necessity calls for the armed service of every citizen in order to preserve the enormous accumulation of the fruits of industry from the aggression of jealous competitors in the new struggle for existence, the struggle for markets.*

*History shows us only one alternative to this necessity, the employment of foreign mercenaries, which led to the ruin of Carthage, and eventually Rome.*

*Thus Nature and History alike speak to us in a clear voice. Fortunate above other nations you have in the past been enabled, as an island race, to escape the sacrifices demanded from other peoples. They have learnt the noble lesson of personal self-sacrifice in many a bitter struggle for existence, in many a season of humiliation; they have seen their territiories invaded, their cities in ruins, their villages in flames, their homes desecrated; they have had to submit to the hard terms of the conqueror, and have groaned under the taxation necessary to pay the huge indemnity demanded as the price of defeat. Well, they have learnt the lesson of preparedness, and stand armed and ready to defend the fruits of their labours. You, on the other hand, know nothing of a struggle for EXISTENCE, if a war carried into your own houses. Supreme beyond all question on the seas, and enjoying internal peace while all the world was at war, you have conquered, colonised and expanded till you own one-fifth of the habitable globe, and you have easily piled up a wealth and commerce that are the envy of less fortunate nations. But now these nations have not only large and splendidly trained armies, but powerful and rapidly growing fleets, which are undermining your maritime supremacy year by year, while you find it ever more difficult to fill the ranks of your small army, or even to supply the men necessary for your fleets. The real sinews of war are, ultimately, men, not MONEY. It is time, high time, for you to face the question: Will you bring the sacrifice of personal service to your country which is demanded as a National Insurance against disaster, or will you risk the loss of all your wealth and commerce, the invasion of your territories, and the inevitable loss of all your colonies and possessions, which such an invasion would entail? If so, future generations will point the finger of scorn at you, as a nation which, while willing to enjoy the fruits of greatness, selfishly refused to recognise the responsibilities which that greatness implies:*

*'A thousand years scarce serve to form a State,*
*An hour may lay it in the dust'.  Byron*

*No man who seriously considers these phenomena can doubt that the moment has arrived when we must make some sacrifice in order to guard that which we, perhaps, have acquired too easily. In other words NECESSITY for Universal Military Training primarily for Home Defence is clear. But, fortunately, this is a case in which virtue brings its own reward. There is no question here of amputating a limb in order to save the patient. Rather is it the application of a TONIC to the body politic, a tonic called for by the symptoms. And we have, as Britons, the privilege of showing the world that we can offer this sacrifice to our country of our own free will. While other peoples (except Switzerland and France) acquiesced in the measures taken by their Governments for the nations good, it lies with the people of England to decide whether they will rise to the great idea of a self-denying ordinance, which shall at once make them truly strong, and give them national security and that lasting peace which Walpole declared to be England's greatest need. Thus, too, we shall acquire that racial immortality which every great people must desire, while if we refuse to accept the clear teaching of the present and the past, we must in our turn inevitably decline and fall as did the great and wealthy Empires that are gone for ever......*

*It perhaps will not be unsuitable to close by quoting some of President Roosevelt's words in his last message to Congress.*

*'It must ever be kept in mind that war is not merely justifiable, but imperative, upon honourable men, upon an honourable nation, where peace can only be obtained by the sacrifice of conscientious convictions or of national welfare. Peace is normally a great deal good, and normally it coincides with righteousness; but it is righteousness and not peace which shall bind the conscience of a nation as it should bind the conscience of an individual; and neither a nation nor an individual can surrender conscience to anothers keeping. Neither can a nation, which is an entity, and which does not die as individuals die, refrain from taking thought for the interest of the generations that are to come, no less than the interest of the generation of today; and no public men have a right, whether from short-sightedness from selfish indifference, or from sentimentality, to sacrifice national interests which are vital in character. A just war is in the long run far better for the nation's soul that the most prosperous peace obtained by acquiescence in wrong and injustice. Moreover, though it is criminal for a nation not to prepare for war, so that it may escape the dreadful consequences of being defeated in war, yet it must always be better remembered that even to be defeated in war may be far better than not to have fought at all. As has been*

*well and finely said, a beaten nation is not necessarily a disgraced nation; but the nation or man is disgraced if the obligation to defend right is shirked.*

*We should as a nation do everything in our power for the cause of honourable peace. We should do all in our power to hasten the day when there shall be peace among the nations, a peace based upon justice and not upon cowardly submission to wrong. As yet, there is no likelihood of establishing any kind of international power, of whatever sort, which can effectively check wrong doing, and in these circumstances it would be both foolish and an evil thing for a great and free nation to deprive itself of the power to protect its own rights, and even in exceptional cases, to stand up for the rights of others. Nothing would more promote iniquity, nothing would further defer the reign upon earth of peace and righteousness, than for the free and enlightened peoples which, though with much stumbling and many shortcomings, nevertheless strive towards justice, deliberately to render themselves powerless while leaving every despotism and barbarism armed and able to work their wicked will. The chance for the settlement of disputes peacefully, by arbitration, now depends mainly upon the possession, by the nations that mean to do right, of sufficient armed strength to make their purpose effective'.*

*In conclusion, I would beg every Reading School boy to use all his efforts to promote the introduction of Universal Compulsory Military Training in our islands and this he can do no better than joining the National Service League.
Yours truly
H.A.Smith-Masters.*

How could impressionable school-boys at the beginning of the war with Britain still controlling much of the world, ignore such sentiments?

But, somewhat mischievously, it does beg a serious question on our part which nonetheless has to be asked....Were the boys who were in their last year during the Autumn Term of 1918 disappointed when the war was over and frustrated that they were never given the opportunity to show their mettle? We would suggest that it would have taken a very brave boy/man to say publically they were not, even if privately they breathed a sigh of relief!!

There had been a similar debate held in 1907. 'This House is in favour of Conscription in England'. It was proposed by Wright who said that the country was not in a fit state to repel an invader; need not follow German and French forms of conscription; the English riflemen should be as good as English Bowmen.

The opposer: Dance, stated that conscription was a form of servitude; England never needed soldiers as long as the colonies remained loyal; war was not the only pursuit for man. Conscription tended to stop civil institutions; a man who works one day commercially cannot become a soldier the next day.

Horne (ma.) said that as the English always boasted that they were ready to serve the country, they should be willing to serve as conscripts; a Cadet Corps was a conscript force. Welling-Laurie (ma.) declared he was going to oppose the motion and that he thought the nation would learn to shoot without becoming conscripts. Wickham said that conscription hindered a man all his life and Day-Lewis (mi.) thought that if conscripts were needed they should be raised from the unemployed!

The Noes won the debate 11-3.

*'But youth's fair form, though fallen, is ever fair,*
*And beautiful in death the boy appears,*
*The hero boy, that dies in blooming years;*
*In man's regret he lives, and woman's tears,*
*More sacred than in life, and lovelier far,*
*For having perished in the front of war'.*

*Tyrtaeus c.600 BC.*
*(translated by Thomas Campbell 1777-1844)*

It is not always possible to locate exactly where the ORs featured below met their deaths. However, as the war was a long swathe of inactivity punctuated by intense military engagement, it is usually possible to put them within a time zone and thereby in proximity to one of these battles. It is also possible to have some idea from the clues provided by the location of the cemeteries in which they were buried or the memorial their names are on. For example, those killed between July and November 1916 and commemorated on the Thiepval Memorial or buried in the nearby cemeteries were almost certain to have died during the Battle of the Somme those on the Menin Gate and at Tyne Cot and in surrounding cemeteries died in the Ypres salient. Others we cannot be so certain about as many cemeteries were adjacent to Casualty Clearing stations some way to the rear of the front line and some bodies were reburied as the same ground was fought over on a number of occasions.

This section is not meant to be a History of the First World War. There are extensive histories available and some of these can be found in the book list. We have included the descriptions of the major battles simply to contexturalise the situation in which many ORs found themselves at this time. As many of these major battles were long and protracted some specific engagements within them have been included at the beginning of each section. Please note that the specific dates in this 'Overview' may be a day or two different from other sources. This has arisen because it was often difficult to ascertain precisely when a battle or attack actually started and finished. Also, in many other sources, some of these smaller skirmishes have been included within the dates of main campaigns and are not listed as individual engagements.

Therefore the overview is just a rough guide to show where and when attacks, both large and small, took place during the time.

Despite the periods of inactivity many ORs did not, or were not able to write to the Magazine. Some of the letters below come via other sources, either family or friends.

(NB: The exact location of the cemeteries and war memorials where ORs are either buried or commemorated can be found at the back of the book. To avoid repetition, the description of the location is provided the first time it relates to a particular individual. This applies particularly to those who were killed during the Battles of Loos and Somme.)

# The Western Front, 1914-15

HOLLAND

● Antwerp

BELGIUM

Cologne ●

● Brussels

Aachen

R.Rhine

Bonn ●

● Liege

R.Maas

GERMANY

ons

Namur

Charleroi

Koblenz ●

R.Sambre

ge ●

LUXEMBOURG

● Sedan

R.Aisne

R.Moselle

● Reims

● Verdun

Epernay

R.Meuse

January 1915
Front Line

September 1914
Furthest German Advance

# 1914

**December 1914. Library Notes:**

*'The 'Illustrite Zeitung' and the lurid supplements of the 'Petit Journal' with which the library tables used regularly to be supplied, are now, owing to the war, no longer forthcoming, to the great regret of those who use the library'.*

Germany faced the problem of fighting a war on two fronts and to overcome this had to attack first in order to gain an initiative. The idea was to contain Russia while at the same time attacking France by sweeping through Belgium, defeating them on the Western Front and using the railways to move troops to the Eastern Front to attack Russia.

At first the plan went well. The Belgian fort of Liege was taken on August 16th and the German 1st and 2nd armies easily defeated the small Belgian army. The latter retreated to Antwerp and the Germans occupied Brussels on the 20th August.

**Overview:**

| | |
|---|---|
| **August  23 – 24** | Mons |
| **August  24** | Audregnies |
| **August  26** | Le Cateau |
| **August  24 – September 5** | Retreat from Mons |
| **September 1** | Nery |
| **September 5 – 10** | Marne |
| **September 14 –15** | Aisne |
| **October 10 – November 2** | La Bassee |
| **October 12 – November 2** | Messines |
| **October 13 – November 2** | Armentieres |
| **October 18 – November 12** | Ypres |
| **October 21 – 24** | Langemarck |
| **October 25 – 30** | Hollebecke Chateau |
| **October 29 – 31** | Gheluvelt |
| **November 11** | Nonne Bosschen |
| **November 23 – 24** | Festubert |
| **December 14** | Wytschaete |
| **December 20 – 21** | Givenchy |

Queuing at the Recruiting Office at Reading Town Hall, August 1914.

## MONS

### August 23-24<sup>th</sup> 1914

Having crossed into Belgium and forced the surrender of the Liege Forts the German Army continued to advance towards Paris. Those regiments of the Belgian Army which had not surrendered retreated to the west to join up with the British Expeditionary Force which was moving east in an attempt to stop the German army achieving their objectives. As the French army were being pushed back in the south and suffering serious losses they were unable to help the Belgians so the main thrust of the German attack was leveled at the small British force.

By August 22<sup>nd</sup> General Smith-Dorrien had moved the II Corps of the BEF to the town of Mons and had established a defensive line.

At dawn on the following day the advanced guard of the German army arrived but were thwarted by the 4<sup>th</sup> Middlesex Regiment. The respite was short. Three hours later the main German force, eight German Divisions, arrived and attacked the northern end of the town. Supported by heavy artillery fire they again attacked the

Retreat from Mons. British soldiers,
September 2nd 1914.

*Ref. Imperial War Museum*

4th Middlesex and the 4th Royal Fusiliers. However, the Germans made the mistake of advancing in close order and were easily repelled by the BEF who were firing so quickly that field officers reported to the German commander, General von Kluck, that all the British soldiers were using machine guns. Smith-Dorrien remarked 'Their losses were very heavy for they came on in dense formations, offering the most perfect targets, and it was not until they had been mown down in thousands that they adopted more open formations'.

Despite holding out for some time the BEF was forced to retreat because of the danger of being overwhelmed by superior numbers of the German forces[1]. Also, the French forces had pulled back and left the British flank very exposed. When Smith -Dorrien was informed that the Belgian Army was also retreating he was left with no option but to do the same.

On August 25th they fell back to Le Cateau and set up defensive lines there.

The force was relieved by Haig's forces which had not yet seen action. On the 26th the Germans attacked again and the situation became critical. Both flanks were under extreme pressure and only the arrival of the French cavalry kept the line together. The British forces withdrew again, this time to St. Quentin. The action at Le Cateau had cost 7,800 casualties from a complement of 40,000.

---

1    The men marched continuously for five days and as a result they were so tired that many were hallucinating. This could account for the vision of the 'Angel of Mons', an angel wearing white and riding a white horse with a flaming sword in her hand facing the German army and forbidding their progress.

An attack by the Belgian army slowed down the German advance and gave the British forces some respite. Then the former, together with the French reserves, managed to push the Germans back far enough to completely halt their progress and give the BEF and Belgian army time to retreat. The Germans, surprised by the situation they found themselves in, altered their line of advance and began to move south towards the River Marne and Paris.

## THE FIRST BATTLE OF THE MARNE

### September 5-10th 1914

By the end of August 1914 the allied armies on the Western Front were all in full retreat back towards the River Marne and Paris. The fall of the city seemed a distinct possibility as the German 1st and 2nd Armies continued to advance.

Field Marshal French, commander of the BEF, made plans for the retreat of British forces to the Channel ports for immediate evacuation if the need arose. In the meantime the city's military commander, General J.S. Gallieni organised the defence of Paris. He consulted with Lord Kitchener about the use of British Forces and was given overall command of the BEF for the defence, and in so doing stopped the British withdrawal.

His plan was very simple. All allied units would counter-attack along the River Marne and in so doing hold up the German advance. Reserve forces would be used to plug holes in the line as well as attack the German flanks.

The battle started mid-afternoon on September 5th, when the French 6th Army came across the German advance guard. The British did not get involved until after an error made by General von Kluck which was to have serious consequences. As the French 6th Army retreated back to the Marne, he had ordered his forces to pursue and destroy it. By doing this he had opened up a large gap on the right flank between his first and second armies. Seizing the opportunity all three infantry corps and two cavalry divisions of the BEF and the French 5th Army, attacked through this gap and attacked the now vulnerable flanks of both German Armies. On September 9th the Germans were driven back across the Marne and on hearing the news the German Chief of Staff, Field Marshall von Moltke ordered the retreat of the German Armies to the River Aisne on September 13th in order to regroup. Officially the Battle of the Marne had finished on September 10th. Never again were the German armies able to get so close to the French capital.

## THE RACE TO THE SEA AND THE FIRST BATTLE OF THE AISNE

### September 14th – October 20th 1914

The Allied armies pursued the German forces to the River Aisne. The latter had taken up positions on the high ground overlooking the river and waited for the allied advance. They had destroyed most of the bridges which meant that the British forces were stuck on the other side. The commanders were desperate to know where and how the Germans were deployed and were hoping that the Royal Flying Corps, newly arrived at Sapenay, would be able to provide them with the information. However, the weather at this time was appalling and some of the aircraft which ventured out were destroyed by the storm. Some had not even left the ground!

On September 12th the allies made their first attempt to get across the river under the same severe weather conditions. The 4th Division made it because the charges laid by the Germans on one of the bridges had failed to explode. General Sir Aylmer Hunter Watson having inspected the bridge, and realising that the conditions made it impossible to disconnect the charges, thought it was worth the risk of surprising the enemy if they crossed it with 'infinite caution'. What this actually meant is described by Lyn MacDonald.

*'Infinite caution meant inching a brigade of some three thousand men across the bridge in silence, on tiptoe and in single file. Infinite caution meant each man keeping his distance and adopting a light, almost mincing tread, placing his feet as carefully as if he were walking on glass. It meant unloading the ammunition wagons and passing the boxes from hand to hand, one at a time across a human chain. It took many hours before the last man was over...'* (Ref. 1914 op cit p301).

It was a great success as some of the Germans in the advanced trenches, surprised by the arrival of the 4th Division, simply fled.

However, the remaining allied forces were still on the other side of the river which acted as a very effective defensive moat. For another four days the BEF tried unsuccessfully to drive the Germans off the high ground. Casualties were high. The First Corps alone lost 3500 men on the Aisne. The Germans had also been badly hit, both by the numbers of casualties and the sense of disillusionment in that the Schlieffen plan had not worked. Von Moltke was dismissed on September 14th and replaced by General von Falkenhayn, but von Moltke was not allowed to leave Supreme Headquarters because the Germans believed that news of his sacking would be a great propaganda coup for the allies and demoralise their own troops.

However, the Germans did have the advantage of retreating towards their reserves and strong entrenchments that had been prepared as they went. In contrast, the

British Army was just holding on with small enclaves of the army separated by huge gaps, no reserves, destroyed bridges behind them and with no possibility of bringing up artillery support until they had been mended.

The swift victory philosophy behind the Schlieffen plan was now in tatters and the only way in which war could be influenced was by one side outflanking the other. However, the 'Race to the Sea' in an attempt to do just that was not an ad hoc, unplanned campaign. Troops were moved unit by unit and often under the cover of darkness in order not to be seen by observers in the German Luftwaffe . They were transported to various railway stations indirectly so that no increase in train traffic would alert the enemy. As a result the lines of both sides extended right up to the English Channel coast.

On September 26th 1914  the Battle of Artois broke out. It was to last for 14 days until the British Expeditionary force took the city. For the next few weeks the BEF, together with the Belgian army, began to take one city after another, usually to be taken back again by the Germans. The towns of Albert, Arras, Vimy, Loos, Festubert and Neuve Chappelle were repeatedly fought over.


## THE FIRST BATTLE OF YPRES

### October 18th – November 12th 1914

Basically the First Battle of Ypres was an attempt by the German Army to remove the British from the Ypres Salient and break through to the North Sea and Channel coasts. However, the war of the quick advance was over and it became one of attrition and the capturing of towns, villages, copses, hills and communication junctions.

On October 23rd, 1,500 German dead were counted on the battlefield around Langemarck. In the main they were untried troops, including a number of student volunteers. Legend has it that the Germans went into battle singing 'Deutschland Uber Alles'. Thereafter, and especially during the Third Reich, the dead of Langemarck came to symbolise youthful idealism and a spirit of self-sacrifice. The dead are today commemorated, in a cemetery shaded by oaks, by group 'tablets' and a memorial surrounding a mass grave.

The war became static. The German hopes of reaching the sea were just as unachievable as the allied hope of pushing the enemy out of Belgium. The battle for Ypres became a conflict for the salient itself, an area of no more than eight miles at its widest.

There was heavy fighting in the area of Wytschaete, Kruiseecke, Neuve Chapelle and Gheluvelt. The latter was thought by the Germans to be essential if they were to advance and take Ypres. Despite four days of German attacks and shelling the village remained in British hands until a renewed attack on the morning of October 31st removed them, but only to have it recaptured in the afternoon! The Germans also broke through the line at Zillebeke to where Irish Guards were immediately despatched to hold the line, which they did successfully until they were driven back by heavy fire on the evening of November 1st.

On November 2nd the right flank of the British line was relieved by the French. Ypres was within range of the German guns and on November 5th the German army made one last attempt to attack the south of Ypres on the Wytschaete Ridge and push through to the coast. However, by this time the Germans were running out of artillery shells and the scale of bombardment was reduced considerably.

On November 11th the Prussian Guard were ordered to take the town of Ypres. Their attack was preceded by the biggest bombardment of the war so far, made possible by deliberating saving shells over the previous few days. For a very short time the Germans broke through the British front line but were driven back.

By the end of the battle both sides had lost around 5,000 killed in an area of just 50 square miles.

**COLVIN Kenneth Colquhoun** b20.7.1878

OR 1889-1895

Pte. 1735, 13<sup>th</sup> City of London Regt.

Educated by private tuition before entering Reading School.

Died of Pneumonia.

There is only one K.C. Colvin in the Commonwealth War Graves Commission register and he was a Lieutenant in the Army Service Corps. However as he is described as 'Died' rather than 'killed in action' this could be the same person, especially as the dates coincide. Lt. Colvin died on Monday September 6<sup>th</sup> 1915 and is buried at Bulford Church Cemetery in Wiltshire. Grave Ref. 4.I.19. Colvin was on the OR list as C.K. Colvin but this is not on the CWGC register either.

From the front, December 1914:

> *'My Regiment has now been out here for five weeks, out of which the right and left half of the Battalions have taken it in turns to occupy the trenches near (we are not allowed to say where).*
>
> *I have read and heard it said that the Germans can't fight. I would advise anyone to try conclusions with the Army Corps who were attacking us; they fought with a desperate courage which is hard to realise unless seen. One night they made a great effort to dislodge us and came on in a solid mass in the face of a murderous fire of both rifles and machine guns. I can only describe the effort as that of corn going down before a scythe. A few came on alone to the very trenches only to be bayoneted there. The cold in the last cold snap has been terrible, some trenches were knee deep in half-frozen slush and snow; many cases of frostbite is the natural result; no sleep, no smoking. I remember one morning, after a terrible night of sleet and rain, the day broke and our coats were frozen stiff; we were a sorry lot and looked in a dismal, utterly-too-fed-up-to-live kind of way at each other. Suddenly some genius (an Irishman) yelled out 'Begorrah! What are you laughing at Bhoys!' It had the immediate result of a roar of laughter – it seems very silly on paper but the way it was said did the trick.*
>
> *I hope people at home realise that every able man must join. I have seen and heard enough horrors to picture what England would be like if the Germans should ever reach there. Rape, murder, fire and sword are only to be expected, and on a worse scale because they hate us so'.*

**GEDGE Joseph Theodore**

OR 1887

Staff Paymaster, Royal Navy.

HMS Amphion.

Killed in action on Thursday 6th August 1914.

MEMORIAL:
Plymouth Naval Memorial, Devon.
Panel 1.

At the very beginning of the war in August 1914, the cruiser HMS Amphion was ordered to patrol the sea-route from Harwich to Antwerp, to keep it free of any enemy shipping. However, unknown to the crew of the Amphion, the German ship Konigin Luise had already laid a mine field across the North Sea shipping lanes. The Konigin Luise was sighted by the Amphion and a flotilla of destroyers and was sunk in the first naval engagement of the war. The survivors were picked up and housed in the mess deck of the Amphion. However, on her way back, the ship struck one of the mines laid by the Konigin Luise. She was the first ship for almost a hundred years to be destroyed by enemy action and the first ever to be sunk by a magnetic mine. One hundred and thirty British sailors and twenty German POWs were killed.

### HURLEY Rowland Charles

OR 1888-1891

Company Sergeant Major. 'D' Company 2nd Battalion Kings Royal Rifle Corps.

Killed in action on Thursday 17th September 1914. Aged 39.

Husband of Molly Hurley of 29 Mead Lane, Chertsey, Surrey. Hurley also served in the South African Campaign.

MEMORIAL: La Ferte-Sous-Jouarre Memorial, Seine-et-Marne, France.

This memorial, situated 66kms east of Paris, commemorates 4,000 officers and men of the BEF who died in August, September and early October 1914 and have no known grave.

### MINCHIN Hubert Charles Loder

OR 1906-1907

Lieutenant, 125th Indian Infantry, Napier's Rifles.

Killed in action on Sunday 20th December 1914.

MEMORIAL: Neuve-Chapelle Memorial, Pas-de-Calais, France. Panel 14.

The memorial is a circular enclosure which contains a column, 15 metres high recalling the pillars of Asokar, surmounted by a Lotus capital, the Star of India and the Imperial Crown. The following inscription is engraved on the Memorial:

*'To the Honour of the Army of India which fought in France and Belgium 1914-1918, and in perpetual remembrance of those of their dead whose names are here recorded and who have no known grave'.*

Hubert was the eldest of three sons of the late Lieut-Col. Hugh Minchin, Indian Army, who followed their father into that branch of the Service, and of whom the youngest was wounded in France in May 1915.

Lieut. Minchin, who was 23 years old, was educated at Bath College, Reading School and Sandhurst. After a probationary year with the Royal Sussex Regiment, he was posted to the 125th (Napier's) Rifles, then at Mhow, with whom he served in the trenches. After the engagement at Givenchy on December 20th 1914, he was reported as missing. Some time later an Indian Officer, on returning to duty from hospital, reported that he had seen Lieut. Minchin struck in the neck and killed instantly, when in the act of personally discharging a machine-gun against the enemy. The India Office later notified his next of kin that he must be believed to have fallen on that day. This is confirmed by the Commonwealth War Graves archive.

---

## TREWMAN Athol.B.

OR 1902-1907

Lieutenant. 1st Battalion, Middlesex Regt.

Died of wounds on 22nd October 1914. Aged 22.

CEMETERY: Haubourdin Communal Cemetery, Nord, France.

Only son of Lieut-Col. G.T.Trewman, late R.A.M.S.C. and Florence M.Trewman of 210 Tilehurst Rd. Reading. Born at Cape Town, South Africa. Athol Trewman died of wounds on October 22nd in hospital at Hauvourdin, Lille, aged 22. He was born at Cape Town on August 26th 1892, and was educated at Reading School and Wimborne School. He joined the 1st Middlesex Regiment in June 1914 from the Special Reserve, and went out to the front at the beginning of the war with the first part of the Expeditionary Force. He had been missing since October 21st and the report of his death was received through the American Embassy in Berlin.

---

## WARNER Evan

Sergeant (8050). 5th Battalion London Regiment (London Rifle Brigade).*

Killed in action on Friday December 11th 1914. Aged 34.

CEMETERY: Lancashire Cottage Cemetery, Ploegsteert, Comines-Warneton, Hainaut, Belgium. Grave Ref. I.C.8.

The Lancashire Cottage Cemetery was first started in November 1914 by the 1st East Lancashire and 1st Hampshire Divisions. It was used as a front line cemetery until March 1916. The Germans also used it during the first half of 1918.

*The London Rifle Brigade served in the Ploegsteert area during the winter of 1914-15. It had been raised in April 1908 as a territorial battalion. It was attached to regular battalions and spent most of its time repairing and extending the defences around Ploegsteert.

# 1915

School Magazine, July 1915:

*'There is a movement on foot for securing the services of the school in the making of munitions during the holidays'.*

*'The School assisted in the work connected with the collection in the town on Wounded Soldiers Day. Fifty boys acted as cyclist messengers under the leadership of Mr Edwards'.*

*'Drawing and Handicrafts exhibition.*
*........It is hoped that under the tuition of Mr F.W.Spring, the Handicraft teacher, the boys will turn their talents to good account by making shells'.*

| Overview: | Western Front | Dardenelles |
| --- | --- | --- |
| January 15 | Givenchy | |
| March 10–12 | Neuve Chapelle | |
| April 17–22 | Hill 60 | |
| April 22–23 | Gravenstafel | |
| April 24–May 4 | St Julien | |
| April 25–26 | | Landing at Helles |
| April 25–26 | | Landing at Anzac |
| April 28 | | Krithia |
| May 6–8 | | Krithia |
| May 8–13 | Frezenberg | |
| May 8–June 30 | | Defence of Anzac |
| May 9–17 | Aubers Ridge | |
| May 24–25 | Bellewaarde | |
| May 15–25 | Festubert | |
| June 4 | | Krithia |
| July 19, 30, Aug 30 | Hooge | |
| August 6–21 | | Suvla |
| August 6–10 | | Sari Bair |
| August 6–10 | | Sari Bair-Lone Pine |
| August 6–15 | | Landing at Suvla |
| August 21 | | Scimitar Hill |
| August 27 | | Hill 60 (Anzac) |
| September 25–Oct 8 | Loos | |
| September 25 | Bois Grenier | |
| September 25 | Pietre | |
| December 19–20 | | Evacuation of Suvla and Anzac |

## THE BATTLE OF NEUVE CHAPELLE

### March 10th -12th 1915

The war that was to have ended by Christmas continued and during the Spring of 1915 the British High Command planned to deliver a knockout blow to the German army which they hoped would ultimately lead to outright victory.

The focus of the attack was a salient of 1,850 metres (2,000 yards) wide by 1,100 metres (1,200 yards) deep around the town of Neuve Chapelle which had been lost to the Germans in October 1914. The aim was to recapture the original British lines, move on to Aubers, less than a mile to the east, continue the attack on to Lille and then to Germany itself.

The attack began on the morning of 10th March with a 35 minute artillery barrage from 342 guns. The direction of fire was guided by 85 reconnaisance aircraft. British and Indian divisions then attacked over a 3,700 metre (4,000 yards) front and only succeeded in achieving their objective after a great deal of hand to hand fighting.

However, to the north of the attack a quarter mile of German trench had not been shelled and allied forces which attacked on this line were confronted with small arms and machine gun fire. All were killed.

British Dead at Neuve Chapelle.
*Ref. Kriegsarchiv Wien.*

Communications were very difficult as telephone lines had been destroyed by German shelling and messages were delivered by hand thus making it difficult to carry out the original plan[1].

However, Haig ordered a frontal attack and almost all who took part were killed or wounded. By the time the battle was over on March 12th the British trenches had been regained but at a cost of 11,200 casualties .

## BATTLE OF AUBERS RIDGE

May 9-17th 1915

The British forces attacked opposite La Bassee and Fromelles on May 9th 1915 to try to gain Aubers Ridge, which had eluded them during the Battle of Neuve Chapelle. During the preliminary barrage only 8% of the shells were high-explosive and the limited time during which the bombardment could take place, less than forty minutes, meant that the damage done to the German lines was minimal. Other shells were too light and others did not explode at all. It was reported by the Germans that some of the shells, which failed to explode in front of their trenches, were made in the USA and contained sawdust!

Consequently, when the British attacked they were facing undamaged trenches and heavy enemy fire. As they were driven back many were killed by British troops in their own lines who mistook them for an enemy counter attack. That afternoon Haig ordered another attack which was decimated by German machine-gun fire. Eventually the commanders persuaded Haig that any further attacks would be suicidal and that they did not have enough artillery ordnance to lay down another barrage. In all, 458 officers and 11,161 men were killed in just one day's fighting.

## SECOND BATTLE OF YPRES

April 22nd–May 25th 1915

This battle can be subdivided into four areas of conflict. Battle of Gravenstafel (22nd-23rd April), Battle of St Juliaan (24th April-4th May), Battle of Frezenberg (8th -13th May) and Battle of Bellewaerde (24th-25th May)

On the 22nd April 1915 the Germans used gas for the first time in an attempt to win outright victory. At Langemark, in the Ypres salient, the Germans discharged 4,000 cylinders containing 168 tons of chlorine onto Canadian, Algerian and French divisions across a four mile front. The Algerians fled leaving a gap in the

---

1   On March 11th a Colonel, in reply to a Company Commander's enquiry about whether or not he should attack, said:' No, it is a mere waste of life, impossible to get twenty yards, much less two hundred. The trenches have not been touched by artillery. If artillery cannot touch them the only way is to advance from the right flank. A frontal attack will not get near them'. Ref. Gilbert op cit. p133.

line of almost half a mile. The Germans, wearing gas-masks, advanced taking 2,000 prisoners and 51 guns in the process. However, because the Germans had not brought up any reserves they were unable to press home their advantage. The situation was not helped by the gas blowing back into the faces of the 'unmasked' German troops remaining in their trenches.

A second gas attack was launched the following day against the Canadians, 2,000 of whom were killed. At Kerselaar, on the junction of the St Julien-Poelcapelle and the Zonnebeke-Langemarck roads stands a very impressive Canadian Memorial commemorating those who died in the gas attacks. The junction is known as 'Canadian Corner'.

Despite renewed German attacks the line held but with very heavy casualties. The Germans spent the next month trying to defeat the defenders in the town of Ypres itself. Civilians were evacuated but in holding the town the British suffered 60,000 casualties against the German losses of 34,933.

## BATTLE OF LOOS

### Sept 25th-28th 1915

After holding the German advance at Ypres, Field Marshall Joffre planned a new offensive which he hoped would break the German lines in three areas: the Champagne Valley, Artois and Loos. The latter would be the responsibility of the British under General Haig.

The first bombardment was along a six-mile front. Using poison gas for the first time, because of a serious lack of artillery shells, the British released 150 tons of chlorine across No-Mans Land from 5,243 cylinders. Although around 600 Germans were killed in this first wave and the British advanced more than 3,700

Refugees leaving Ypres. *Ref. M.Pol.*

metres at one point in the line, the momentum of the attack slowed down as the gas was blown back into the faces of the advancing troops.

On September 27th the British attacked again but were faced with dozens of German machine-guns which simply traversed the lines of opposing forces walking towards them, causing considerable carnage. Whole battalions were wiped out. The affect of the German machine-guns was so devastating that they called the battle 'Der Leichenfeld von Loos' (Field of Corpses of Loos).

The death toll was greater than any other battle so far. The list of casualties filled four columns in the Times. *(Ref. Gilbert op cit p198).* Of the 10,000 British soldiers who took part in the Battle of Loos, 385 officers and 7,861 men were killed or wounded.

**AYRES Giles Frederick**

OR 1897-1901

2nd Lieutenant. 3rd Bn. Lincolnshire Regiment/ Dorsetshire Regiment.

Killed in action on Sunday 9th May 1915. Aged 30.

He was the only son of Mr and Mrs Frederick Ayres of Caversham.

MEMORIAL: Ploegsteert Memorial, Comines-Warneton, Hainault, Belgium. Panel 3.

The Ploegsteert Memorial records the names of 11,447 British soldiers who died in the Caestre-Dranoute-Warneton area north of the line and Haverskerque-Estaire-Fournes to the south and who have no known grave. Many fell in the Battle of Lys.

The major battles in this area were those around Ypres and Messines.

Ayres entered Reading School in April 1897 having been privately educated by a Miss Burgess. He left at Christmas 1901 and in the Valete is listed as being a member of the 2nd XV.

He was married in December 1914.

*'Ayres-Pitman. On the 5th December at St. Giles Church Reading, quietly by the Rev. Fitzwilliam G.C.Gillmor, Vicar. Giles Frederick Ayres, 2nd Lt. 3rd Battalion Dorset Regt. only son of Mr and Mrs Frederick Ayres of Harlech, Caversham, to Marjorie Pitman, eldest daughter of Mr and Mrs Warren H. Pitman of Chedworth. Northcourt Ave'.*

Like many other 2nd Lieutenants during the war, Ayres was killed leading a charge on May 9th 1915.

The letter announcing his death received by Mrs Giles Ayres was signed by Capt. J.A.Griffin, 2nd Lincolnshire Regiment to which unit he was attached. It stated:

*'.....He was killed in action on the morning of 9th May whilst leading his men in an attack on the German trenches.*

*It may be some consolation to you in your terrible loss to know that he was shot through the heart, death being instantaneous.*

*He was a very popular officer and his death is deeply regretted throughout the regiment'.*

Full particulars of his last moments are not to hand. But it is evident from the foregoing and from one's knowledge of his character that he did not shrink from duty when his life hung in the balance, but faced his task with grim resolve and lion-hearted courage.

Lieut. Giles Ayres had hosts of friends and well-wishers in Reading, where he assisted to control a leading business house, and doubtless where he would have become a prominent figure in public life if he had been spared. He belonged to a family which has been engaged in business in the town upwards of a century. He was the only son of Mr and Mrs Frederick Ayres, and was named after his uncle, Captain Giles Ayres who served in the South African War with the Berkshire Yeomanry and whose death in January 1907 robbed the district of one of the best sportsman and kindest benefactors.

Peculiar pathos attaches to his last letter to his family in Reading. It was written on Saturday May 8th the eve of the great advance, in which he fell while gallantly leading his men in an attack on the German trenches. From his last letter we are privileged to take the following extracts:

*'Just a line to tell you the day has arrived. Tomorrow we go into our position, and there is going to be a tremendous attack. You will read about it in the papers. Oh may it be a success! Of course I ought not to write about this, but it matters not; it will either be good or bad by the time you receive this letter and I expect it means that I shall either be on my way home wounded or I shall remain here for ever....the first I hope. I do so want to see you all again. I am going over the parapet with a shout of 'School' on my lips and then pray God's will be done!*

*I am writing in a little out-house where I am sleeping on straw tonight. Please do not send another parcel until you receive a postcard from me to let you know the result. I do not know what else to write about, except to say several fellow officers in the Dorsets have been wounded or killed. Well I must close, as I have heaps to do, and must try to get some sleep tonight. I am thinking of you all. If the worst comes to the worst, tell any young fellows in Reading who can, and there are many, that they must come out and take our places'.*

In another letter Lt.Ayres wrote:

> *'It is a terrible business and we are nothing better than worms, dug in and stopped here, but hope that happier times are in store and very soon. We all hope and pray for it every day. I don't think the people at home realise what a gigantic task we have; but we mustn't grumble, but do it'.*

## BELCHER Gordon

Master 1907-10.

'3rd Battalion Royal Berks Regt. has been restored to the establishment with the rank of Captain'.

July 1915.

'Captain Gordon Belcher. 3rd Battalion (attached 1st) Royal Berkshire Regt. The Vicarage, Bramley, Hants'.

Killed in Action on Saturday 15th May, 1915. Aged 29.

CEMETERY: Rue-des-Berceaux Military Cemetery, Richbourg-L'Avoue, Pas-de-Calais, France. Grave Ref: I.A.5.

The cemetery was first established in January 1915 and used until February 1917.

Belcher was an MA Cambridge and had been an assistant master at Brighton College, where he held a commission as Lieutenant in the school contingent of the OTC. He received his commission in 1910 and was promoted lieutenant in 1912. He was on the seconded list at the outbreak of war, when he rejoined the 3rd Battalion Royal Berkshire Regiment. He saw fierce fighting in the autumn of 1914 and was mentioned in Sir John French's despatch of January 14th 1915, together with several brother officers, and was awarded the Military Cross. In the same month he was gazetted Captain. He was well known to followers of cricket as a player for Berkshire County Cricket Club for whom he did useful service with bat and ball.

In August 1914 the 1st Battalion Royal Berkshire Regiment was based in Aldershot at the Mandora Barracks and was part of the 6th Brigade, 2nd Division. It left for France on August 13th, landing at Rouen. On December 13th, 1915 the battalion was transferred to the 99th Brigade in the same Division.

Its first action of any significance was at the Bridge on the Sambre, August 25-26th 1914. After being involved in the retreat from Mons and then the counter-attack, the battalion crossed the Marne and then later the Aisne on September 14th. It was then based at La Metz Farm. From October 22nd - November 13th the 1st Battalion was involved in the 1st Battle of Ypres. It then went into the Divisional Reserve and spent the winter of 1914/15 in this role. During 1915 it took part in attacks at Ducks Bill, February 20th, The Keep, March 10-11th, and Richebourg, May 15th. It would seem that Belcher was killed in this engagement, although the records state that reserves from the 3rd Battalion did not reach the 1st until May 16th.

## BLACK Francis

OR 1909-12

Pte. 5827 18th Battalion, Royal Fusiliers.

Killed in action in France on Thursday 2nd December 1915. Aged 22.

Only son of the late Claude Black F.G.S. M.I.M.M. and of Mrs Black, Reading.

Black had been a Prefect and Captain of the 1st XV in 1911. He then travelled to Canada.

MEMORIAL: Loos Memorial, Pas de Calais, France. Panel 25-27

The Loos Memorial forms the boundary of the Dud Corner Cemetery. Both commemorate the lost and those killed during the Battle of Loos. It stands on an original German redoubt which was captured by a Scottish Division on the first day of the battle. It commemorates over 20,000 officers and men who were killed in the area from the River Lys to the southern boundary of the First Army, east and west of Grenay, who have no known grave.

Captain 1st XV 1911
'A Centre three-quarter. The best tackler in the team. Has had little opportunity of attacking, but is inclined to play too close up to the scrum. Kicks fairly well'.

## BLAZEY John William Victor b25.4.1897.

OR 1909-13

2nd Lieutenant. No.2492 'A' Company 1st Battalion Royal Berkshire Regt.*

Killed in action on Sunday 26<sup>th</sup> September 1915.  Aged 18.

MEMORIAL: Loos Memorial, Pas de Calais France, Panel 93-95.

1<sup>st</sup> XI 1912
'A greatly improved bat with plenty of defence, but will have to learn to drive. His slow bowling has not been much needed this year. A good and keen field'.

*The 1<sup>st</sup> Battalion Royal Berkshire Regiment was heavily involved at the Battle of Loos, loosing 288 men in one day. Blazey died on the second day of the engagement.

Blazey entered Reading School in January 1909 as a 'Freeplacer'. He had been previously educated at Redlands Council School, Blenheim Gardens, Reading.

His father, John Arthur Blazey was a tailor and, with Mary Emily Blazey, lived at 34 Bulmershe Rd. Reading

He wrote the following to the Magazine, July 1915:

> *'I thought you might like to have a line telling you a few experiences to date of trench warfare and life in general out here. First of all, I do not wish to convey the impression which one would gather from reading Reading local papers, i.e. that we have been in action, but we have had several sufficiently exciting and nerve-racking days for most people's liking. So far, it has generally been on Sunday that we have been particularly 'favoured' with shell-fire and it is from these bombardments that our few casualties, for the most part, have occurred.*
>
> *Although we are in quite an advanced part of the line, it is at present comparatively quiet, the object being, I think, to push up our immediate flanks until they are on a level with us. This policy is succeeding if the reports we hear are true, but the process is of necessity very slow.*
>
> *Our life consists of four days in the trenches, followed by four days in support about a mile behind the firing line, and this second period is taken up with nearly unending fatigues, such as taking rations up to the half battalion doing duty in the trenches, digging fresh trenches, and above all, making ourselves generally useful.*
>
> *The two first-mentioned jobs are quite as dangerous as, if not more so, than being 'in' as we call it, for the Germans have machine guns trained on all roads leading trenchwards, and at frequent intervals 'let rip' in the hope of catching one of our parties. There are hundreds of stray bullets flying about too and every now and then someone gets one, and if the wound is not too serious, is talked about as being a 'lucky devil', and other things, for it means a*

*holiday in England. But the spirits of all concerned out here are tip-top, and although few venture opinions as to the duration of the war, optimism reigns supreme. And that, to my mind, is a great factor in our favour.*

*I'm afraid I'm now the only O.R. left in this Battalion.*

*I've every reason to believe that my application for a Commission would have materialised some time ago had I let it continue, but seven months training in England was so wearying that I jumped at the idea of coming out here and cancelled the application. And I must say I don't regret it in the least, for on the whole one couldn't wish to run across a better lot of fellows.*

*It was with deep regret that I heard of the death in action of Lieutenants Hawkins and Giles Ayres, also of Captain Belcher; but it is certain that each one died as an Englishman should, and no greater tribute could be paid to anyone. Likewise, I was glad to hear that Wells and Baseden are progressing favourably; of course it is inevitable that the old School should suffer some losses, but that they may be as light as possible is the only thing to hope.*

*To turn to a lighter subject. I hope the XI will do really well again this season, young though the talent may be! It is a noticeable fact that all the casualties connected with the School, so far as I know, have happened to those who were to the front in sport, and every branch of athletics will be hard hit before this war is over, I fear.*

*Please give my kind regards to all those masters whom I know and tell Mr Crook that my OTC training has served me in good stead'.*

Dec 1915

*'Information has been received by his parents, who reside at 34, Bulmershe Rd. Reading, that their son, 2nd Lieutenant J.W.Blazey, was killed in action on September 28th. Aged 18. Lieut. Blazey was an Old Boy of Reading School and was a member of the Officer's Training Corps; he won his colours in Cricket and was a member of the Rugby XV. He was engaged in the Continental Office at Messrs. Huntley and Palmers. He joined the Army as a private early in August 1914, and after going to the Front in March he returned home last August and received a Commission. Information shows that his Company were ordered to make an attack in the recent advance. The assault was met by a strong force. 2nd Lieutenant Haigh, 68 Hamilton Rd. Reading, who has been wounded, says that he saw Lieut. Blazey and a little band of men, surrounded by superior numbers of Germans and that there was little hope of them escaping alive'.*

**COLLIER George William**

OR 1897-1902

Lance Sgt. 13254. 8th Batt. The Buffs, East Kent Regiment.*

Killed in action on Monday 27th September 1915. Aged 32.

Son of Mrs E.P.Collier, of 'Westgrove', Grovelands Rd. Reading and the late E.P.Collier; husband of Florence E. Burgess (formerly Collier) of 254, Shinfield Road, Reading.

MEMORIAL: Loos Memorial, Pas de Calais, France. Panel 15-19.

*The 8th Battalion had been established in Canterbury in September 1914 as part of Kitcheners 3rd New Army. In August 1914 it had been attached to 72nd Brigade and in October 1915 with the 17th Brigade. It was disbanded in France, February 1918.

**COHEN H.**

OR 1908-12

2nd Lieutenant. 8th Battalion Royal Berkshire Regt.*

Killed in action on Sunday 18th July 1915

CEMETERY: Golders Green Jewish Cemetery, Middlesex.
Grave Ref: West 17.26.

*The 8th (Service) Battalion, Royal Berkshire Regiment was formed at Reading in September 1914 as part of Kitchener's 3rd New Army.

**CORRY Roland Longman**

Sergeant. 1299. Honourable Artillery Company.

Killed in action on 24th September 1915. Aged 25.

Son of William Longman and Annie Corry of St.Katherines, Caterham Valley, Surrey. Before the war he was a Civil Engineer on the Staff of the Thames Conservancy. He joined the H.A.C. as a volunteer in August 1914 and was offered a commission the day before he was killed.

CEMETERY: Brandhoek Military Cemetery, Ypres, West-Vlaanderen, Belgium. Grave Ref: I.D.6

Corry left school in 1908 while in the fourth year. Even so he played Cricket for the 1st XI and Rugby for the 1st XV in 1907. In the former he was described as:

'A good slow bowler, when he gets his length, the ball having a deceptive flight and breaking just enough. As a bat he is far too stiff and does not open his shoulders'

and in the latter as:
'A greatly improved forward. Tackles and dribbles well. Good on the line out and at opening the game out from a forward rush'.

During the First World War, Brandhoek was within an area of comparative safety from shell fire which extended beyond the Church at Vlamertinghe. Field Ambulances were posted there throughout the war and the Military Cemetery was opened in May 1915 in a field next to the dressing station. It closed in July 1917 when the new Military Cemetery was opened nearby.

**EDWARDS Harold Ethelstan**

OR 1905-07

Lieutenant. 3rd Battalion attached 2nd Battalion Royal Warwickshire Regiment.*

Killed in action on Saturday 25th September 1915. Aged 20.

MEMORIAL: Loos Memorial, Pas-de-Calais, France. Panel 22 to 25.

Son of Mrs Edwards, Pensbury, Erleigh Road, Reading.

* The 2nd Battalion had been in Malta in August 1914. It returned to the UK in September and joined the 22nd Brigade. 7th Division. The 3rd (Reserve) Battalion remained in the UK throughout the war.

During the Battle of Loos the 7th Division took part in the initial assault north of the Vermelles-Hulloch road. It was affected by the drifting of British gas and was decimated by German machine gun fire and artillery. The Division managed to gain their objective, which was a series of quarries and only failed to breach the third German line because the men were very tired.

**FORSS Francis Stephen Arthur**  b7.10.1894.

OR 1909-13

Sgt. Australian Forces, Gallipoli.

Entered Reading School in January 1909.

Educated at Maidenhead College.

Father: Solicitor F.J.C. Forss, Churchgate House, Maidenhead.

Awarded Medaille Militaire.

Shooting VIII 1910-13.

'Probably the best shot in the team. He worked very hard at the backward shots and was a very efficient Secretary'.

(Letter to magazine December 1915 from his father)

> *26th November 1915*
>
> *Dear Sirs,*
>
> *As the doings of Old Boys are of interest to the readers of your Magazine, I send a copy of the 'Daily Telegraph' of the 18th instant giving an account of the sinking of a British Transport off Mudros. The Press Bureau statement, which appeared in the Daily Telegraph of the 12th instant and other Morning Papers, was as follows:*
>
> *'The War Office announces that on September 2nd, 1915, the Transport 'Southland' [1] from Alexandria was torpedoed in the Aegean Sea but reached Mudros under her own steam at 10pm the same day'.*

[1]  The 'Southland' (12,200 tons) was originally called the 'Vaderland' and had been built at the John Brown shipyard in Glasgow for the 'Red Star Line' She was launched in 1900 and made her maiden voyage from Antwerp to New York in December of the same year.

The 'Vaderland' arrived in New York a few days after war was declared and she was placed at the disposal of the White Star Line, making a return trip to Southampton on September 3rd 1914. She remained as a passenger vessel on the Liverpool-New York route and Canadian-Dominion service for several months until, in 1915, she was renamed the 'Southland' (because the 'Vaderland' was too Germanic) and taken over as a troopship.

The ship is also mentioned in the diary of an anonymous Australian soldier who states on January 3rd 1916 'The Southland is again in Harbour (Mudros) and is leaking badly'.

In August 1916 the 'Southland' returned to the White Star Line and was on the Liverpool to Canada route which took troops eastbound and passengers westbound. On June 4th 1917, while on a journey from Liverpool to Philadelphia, she was hit by two torpedoes from a German U-boat (U70) and sank off the coast of Ireland. Four members of the crew were killed.

(Ref. 'Merchant Fleets' Haws, 'North Atlantic Seaway' Bonsor, 'Wartime Distasters at Sea'. Williams.)

*The above mentioned account was contained in a letter written by Sergt. F.S.A. Forss to his mother and myself. Having been nominated by Dr. Eppstein, your late Headmaster, for entry into Sandhurst, Forss was examined by the Army Council Medical Board and rejected as being 'unfit for medical service owing to defective vision'. This was in January 1913. Notwithstanding such defective vision, one eye I believe not being quite up to the then Military standard, he made, in the same year, as I think you will find recorded in your Magazine, shooting for the school at Bisley in the Ashburton Shield, 33 out of 35 at the longer range, and, as regards shooting at our local rifle club range, he 'cleared the board'. However, this was before the war when the Army did not matter. Not being good enough for our Army he went out to Australia on the same liner as Brigham, another old boy, who I am glad to hear is recovering from a serious wound and in England again, and was during our winter 1914-15 on the farm of a cousin up-country from Melbourne. In February last he joined the 3rd Australian Expeditionary Force. Thanks, no doubt, to his training in your excellent OTC he was promptly made a Corporal and soon after a full blown Sergeant in the 'C' Company 21st Battalion, 6th Infantry Brigade, 2nd Division. After spending some time in camp at Broadmeadows near Melbourne his Battalion left for Heliopolis Camp outside Cairo, where they were stationed for several months; leaving Alexandria on board the 'Southland' at the end of August.*

*He is now in the trenches 'in a little dug-out somewhere in Gallipoli' and states that 'the Turks are about 50 yards away but we don't trouble much about them'.*

In 1915 the Greek government, although not totally committed to the war, had allowed the use of the Islands of Imbros, Lemnos and Bozcaada as forward bases in the attempt to take Constantinople from the Turks, their old enemies. Destoyers and Battleships had gathered in the ports of Tenedos on Bozcaada and Mudros on Lemnos. The small ships and boats that would take the troops from the ships through the shallows to the shore had been towed across the Mediterranean to Lemnos. This daily traffic of ships made the preparations difficult to conceal and the Turks soon became aware of what was going on.

Daily Telegraph. November 18th:

*'AUSTRALIANS' COOLNESS ON SINKING TRANSPORT'*

*(Written by Sergt. F.S.A. Forss. O.R.)*

The following passages from the letter of an Australian soldier who was on board a British Transport which was torpedoed some time ago in the Aegean give a simple account of the extra-ordinary coolness, bravery and discipline shown by Australian troops on board the vessel.

'All went well until we were twenty-five miles off the base where troops get into smaller steamers to be brought on here, when suddenly, at eleven minutes to ten in the morning just as I was about going to my troop deck for morning inspection (I was a troop deck Sergeant), a supposed Austrian submarine sent a torpedo into us, which caught us on the port side, between Nos. 2 and 3 holds, which were about the centre, or a little to the rear of the centre, of the forward well deck. At that time, luckily, most of the troops were on their respective parade decks, as morning parade started at 10 a.m. Immediately they all fell in, and the company nearest the boats were got quickly and quietly away, no disturbance or rushing being shown by the troops in any way.

I helped to get away two collapsible boats and then went port side, where I helped with four others. I took a moment off to see how 'C' Company was getting on, this was at least forty minutes after we were hit. Looking down from by the bridge to the well deck I saw the whole company formed up in four lines, with their belts on and their packs and equipment at their feet. No noise whatever. Some of the men were taking off their boots and puttees; others their coats; others were smoking and joking. It was a fine sight. After a while 'C' Company came up in a single file and got away quietly, and having run short of fags (the third officer on the boat, and a fine chap, had half mine) I ducked down for some more, and when I came up the last boat was just going, and, as the captain of the boat thought he could get the boat beached, the adjutant, Captain......, called for volunteer stokers. I put my nose in as usual.

## WORK IN THE STOKEHOLD

We stripped, except for our breeches and boots, and went below, ten, including Lieutenant........, and myself. We started with a steam pressure of 80lb, and had to get it up to 200lb., before the engines could be started. We slaved away, stoking twenty-four fires between us, and it seemed ages before the 200lb mark was reached. Then the pumps were started and soon after the engines went 'slow ahead'.

The Captain sent us down bottles of soft drinks in a bucket of ice, which were very acceptable, and after doing a 'watch' we were relieved by stokers of torpedo-boats, so we all went up on deck and a fine sight we looked covered in perspiration and coal dust. It was a fine sight. All round the boat, which had a fair list, were a string of torpedo boats, cruisers, and gunboats, here and there a hospital boat, and two or three cargo boats going off in the distance, making for Mudros, which is the base I spoke about earlier in the epistle, and which Captain.......has just told me I may mention. We then, after having a bit of a rest and a wash, started piling up all the rifles we could find, about 1500, and about four o'clock someone mentioned that we had had no grub since 8 a.m., so we went and foraged below and had a snack, and one chap was appointed cook, and had two to help him, and we arranged to have dinner at 7.30 p.m. Then up *on deck we went and did a bit more stacking of rifles, and at 7.30 we went down in the officers saloon, and there was spread almost everything our cook could lay his hands on.*

*We set to and demolished chicken, green peas, and 'spuds' as if we had never seen such things, and about eight p.m., the chief officer limped down; he had knocked his ankle earlier in the day, and told us that we were beached safely. So gently was it done that we had not noticed our stopping at all.*

*Then the rest of the ship's officers who had not left the ship, the second and third officers, chief engineer, and three or four other engineers, and the boatswain and one or two others, all sat down for the first time, and ate and talked of the day's proceedings. We turned in about 10.30.*

*Altogether about thirty or thirty-five were killed or drowned out of close on 2000. We lost our brigadier-colonel, as I expect you will have heard by now; his boat was upset, and he died from shock and exposure, I fancy. Later in the morning a fatigue party came on board and collected all the kit and placed it in lighters and took it to the......a boat of 1,800 tons, a Cunarder, I fancy, where the battalion was being refitted. This went on for about four days, and all the time our little party remained on the stranded troopship, and were the last to leave. After outfitting, which took about two more days, we got into small steamers one afternoon, and arrived off the coast here at.....'*
(December 1915).

---

### FROST Kenneth

OR 1905-6. (Left in the third year).

2nd Lieutenant. 1st Battalion, Queen's Own Royal West Kent Regt.

Killed in action on Monday 22nd February 1915. Aged 23.

Son of Ralph Frost, 13 Wandle Road, Wandsworth Common, London.

MEMORIAL: Ypres (Menin Gate) Memorial, Ieper, West Vlaanderen, Belgium. Panel 4 and 47.

Since July 1st 1928 the Last Post has been played at 8pm beneath the arches of the Menin Gate every day, (except during world war two where it was played at Brookfield Cemetery in London, until September 6th 1944 when part of Ypres was liberated.) The tribute is in honour of the memory of the soldiers of the British Empire who died in the Ypres Salient 1914-18 and who have no known grave. In total around 100,000 men were never found. 54,896 are commemorated on the Menin Gate, the remainder are on the Memorial to the Missing at Tyne Cot cemetery. The latter, which contains 11,908 graves and is the largest British military cemetery in the world, takes its name from a small collection of buildings on the Broodseinde Ridge. The story goes that it was named by the 50th Northumbrian Division who were in the area during the Battle of Passchendaele, but it was marked as Tyne Cot on British maps long before 1917.

The 1st Battalion Royal West Kent was raised in Dublin in 1914 as part of the 13th Brigade 5th Division. As part of this Division Frost would have seen action in the Battle of Nonne Boschen on the 11th November 1914. Their next engagement was the attack on Hill 60 in April 1915 but he had already been killed by this time.

## GREGORY P.P.

OR 1912-1914

Gentleman Cadet. Royal Military College.

Killed in action on Sunday 26th September 1915.

1st XI 1912
'A very erratic bowler who, fortunately, has found his form in the school matches, particularly against Whitgift. Must aim at more steadiness in run and accuracy in length. A good field'.

CEMETERY: Sandhurst Royal Military Academy Cemetery, Berks. Grave Ref. 569.

## HARRIS Percy Cuthbert

OR 1898–1905

Captain. Suffolk Regt.

Killed in action on Tuesday 16th February 1915.
Aged 26.

Son of Capt. J.E. Harris (late Suffolk Regt.) and Mrs Harris of The Shade, Shamford, Hinckley, Leicestershire.

MEMORIAL: Ypres (Menin Gate) Memorial, Ieper, West Vlaanderen, Belgium.

Took the Army Qualifying Examination in 1904. Member of the 1st XV in 1904 and 1905. Described as a light but hard-working forward who was a splendid tackler and good at falling on the ball.

The Menin Gate is one of four memorials to those listed as 'missing' in the Ypres Salient. The salient stretched from Langemarck in the north, to the north of Ploegsteert Wood in the south. However, the shape of it varied throughout the war.

## HOLTOM. E.C.

OR 1897-1902

*'Uncertainty as to the fate of Surgeon E.C. Holtom of HMS Goliath[1], elder son of Mrs Holtom of 23, Junction Rd. Reading, has been dispelled.*

*The Admiralty informed Mrs Holtom on November 29th that he was 'reported missing but probably prisoner in operations against the enemy yesterday'. The operations referred to were off German East Africa. Captain Ritchie, of the 'Goliath', who has just arrived in England, reports that he saw Surgeon Holtom being rowed by natives in a boat, the Germans firing at him from under the white flag. He fell back in the boat and was taken to a German hospital ship.*

*The Admiralty now state that, according to the Governor of German East Africa, Surgeon Holtom is imprisoned in a healthy locality and is quite well and well looked after. It is hoped that the Government will arrange an exchange of doctors who are prisoners of war, and in that case Surgeon Holtom will be liberated.*

*He was educated at Reading School and formerly served on HMS Thistle on the China Station'.*

Dec 1918
*'Surgeon E.C.Holtom, stationed at Chatham, has been promoted to the position of Staff Surgeon (Lieut. Commander) in the Navy.*

---

1    HMS 'Goliath' was one of six 'Canopus' Class of Battleship. It was 12,950 tons and had a crew of 682 men. It was launched on March 23rd 1898 and commissioned two years later, almost to the day at Chatham. It was originally designed for service in the China Seas and had a shallow enough draught to enable her to go through the Suez Canal. It remained in the Far-East until 1903 when it returned to join the reserve at Portsmouth in 1904 and the Mediterranean Fleet in 1905, transferring to the Channel Fleet in December of the same year.

It was mothballed in 1913 but brought out again in August 1914 to join the Battle Squadron based at Devonport. It was later transferred to Loch Ewe for defence of the Grand Fleet anchorage. In September 1914 it was sent to the East Indies on escort duty and engaged the German light cruiser 'Konigsberg' in the Rufigi River, East Africa, in November. As the ship was then sent to the Dardenelles in 1915 and was damaged on April 25th and again on May 2nd, one can assume that Holtom's captivity was linked in some way with the Rufigi River incident. The ship was eventually sunk by torpedoes from the Turkish torpedo-boat 'Muavanet', May 13th 1915.

*He has written a book which is being published by Hutchinson and Co. of London under the title of 'Two Year's Captivity in German East Africa'. Mrs Holtom, of 23 Junction Rd, Reading, the mother of Surgeon Holtom has received a letter from Queen Alexandra, in which she says she has ordered a copy of the book'.*

## HORNE Joseph William

OR 1906-09

Entered School Sept.1906. School Prefect 1909. Secretary of the Games Committee 1909. Member of the Debating Society.

Before entering Reading School as a Reading Education Committee Scholar, Horne had been educated at Ascham House, Reading.

He left the school in1909.

In April 1910 he won an Academic Clerkship at Magdalen College, Oxford to the value of £115 perannum for six years.

Cricket 1st XI 1909. 'A useful left-hand bowler, but tires rather early. Has made a few runs, but must learn to field better'.

Rugby 1st XV. 1909 described as 'A fair forward who was never very prominent either in the scrum or in the loose. Will improve with more knowledge of the game'.

*Broken Hill*
*Northern Rhodesia*

*October 27th. 1915*

*Africa so far has agreed with me very well. I was in Livingstone for about three months but was glad to get away as it was stuffy and suburban. Ever since June 1914, I have been stationed here and enjoy life immensely. Administratively this is an important place, being the magisterial centre of the most important district in the Country, a district about as big as England, Scotland and Wales, with five sub-districts and with the Belgian Congo as its northern border, and Broken Hill is also a sort of railhead, as although the line goes on to Karnbove, all the main roads for up-country stations leave the line here.*

*For this reason Broken Hill has, since the war started, been a military base. All stores for the forces on our border leave the line here and start their 600-mile journey by carrier. Consequently this place has been a mass of black and odoriferous humanity for months. We have often had over 2,000 natives on the Station , and it takes us all our time to manage and feed them and get them away with their loads. We have sent away about 9,000 boys in the last three months with all sorts of food, equipment and munitions for the small force defending the border. It has all been very interesting and is, in a way, history. Natives have never before been called out to this extent to help the Government, and they have taken it remarkably well considering that they simply hate carrying loads, and small blame to them too, doing 20 miles a day with 60lbs on one's head for 10/- a month is rather an over-rated pastime.*

*It is good to see from the Magazine how the school is taking part in the war. I only wish I were on active service, but people on the District Staff could not possibly be spared. One has to remember that natives in this country outnumber the white men probably by 1,000 to 1, and though they are quite a good contented crowd they have to be watched.*

*This is a great country, and the life, for an irresponsible bachelor, is in many ways ideal.'*

## THE STORES FOR THE FORCES ON OUR BORDERS

It was General Paul von Lettow Vorbeck in Tanganyika who was giving J.W. Horne so much trouble in Broken Hill. It is no surprise that a man who is alleged to have told Hitler to "go away" in military language would cast such a long shadow during WW1. When that war started he had trained 1,156 Tanganyikans to fight. He called them Schutztruppe. With these and 300 German officers he waged a guerrilla war in East Africa which tied up 5,000 British, South African and Indian troops for the duration. He adopted an "Ice Cream policy", that is when his soldiers felt the heat they melted away into the bush. He and his soldiers made strategic withdrawals right through Tanganyika, Portuguese East Africa and Northern Rhodesia. He did not capitulate until three days after the Armistice was signed in Europe. He did so at Abercom in J.W. Horne's own territory in Northern Rhodesia.

He not only tied up 5,000 allied troops but forced recruitment meant that over one third of the adult males in Northern Rhodesia were engaged in carrying military stores. In British East Africa an ordinance signed in 1915 made all males between the ages of 17 and 45 liable for military service. In all over 50,000 African troops and 1,000,000 carriers were engaged in the conflict and more than 100,000 of them died.

He earned the grudging respect of his enemies. Even Phillip Percival, the famous white hunter, who had fought against him, acknowledged that he was a good general. The British respect some of their enemies if they fight well and honestly, but lose in the long run.

***

**HOWELL Roland Basil**

OR 1909-12

2nd Lieutenant. 4th Battalion North Staffordshire Regt.*

Killed in action on Saturday 2nd October 1915. Aged 20.

MEMORIAL: Loos Memorial, Pas-de-Calais, France. Panel 103-105.

January 1917
*'It will be remembered that in October 1915 Mr Howell's elder son, 2nd Lieut. Roland Basil Howell, was reported 'wounded and missing.' Nothing has since been heard of him, and any hopes of his being alive hang on the very slenderest thread. On the 16th of last month the War Office wrote saying that they were now forced to believe he was killed.*

*Lieut. Basil Howell was born October 1895 and received his Commission in the 4th North Staffordshires three months after the war started. He was attached to the Northumberland Fusiliers (the Fighting Fifth), and went to the front in May 1915.*

*Reports received from the front show that on the night of October 1st-2nd, 1915, the battalion to which Lieut. Howell was attached were in severe action. After all the other officers of the company were killed he gallantly led a bombing party to attack a German trench, but was never seen again. Every possible enquiry was made through the War Office, the American Embassy, the Red Cross and the wounded men who returned to England. Many references were made by the latter to the respect and love they had for the brave young officer.*

*Like his brother, he was educated at Reading School and St Laurence College, and had started his training to follow his father's profession. For many years he was an enthusiastic scout, and took a big share in starting the South Reading Troop'.*

* The 4th Battalion North Staffs was raised in Lichfield in 1914 and in June 1917 was attached to the 67th Division.

***

## HAWKINS Oliver Luther

OR 1905-11

2nd Lieutenant. 3rd Battalion East Yorkshire Regiment.*

Died of wounds near Ypres on April 26th 1915. Aged 22.

CEMETERY: Hazebrouck Communal Cemetery, Nord, France. Grave Ref. II.E.28

From October 1914 until September 1917 Hazebrouck was the site of many Casualty Clearing Stations and Hawkins would have been sent down the line to one of these when wounded in 1915. British burials in the Communal Cemetery began in October 1914 and continued until July 1918.

He was one of the most popular boys of Reading School (1905-11) of which he was for several years Captain. He twice won Lord Roberts' prize and gained distinction in cricket and football. On leaving school he studied at Marburg University Germany, and in 1913 he went into residence at Jesus College Cambridge, where he joined the OTC. On the outbreak of war he obtained a Commission.

1st XV 1911

'Has played in three positions during this term, wing, outside half and centre. Did not use his pace sufficiently either in attack or defence, but scored five tries against Sutton Courtenay. Poor Kick'.

## HAYNES William Gray

OR 1899-08

Lieutenant. 8th Battalion, Royal Berkshire Regt.

Killed in action on Saturday 25th September 1915. Aged 24.

CEMETERY: Bois-Carre Military Cemetery, Haisnes, Pas-de-Calais, France. Grave Ref. A.19

The actual village of Haisnes remained under German occupation until 1918, but some areas had been captured by British forces during the Battle of Loos. The cemetery, named after a wood a few hundred yards to the south-west, was started in September 1915.

Son of William and Annie Haynes of 5 Alexandra Rd. Reading.

He was known to all his friends as Billy. In 1907, he beat the school record for the mile by 2.6 seconds to reduce it to 5 minutes 1.2 secs. and presented a trophy for an annual mile race.

An all round sportsman he played for Berkshire Wanderers RFC and for Reading Hockey Club. He had been a member of the 1st XI Hockey (1908) ('Inside Right. Plays with plenty of dash. Is inclined to hit and run. A good shot. Lacks combination with his partners') and the 1st XV (1907) ('Left Centre. Has not come on as well as expected. Passed poorly and frequently missed his man. Good Kick.)

He worked for his father in the family Ironmongery business in Duke St.

In 1911 he joined the Territorial Army and became a 'crack shot' with 4th Battalion. Royal Berkshire Regiment.

At the outbreak of War he was promoted to the rank of Corporal and in December 1914 was commissioned as 2nd Lt. 8th Battalion and promoted Lt. when he reached France in August 1915.

Writing to Mr and Mrs Haynes, Major Bartlett said:

> *'His death was a great blow to us all. Not only have we lost a charming companion, but a real good officer. He was a natural leader of men and the men of his platoon were devoted to him. When he came to us from the 4th Batt., he came with a reputation which he certainly increased each day he was with us'.*

He was killed on 25th Sept. 1915 when hit by machine-gun fire in front of the German wire. He was buried on the 26th Sept. at Vermelles but his body was later transferred to Bois Carre Military Cemetery near Hulluch. *(Ref. Responding to the Call. Op.cit)*

> *9th November 1914.*
> *'A' Company 4th Royal Berks. Regt.*
> *Chelmsford*
>
> *Dear Captain Crook,*
>
> *Having seen the paragraph in the Reading Standard concerning O.Rs serving in His Majesty's Forces, I write to let you know that there are five of us in the 'A' Company of the 4th Royal Berkshire Regt., Sgt G.R.Dowsett, Ptes G.W.Blackall, J.W.Blazey, R.G.Holtum and myself with Corporal's rank.*

*Although this, in its original establishment was a Territorial unit, we have all signed for foreign service and hope that we may be able to do our bit when our turn comes, for the honour of the School and our Country. Pte. C.D. Balding was in this battalion, but he has been transferred to a Reserve Home Service Company because he did not volunteer for Imperial Service with the rest of us.*

*For the last two or three years it has been my privilege to arrange the O.R. XV to play the School, this year I shall be unable to do so, I doubt if it will be possible to raise a team at all; there should not be many able-bodied O.R.s about except those serving; anyone fit to play Rugger should, except in exceptional circumstances, be doing his share in some branch of the forces.*

*I have had two games of Rugby down here, one a practice and the other a match, 4th Royal Berks v 10th Essex Regt. Lieut R.W.Poulton-Palmer, of international fame, was captain of the Berkshire team, which included three O.R.s Blazey, Blackall and myself. We won by 16 points to nil after a fast and open game.*

*We were exceedingly sorry to learn of Dr. Eppstein's departure from the School. We were pleased to hear of Mr Keeton's appointment as his successor. I doubt whether Mr Keeton would remember me; when he was at the School before, I expect that I was a slacker in the second or third division game. I shall never forget the way in which he used to dribble a ball, no, nor the way in which he used to drop on us for walking on the grass sides down the drive.*

*Kind regards to Mr Newport and other members of the staff.*

*Yours sincerely,*
*W.G.Haynes.*

The Haynes ironmongery business. Duke Street, Reading.
*Ref. Berkshire County Libraries*

**HOWKINS George Addington**

OR 1903-06. (Left in his second year).

2nd Lieutenant. 12th Battalion Northumberland Fusiliers.*

Killed in action. Saturday 25th September 1915. Aged 21.

Son of John Thomas and Emily Addington Howkins of Sindlesham, Wokingham, Berks.

MEMORIAL: Loos Memorial, Pas-de-Calais, France. Panel 20 to 22.

* The 12th Battalion was established in Newcastle in September 1914 as part of Kitchener's 3rd New Army. It was attached to 62nd Brigade, 21st Division, later in the same month. This Division was assembled around Tring and crossed to France between the 2nd and 13th September 1915. Having been in France only a few days long marches brought it into the reserve at the Battle of Loos. GHQ planning had left it too far behind to be a useful reinforcement but when in went into action at the end of September it suffered tremendous casualties.

**LOUTH Harold George**

OR 1900 - (Not listed)

Not Commemorated on the War Memorial but instated in 2001.

Pte. 2094. 4th Battalion, Seaforth Highlanders.*

Killed in action on Sunday 9th May 1915.

Son of the late George Edward and Mrs Louth, Western Elms Avenue, Reading.

MEMORIAL: Le Touret Memorial, Pas de Calais, France. Panel 38 and 39.

The Le Touret Memorial contains the names of over 13,000 men who were killed in the area around Le Touret before September 1915.

* In November 1914 the Seaforth Highlanders landed at Le Havre and on the 12th December 1914 joined the Dehra Dun Brigade, 7th Meerut Division on the Western Front.

**HEDGECOCK S.E.**

Lieutenant. Welsh Regiment Pioneers, elder son of Mr and Mrs E. Hedgecock, 2 Shinfield Rd, Reading has been appointed Captain.

Was invalided home with enteric fever. Educated at Reading School and King's School, Canterbury.

**JOHNSTONE J.C.**

Left School in 1912. Had been a Prefect, secretary of the debating society. Became a 'White' Scholar at St. John's College Oxford.

'St Johns and Devons Cyclist Batt. is to be congratulated on becoming a full lieutenant. Nothing else is known of him'.

December. 1915.
*'was lately engaged in hunting German spies in Portsmouth. Since then he has been seen in Reading, when he was, it was rumoured, en route for somewhere in France'. (Oxford OR).*

## McILROY W.E.C.

Lieut. Oxford and Bucks Light Infantry, second surviving son of the late Mr W. McIlroy, Holybrook House, Reading and of Mrs McIlroy, Newbury.

Wounded while in France and was transferred from a hospital in Rouen to Manchester, where he is making satisfactory progress. Lieut. McIlroy, who was educated at Reading School, enlisted in 1914 and went to France in July 1915. His two brothers are serving.

Left School in 1911. Had been a member of the 1$^{st}$ XV in 1910. Described as

'A useful forward, doing his share of work in the scrums, and fairly fast in the open. Should practise following up more. Poor tackler'.

2$^{nd}$ Lieutenant H.G.P.McIlroy, the eldest, joined the Oxford and Bucks Light infantry in 1914 and went to France with that regiment early in the following year. Shortly afterwards he returned home to take up a Commission and was attached to the East Yorks Regiment. He spent the greater part of last autumn and winter on the East Coast as a machine gun instructor, and during the air raids was in charge of anti-aircraft guns. He returned to France last May.

Sapper R.F.McIlroy, R.N., D.E., the youngest, went to Gallipoli last summer, and after the evacuation of the Peninsular spent many months on Greek Islands in the Aegean Sea. He was wounded there in the foot and arm. In May he was transferred to France.

1$^{st}$ XV 1914
'Left Wing Three-Quarter. Used his pace well with a clear course, but was too much inclined to slow up and be tackled. Weak defence. Must learn to kick with both feet'.

## MOODY WARD Richard Guy Torrington

OR 1895-96

Captain. 2<sup>nd</sup> Battallion, Royal Berkshire Regiment.*

Killed in action on Sunday, 9<sup>th</sup> May 1915.

MEMORIAL: Ploegsteert Memorial, Comines-Warneton, Hainault, Belgium. Panel 7 and 8.

The Ploegsteert Memorial records the names of those who died in the Caestre-Dranoute-Warneton area north of the line and Haverskerque-Estaire-Fournes to the south and who have no known grave.

The major battles in this area were those around Ypres and Messines.

* In August 1914 the 2<sup>nd</sup> Battalion Royal Berkshire Regiment was based in Jhansi, India in the 5<sup>th</sup> Mhow Division. On August 20<sup>th</sup> 1914 it sailed for England arriving on October 22<sup>nd</sup>. It was assigned to the 25<sup>th</sup> Brigade, 8<sup>th</sup> Division based at Winchester. The Battalion left for France on November 5<sup>th</sup>, 1914 landing at Le Havre.

## SHARP P.M. (Lieut.)

OR 1914

Captain of School. Captain of the Shooting VIII.

'Has been a most disappointing shot all through the year (1913) but selected a very strong team and coached them most untiringly and carefully. Much of the credit for the success at Bisley attaches to him'.

*October 15<sup>th</sup> 1915.*

*When you first come to the front and everything is new, you are deluged with letters from home and everywhere, and, I spent a whole month answering letters. After that, when one gets accustomed to the life and even inclined to boredom, letters are welcome, and so, consequently, people at home stop writing.*

*You will doubtless have heard from my father that I have been in France very nearly three months. At first we were billeted near General Headquarters and then moved up to the 2<sup>nd</sup> Army. For a week or so we were in reserve and were pushed up into support at Armentieres. There we dug every night and in the day* *where possible. The enemy were very vigilant and used to turn machine guns on to us for ten minutes at a time, or treat us to a salvo of shrapnel. Our casualties were very slight, and the digging parties I took, which were always all-night turns, never suffered one killed or wounded, thank goodness. We then went into the trenches at Armentieres, and my Company got a bit only 80 yards from the Germans. Our left was on a river, and so strange is this war that we were actually able to enjoy the luxury of a bathe, less than a hundred yards from the enemy. Traverses and various devices screened us from view. They had a horrible knack of sending over things we called sausages. These consist of a thin cylindrical shell, about 1 foot high entirely filled with Lyddite. These 'sausages' are fired by a trench mortar of sorts and their maximum range is about 500 yards. They go up like a rocket and then drop vertically. You run like a hare as you can see them quite easily. They burst on percussion with a terrible noise, and though their effect is local it is immense. Men are literally blown up and deposited 30 yards away, and there were many ghastly cases of 'buried alive'. We then got a shift suddenly and came down south to the 3rd Army. I musn't tell you where we are now. This great advance was north of us and the din was awful. I was out of the trenches in Divisional Reserve at the time, and instead of resting, as per programme, we were hurried hither and thither to places where they might need us.*

*Our programme as a Battalion is 12 days in the trenches and 12 days out. As a Company, 6 days in the firing line, 6 days in the ruined village behind, in support, and 12 days rest. Life is therefore fairly easy. In the trenches one gets little or no sleep, 4 hours in 24 is a very full allowance. We all have to be in the trenches for an hour before dawn, and an hour after sunset. These periods are known as 'Stand To'. At night there is a lot of work to be done; repairing damage to trenches done by enemy shells, putting new wire of the barbed variety out in front, or patrolling the space between the German and the British lines. This is done every night, and I have been out several times. It is rather exhilarating. There is always one officer on duty in the fire trenches of a Company. In the ruined village we have an easier time, although our men have to find constant fatigues for the Royal Engineers, cleaning the communicating trenches, improving fire trenches etc. In reserve we do a lot of digging, bombing and practise attacks; but generally after 3pm we are free to rest or to do what we will in a deserted and, at any time, poky French village. This time I was sent on to billet the Battalion, and succeeded in satisfying the C.O., Adjutant, Officers and Men, a hitherto unaccomplished feat! Everyone grouses at billets. For my own Company I chose an empty farmhouse. The men are billeted in barns and we are in the bare rooms. Today, Sunday, is a day of rest, and I sit out of doors in the hot sunshine, with a manure-heap in front, the ever present symbol of a French farmhouse, on which ducks, geese and hens are all disporting themselves.*

*I am awfully sorry to see that Harold Edwards and Billy Haynes have fallen in this last attack. With the deaths of Trewman and Hawkins, both of whom were great friends of mine, this makes a big gap in the circle of school friends that mean so much.*

***

### SALMON Ronald Stuart

OR 1905

Rifleman 3061. 1st/21st Battalion, London Regt. (First Surrey Rifles).

Killed in action on the night of Tuesday 25th May 1915 in France, while rescuing wounded comrades. Aged 21.

MEMORIAL: Le Touret Memorial, Pas-de-Calais, France. Panel 45.

'Among the names mentioned by Sir John French in his final dispatch for gallant and distinguished conduct in the field was that of Pte R.S. Salmon of the London Regt. son of the late Mr E.H. Salmon of this town and Mrs Salmon now of High Wycombe. His death at the front was reported some time since, but the posthumous honour is some consolation to his relatives'.

***

### WHITTAM Matthew John Goldsborough

OR 1905-08

Lieutenant. 8th Battalion Duke of Wellington's (West Riding Regt.)*

Killed in action on Wednesday, 11th August 1915. Aged 21.

CEMETERY: Lancashire Landing Cemetery, Turkey. Grave Ref. K.18.

John Whittam who died of wounds received in action in Gallipoli on August 11th was gazetted to a Commission in the 8th Duke of Wellington's Regiment in September, 1914 and made Lieutenant in February 1915. He was the only son of the Rev. W.G.Whittam and Mrs Whittam, St Luke's Vicarage, West Norwood, and was 21 years of age. Educated at Reading School and St. Paul's School, he was elected to a Pauline Exhibition at Corpus Christi College, Cambridge, and when the war broke out had been at Cambridge for two years. He took a prominent part in college athletics.

***

The Dardenelles campaign was planned to remove Turkey from the war and reopen the supply lines to Russia. It originally involved an Allied fleet forcing its way through the Dardenelles to gain access to the Black Sea and at the same time targeting Constantinople. From the very beginning it was mishandled and the campaign became one of the most mismanaged military operations in history. After the Naval assault failed it was decided to land a force on the Gallipoli peninsular to advance towards Constantinople. However, the difficult geographical conditions meant that the troops, made up from British, ANZAC units and a small force of French, could only assemble slowly which gave the Turkish and German armies time to reinforce their defences.

On the 25th April 1915, the 29th Division landed troops on five small coves, labelled 'S', 'V',' 'W','X','Y', at or near the southern end of the Gallipoli Pensinsular. The landing at Ghurka Bluffs ('Y') was carried out by the King's Own Scottish Borderers and the Plymouth Battalion of the Royal Naval Division, but they had to retreat and were forced to re-embark on the 26th April. The 2nd Royal Fusiliers landed at 'X', followed by the 87th Brigade. The 1st Lancashire Fusiliers landed at 'W' under very heavy fire but managed to work their way through the beach defences to the edge of the cliff. They and the 88th Brigade established themselves on the hills of Tekke Burnu and Helles Burnu. The beach became known as the Lancashire Landing.

Rows A-J and part of L in the Lancashire Landing Cemetery contain the bodies of men killed in the area between the landings in April 1915 and the evacuation in January 1916. Row K, where Whittam can be found, was created after November 1918 and contains the bodies of men who had previously been buried in smaller cemeteries on islands in the Aegean. Dates would suggest that Whittam may have originally been interred in the Kephalos British Cemetery on the island of Imbros.

* The 8th Battalion was formed in Halifax on August 21st 1914 under Army Order 324 which authorised the formation of six new Divisions as part of Kitchener's 1st Army. Later in the same month it was attached to 34th Brigade, 11th Northern Division. It comprised entirely of volunteers. To begin with it had no equipment or weapons of any kind, but the recruits were considered ready for action in the spring of 1915. It was then ordered to reinforce the garrison at Cape Helles, Gallipoli. It sailed from Liverpool on July 1st 1915 and landed at Mudros on the 18th, after a stop over in Alexandria. Between July 20-31 it embarked at Cape Helles and went into action at Suvla Bay on August 7th.

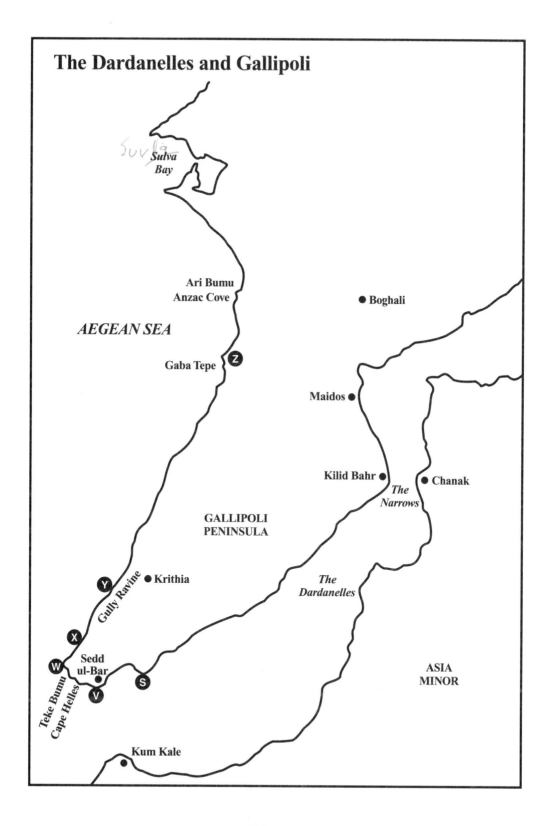

# The Dardanelles and Gallipoli

Suvla

*Sulva Bay*

Ari Bumu
Anzac Cove

● Boghali

*AEGEAN SEA*

Gaba Tepe **Z**

Maidos ●

Kilid Bahr ●   ● Chanak

*The Narrows*

**GALLIPOLI PENINSULA**

**Y** Gully Ravine   ● Krithia

*The Dardanelles*

**X**

**W** Sedd ul-Bar

Teke Bumu
Cape Helles   **V**   **S**

**ASIA MINOR**

Kum Kale
●

December 1915

Lecture on Serbia

On Saturday November 20th 1914 a Mr Henman, Special Commissioner of the Committee of English Farmers who had been assisting Serbian Agriculture, gave a lecture to the school on the present state of Serbia.

' *He began by a geographical description of the country, showing us where the Allied Forces then lay, and the position of the main roads and railways. He had started on his tour from Salonika, and gradually moved north visiting Belgrade itself, and Shabatz.*

*He gave a vivid account of the terrible condition of the roads, and said that he himself had seen no fewer than sixty Austrian guns which had been captured by the Serbs through being stuck in the mud. The advance of the enemy would undoubtedly be seriously hindered by the extreme difficulties of communication both by road and rail.*

*One of the brightest spots in Serbian national character is their home life. When a man's sons grow up for instance, the new homes which are formed on their marriage are, in most cases, built quite close to that of the old father and mother, who still retain the obedience and respect of their children. Though poor, they are thoroughly honest. The sum of £1,000 which had been sent for their relief, was returned at once by them when they found they could not apply as it had been intended by the donors; and this when they were in he direst straits, and money was exceedingly scarce.*

*The terrible atrocities which have been committed, especially in the North, were the work of the pure German and Magyar sections of the Austro-German invading force. The beautiful town of Shabatz, the centre of a once flourishing agricultural district, has been completely destroyed, and has been the scene of hideous massacres, which the Austrians affirm is a deliberate revenge for the murder of the Archduke at Sarajevo. Belgrade too, a lovely city, which was full of fine modern buildings, has been reduced to ruins by the heavy gun fire of the enemy.*

*Another most interesting feature of Serbian life is their love of music. Folk songs and national songs are very popular. Some of the latter are woven round the legend (in many ways similar to that which the Germans tell of Barbarossa) that King Marco on his horse Sharatz will return in Serbia's darkest hour and fight for them as he did nearly five centuries and a half ago.*

*Mr Henman then described the splendid work of Mrs Stobart's Nursing Mission. The condition of the hospitals out there was dreadful, and even at the best, disease was rampant. The peasants for miles round bring their sick to the British hospital, for the British doctors to prescribe for them. One little girl had walked for four hours to get medical advice for her mother who was dangerously ill. Their faith in the British is marvellous, in fact, scarcely credible. It is our duty to live up to that great reputation and to see to it that Serbia is adequately supported in this her time of trial'.*

On the same page someone gave a long description of their holiday in the Lake District which involved burst tyres, punctures, a broken three-speed and complained about 2d bottles of lemonade being sold for 6d. Was there really a war going on!?

# 1916

*'With the wrecks of our attack; the bandoliers,*
*Packs, rifles and bayonets, belts and haversacks,*
*Shell fragments, and the huge whole forms of shells*
*Shot fruitlessly – and everywhere the dead.*
*Only the dead were always present – present*
*As a vile sickly smell of rottenness;*
*The rustling stubble and the early grass,*
*The slimy pools – the dead men stank through all,*
*Pungent and sharp; as bodies loomed before,*
*And as we passed, they stank; then dulled away*
*To that vague foetor, all encompassing,*
*Infecting earth and air.....'*

From 'The Night Patrol'. Arthur Graeme West.

The allies were losing so many men that compulsory military service was introduced into Britain for the first time on February 9th 1916.

Overview:

| | |
|---|---|
| January 8 – 9 | Evacuation from Helles |
| March 27 – April 16 | St Eloi Craters |
| June 2 – 13 | Mount Sorrel |
| July 1 – November 18 | Somme |
| July 1 – 13 | Albert |
| July 1 | Beaumont Hammel |
| July 1 | Schwaben Redoubt |
| July 14 – 17 | Bazentin |
| July 15 – September 3 | Delville Wood |
| July 19 | Fromelles |
| July 23 – September 3 | Pozieres |
| September 3 – 6 | Guillemont |
| September 9 | Ginchy |
| September 15 – 22 | Flers Courcelette |
| September 2 – 28 | Thiepval |
| September 25 – 28 | Morval |
| October 1 – November 11 | Ancre Heights |
| November 13 – 18 | Ancre |

## THE BATTLE OF THE SOMME

### July-November 1916

The purpose behind the Battle of the Somme was to break through the German lines in order to allow a Cavalry attack which could move forward quickly to exploit whatever breakthroughs had been achieved.

At dawn on July 1st 1916 the allies launched an artillery barrage of around 250,000 shells in just one hour that was so intense it could be heard in London. At 7.28 a.m. ten mines were exploded under the German trenches and at 7.30 the allies attacked along a 25 mile front.

First day of the Somme. Still from moving picture.

*Imperial War Museum*

The British Commander, Sir Henry Rawlinson, was so convinced that there would be no German resistance, he ordered the men to attack in parade formation. The vast majority of them also carried about 28kgs weight of equipment including 'a rifle, ammunition, grenades, rations, waterproof cape, four empty sandbags, a steel helmet, two gas helmets, a pair of goggles against tear gas, a field dressing, a pick or shovel, a full water bottle and a mess tin'. *(Ref. Gilbert op cit p259).*

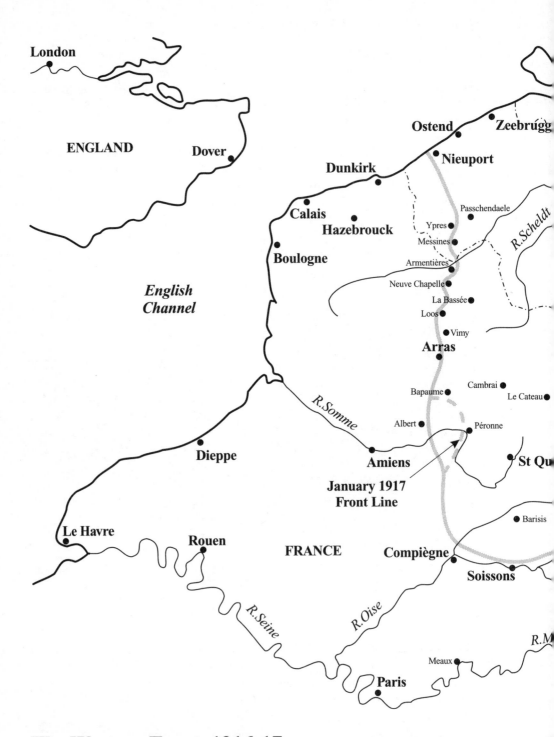

**The Western Front, 1916-17**

Trench at Thiepval. Soldiers resting, August 1916.

*Imperial War Museum*

Hundreds of German machine guns, many in armoured emplacements, had not been affected by the bombardment. Consequently, as the allies advanced they were mown down. This was made easier by the fact that many of the troops were having to funnel through small gaps in their own wire. Thus, all the German gunners had to do was concentrate their fire on these areas. Rawlinson considered calling off the attack, but he was ordered to continue by Haig. On that first day the German-held areas around Mametz and Montauban and the Leipzig redoubt were captured. But the cost in human life was devastating. On the first day the British lost over 1,000 officers and 19,240 men killed. 35,494 seriously wounded, 2,152 missing, 585 taken prisoner. The Ulster Division lost 5,600 men before midday!

Haig refused to accept defeat on the Somme and continued the campaign for another four months. By November the allies had gained 125 miles at a cost of 419,654 British casualties, 95,675 dead,[1] and 200,000 French casualties, 50,729 dead. The Germans lost 164,055 killed out of a total of 450,000 casualties.

1   The British official war history states that the figures cannot be considered as totally accurate because 'The clerk-power to investigate the exact losses was not available'. If one adds the number of casualties at Verdun to those of the Somme the five month death toll was 960,459 men. This works out at approx. 6,600 killed per day, 277 every hour nearly 5 men a minute. (Gilbert op cit p300).

Ammunition Limber. November 1916. Near Flers on the Somme.
*Imperial War Museum.*

## ALLNATT Norman Reginald

OR 1902-04

Pte. No.19462  Rifleman. London Rifle Brigade/26th Battalion, Royal Fusiliers.*

Killed in action on Friday 15th September 1916. Aged 29.

MEMORIAL: Thiepval Memorial, Somme, France. Pier and Face 8C, 9A and 16A.

Son of Blake Pearman Allnatt and Eliza Matilda Allnatt of 'Homeland', Woodcote Road, Caversham, Reading.

* This Battalion was formed in London in July 1915 by the Lord Mayor and the City of London from Bank Clerks and Accountants.

**APPELBEE T.**

OR 1909-12

2nd Lieutenant. 15th Battalion, West Yorks Regiment (Prince of Wales's Own).*

Killed in action on Sunday 20th August 1916.

CEMETERY: Le Touret Military Cemetery, Richebourg- L'Avoue, Pas de Calais, France. Grave Reference: IV.B.1.

The cemetery in which Appelbee is buried was used continuously by field ambulance and fighting units until March 1918 when it was over run by German forces.

The Le Touret memorial on the same site commemorates the 13,000 men who died in this area of France before September 1915.

* The 15th Battalion West Yorks were the Leeds Pals formed by the Lord Mayor and the City of Leeds in September 1914. In June it was attached to the 93rd Brigade 31st Division. They suffered severe casualties on the 1st July around Serre.

**BANKS Walter Ralph**

OR 1898-1904

Private PS/42. 19th Battalion, Royal Fusiliers.*

Killed in action on Sunday 2nd January 1916. Aged 28.

CEMETERY: Woburn Abbey Cemetery, Cuinchy, Pas de Calais, France.
Grave Ref. I.H.17.

This cemetery was used by both field ambulances and fighting units between June 1915 and January 1916. It was closed because of its exposed position. It gets its name from a house on the east side which was used both as a Battalion HQ and a dressing station.

Son of Jane A.B. Banks of 37 Hamilton Rd. Boscombe, Bournemouth, and the late Edward Howard Banks. (Paymaster in Chief, R.N.)

Banks entered Reading School in April 1898, having been previously educated at Worcester Lodge, Reading. He was a Corporation Scholar and a School Prefect and had gained a distinction in his Higher Certificate in German.

Before the war he was an examiner in the Exchequer and Audit Department at the Admiralty and joined up in September 1914. At the time he was reading for Holy Orders and had hoped to have taken his final Exam in October 1914 before proceeding to a Theological College.

He was killed during a very heavy bombardment of trenches while serving as a member of the No 42 D. Company 19th Battalion Royal Fusiliers.

* The 19th Battalion (2nd Public Schools) was formed in Epsom on September 11th 1914 by the Public Schools and University Mens Force. On June 26th it was attached to 98th Brigade, 33rd Division. On February 27th 1916 it was transferred to GHQ and disbanded in April 1916 with many of the men being commissioned.

## BASEDEN Eric

OR 1908-13

Lieutenant. 3rd attached 2nd Battalion, Royal Berkshire Regt.

Killed in action on Thursday 26th October 1916. Aged 22.

Son of William Henry and Florence Ada Baseden, of 'Grovelands' The Grove, Caversham, Reading.

CEMETERY: Bancourt British Cemetery, Pas de Calais, France. Grave Ref:IV.K.4.

This cemetery was created by the New Zealand Division in September 1918. The remainder of the graves contain bodies which were brought from other cemeteries. Baseden would originally have been interred in one of the following.

Bapaume Road Cemetery, Beaulencourt which contained the graves of 20 British soldiers who died in October 1916, Beaulencourt Road Cemeteries (3 of them) which contained the bodies of those killed during the Autumn of 1916 and April 1917 or Cloudy Trench Cemetery, Guedecourt, which contained the graves of 40 soldiers who died between October and November 1916.

Member of the 1st XV from 1910-12
'Scrum-half. Was moved to this position from forward soon after the beginning of

term. Inclined to be slow at getting the ball away, only being able to pass in one direction, but very frequently gained ground by dribbling from the scrum. Fair defence and a good place kick'.

1st XI Captain. 1913
'Has not had much success in batting or bowling, but is an excellent field. He has captained the team with judgment and has set an excellent example of keenness, both on and off the field'.

Mr and Mrs Baseden have been much touched by the very many expressions of sympathy they have received in the death of their son, Lieut. Eric Baseden, Royal Berkshire Regiment.

The Colonel wrote:

> *'It is with deep regret that I inform you that your son, Lieutenant Eric Baseden, was killed in action in the recent fighting while gallantly leading his platoon. I deeply sympathise with you in your sad loss. He was a most excellent officer in every way, and I can ill afford to lose him.'*

Lieut. Mackinlay of the Signal Company, wrote:

> *'Although I have only known your son for six months or so, we saw a good deal of each other and had become great friends. He was attached to this company until recently, and worked with me for several months preparing for the 1st July. I count it a great privilege to have regarded him as one of my friends. He was always so cheery and bright in difficult times, and took his hardships and disappointments like a man. If he had not been such a good fellow he would have been seconded to Signals some time ago. We all tried hard to get his papers through, but his battalion, knowing what they would lose if they lost him, refused to sanction, and he returned to lay down his life as cheerily as one would expect who knew him.*

> *I know what a disappointment the refusal of his transfer was to him, but I admired him even more than before, if that were possible, for the way he took it. His battalion went over the parapet two days after I saw him last, and he came through safely. Then his battalion were withdrawn to support trenches a few hundred yards back....Eric was killed instantaneously by a shell while in the trenches, and was buried by his men immediately behind the trench. I find it hard to realise that he is gone. I sympathise most deeply with you. You have lost a son and I have lost a very dear friend.'*
> December 1916

## BLISS Arthur Joseph

OR 1903-05

2nd Lieutenant. 4th Battalion Attached 7th Battalion, Leinster Regiment formerly Royal Army Medical Corps.*

Killed in action on Saturday 9th September 1916. Aged 28.

MEMORIAL: Thiepval Memorial, Somme, France. Pier and Face 4C.

The Thiepval Memorial serves two purposes. It commemorates the Anglo-French Somme offensive in 1916 and it has on it the names of 73,000 British and South African troops who had no known grave and who died on the Somme between July 1916 and March 1918.

The memorial, designed by Sir Edward Lutyens is 150 feet high. It has sixteen piers on which the names are inscribed. It is the largest British war memorial in he world. It was unveiled on 31 July 1932 by the Prince of Wales and the President of France. It was not without its critics. Some believed that the money could have been better spent on alleviating the poverty which many ex-soldiers found themselves in during the 1930s.

'Younger son of Mr Joseph Bliss, solicitor, of High Wycombe. Born 1888, he was educated at the Wycombe Royal Grammar School and at Reading School. He was afterwards articled to his father and was admitted a solicitor in 1911. He enlisted on August 7th, 1914 in the R.A.M.C., and in April 1915, he was given a Commission in the Leinster Regiment'.
December 1916.

* The 7th (Service) Battalion was formed at Fermoy, Ireland in October 1914 as part of Kitchener's 2nd Army. In September 1914 it was attached to 47th Brigade, 16th Irish Division. It was disbanded in France on February 14th 1918. The Battalion fought at the Battle of Guillemont which would tie in with the dates of Bliss' death.

## BLYDE W.A.

'The gallantry of 2nd Lieut. W.A. Blyde in Gallipoli won him sergeants stripes on the field, and last month he received a commission. The deed which has won this well-deserved recognition was as follows: 'On the night of August 25th he was out with a covering party, from which becoming separated, he was lying alone in a gully, when he was attacked by two Turks. He shot one at a distance of twenty yards, and killed the other after a fierce struggle'.

(He was later invalided home. Dated April 1916. Employee at the Sun Fire Office, Reading branch in civil life).

Awarded DCM.

1st XV 1911
'A light forward. Always played a fair game without being at all brilliant. Likely to improve next year.

## COLLINS D.

OR 1892-97

Corporal 1758. 7th Regiment, South African Infantry.

Killed in action on Sunday 12th March 1916. Aged 28.

CEMETERY: Taveta Military Cemetery, Kenya. Grave Ref: VII A.16.

At this time a continued campaign was been fought by South African detachments, together with Belgian and British, against German forces in East Africa. One can only assume that Collins was killed in this campaign, hence his burial in Taveta Cemetery.

Son of Mr E.F.and Mrs S.A.Collins, of 6 Adderley St., Cape Town, South Africa. Born in Reading, Berks.

## COSTIN W.C.

December 1916

Awarded Military Cross.

'2ⁿᵈ Lieut. (Temporary Lieut.) W.C.Costin, Gloucester Regt. For conspicuous gallantry during operations. When enemy penetrated our front line he pushed forward to a point where he was much exposed, and directed an accurate fire on the trench with his trench guns. It was largely due to his skill and courage that we recaptured the trench. An Old Boy of Reading School, he won a scholarship at St. John's College, Oxford'.

## COWAN D.T.

OR 1914

2ⁿᵈ Lieuenantt. Argyll and Sutherland Highlanders.

Awarded Military Cross.
(December 1916 Magazine.)

1ˢᵗ XI 1912
'Has been invaluable as a wicket keeper, and promises to become really good. His batting is improving in proportion as his fear of the fast ball on the leg decreases'.

## EDWARDS F.A.L.

OR 1904-1911

Temporary 2ⁿᵈ Lieutenant. 5ᵗʰ Battalion Royal Berkshire Regiment.*

Killed in action on Thursday, 10ᵗʰ August 1916.

CEMETERY: Puchvillers British Cemetery, Somme, France. Grave Ref. III.A.5.

The 3ʳᵈ and 44ᵗʰ Casualty Clearing Stations (CCS) were established in Puchvillers in June 1916 prior to the opening of the Somme offensive. Many of the graves in the British cemetery contain the bodies of men wounded in action and then dying at the CCS.

Had been a Prefect and a member of the Football and Hockey Clubs in 1910-11.

'Awarded Military Cross for conspicuous gallantry during operations. When the enemy twice attacked under cover of liquid fire, 2nd Lieut Edwards showed great pluck under the most trying circumstances and held off the enemy. He was badly wounded in the head while constructing a barricade within twenty five yards of the enemy'.

(2nd entry)
'Died of wounds on August 10th. He was 23 years of age and younger son of Capt. H.H. Edwards, Royal Navy, and Mrs Edwards, of Broadlands, Cholsey. He was educated at Reading School and the City and Guilds College, Kensington. He had been on active service for 10 months. His Adjutant wrote: 'He was the bravest of men in the trenches. All the men say he was simply wonderful on the morning of August 8th. We lost a very gallant soldier and a lovable man'.
(December 1916 Magazine)

* The 5th (Service) Battalion Royal Berkshire Regiment was formed at Reading on August 25th 1914 as part of Kichener's 1st New Army. It was assigned to 35th Brigade, 12th Division based at Shorncliffe Camp in Kent. On March 1st, 1915 it moved to the Malplaquet Barracks in Aldershot for final training and left for France on May 31st, landing at Boulogne. The Battalion was on the Somme from July 1st-24th and again from September 11th to October 2nd 1916. It would seem that Edwards was wounded during this first engagement.

On February 6th, 1918 the battalion was transferred to the 36th Brigade, 12th Division.

**FULLER Cyril John**

OR 1909-12

2nd Lieutenant. 6th Battalion, Royal Berkshire Regt. *

Killed in action on Saturday 22nd July 1916. Aged 19.

Son of John H. and K. Fuller, of 'Hartleigh', Eastern Ave., Reading.

Member of the 1st XV 1912. 'A very useful forward, working well in the scrum. Has come on greatly at tackling, frequently stopping a forward rush'.

CEMETERY: Dive Copse British Cemetery, Sailly-le-Sac, France.
Grave Ref. II.B.27.

In June 1916, before the attack on the Somme, the area north of Dive Copse was chosen as the site of a number of field ambulances. These later became the XIV Corps Main Dressing Station. The cemetery gets its name from a nearby wood on the Bray-Corbie road which itself had been named after the officer commanding the Dressing Station. The cemetery was used by the staff of the dressing station. Fuller is buried in Plot II which contains casualties from the first three months of the fighting.

Of four officers of his company who took part in the advance of July 1st he alone came through without a scratch. On July 10th he wrote to his parents:

> *'We were the leading battalion in the attack. Our prisoners were all well equipped. They appeared to have just come back from a rest, for in their trenches there were great coats, tunics and general clothing in top-hole condition. They had enough stores to refit a company and possessed remarkable dug-outs'.*

On July 18th he wrote:

> *'I have three slight wounds and do not expect to go into hospital. The Huns' shell fire was terrific, but we were congratulated by the Brigadier for our good work. Our fellows are fighting very bravely: I know they will do well'.*

Magazine:
'Educated at Reading School, Lieut. Fuller won his colours and was a member of the OTC. He enlisted early in the war and underwent his training with 2nd Lieut. H.P. Sadler, who, alas! has also made the supreme sacrifice. They received their Commissions at the same time, but were separated at the front. An all round athlete, Lieut. Fuller was a member of the Reading Rowing Club and a keen motor cyclist. In civil life he assisted his father in the business of oil and colour merchant, Minster Street, Reading. A brother Lce-Cpl H.J.Fuller, was wounded while in the King's Royal Rifles and has been discharged from the Army and is doing his bit in the Marine Transport'.

* The 6th (Service) Battalion was raised in Reading on August 25th 1914 as part of Kitchener's 2nd New Army. In October of the same year it was assigned to the 53rd Brigade in the 18th Division based at Colchester. In May 1915 it moved to Salisbury Plain for final training. On July 27th it sailed for France, landing at Boulogne.

The Battalion was heavily involved during the Battle of the Somme. On the first day it attacked Montauban, an action which cost the lives of 7 officers and 71 other ranks, with 254 wounded and 11 missing. The Battalion was disbanded in France on February 12th, 1918, the remaining men being transferred to the 1st, 2nd and 5th Battalions.

## GRIFFITHS H.C.L.

OR 1906

Captain. 9th Seaforth Highlanders.

Letter to Headmaster. This is his description of a German Trench:

*'One of these dug-outs had been constructed right underneath a large farm that I had to put into a state of defence in the village of L......, and had rooms bordering on the main shaft large enough to accommodate a hundred men. We were almost the first to enter this 'palace' and discovered several good souvenirs. Every man in my platoon came home with a helmet.'*
December 1916 Magazine.

1st XV 1905-6
'Should make a good half-back; has some idea of openings and runs straight'.

## GUILLE Harold

OR 1900-02

Pte. 442387. 7th Battalion Canadian Expeditionary Force, British Columbia Regt.

Killed in action on Saturday, 15th April 1916. Aged 31.

CEMETERY: Railway Dugouts Burial Ground, Zillebeke, Ieper, France.
Grave Ref: VI.E.30.

Approximately 1.5 miles west of Zillebeke the railway runs on an embankment which overlooks a farm known to the British Army at the time as 'Transport Farm'. Burials began on this site from April 1915 and continued until November 1918. It was used a lot during 1916 and 1917 when the Advanced Dressing Stations were situated in the embankment and the farm buildings. Guille would therefore have been brought back to this site.

Youngest son of Mr and Mrs G.C.Guille, 28 Castle Crescent, Reading.

'Died on April 15th 1916, aged 31. Educated at Reading School, for the last 12 years he was in British Columbia with his brother, E.E. Guille, who came over with the 1st Contingent and has been wounded twice. Harold, who has been at the front only a month, leaves a wife and a child'.

## HAIGH R.

OR 1907-1914

2nd Lieutenant. 1st Berkshires.

'Son of Mr William Haigh, of Llanarth, Hamilton Rd. Reading. and of University College, was wounded in the foot at the outset of the attack on September 28th. He is making excellent progress. Lt. Haigh was educated at Reading School where he was a member of the Officer's Training Corps, and joined the Royal Berks. on leaving Sandhurst in February'. (December 1915).

April 1916: Appointed Lieutenant, September 27th 1915.

1st XV 1911
'Not a great player as he tackles high and when in possession either runs across the field or puts his head down and dashes into the thick of it'.

## HOWELL Norman Asquith

OR 1907-10

2nd Lieutenant. 6th Battalion King's Shropshire Light Infantry.*

Killed in action on Saturday 23rd December 1916. Aged 19.

CEMETERY: A.I.F.Burial Ground, Flers, Somme, France. Grave Ref: III.M.I.

The village of Flers was captured on the 15th September 1916 during the Battle of Flers-Courcelette when New Zealanders and members of the 41st Divisions entered the village behind tanks. It was retaken by the Germans in March 1918 but regained in August of the same year. The cemetery was started by Australian medical units, housed in nearby caves, in November 1916. It was enlarged after the Armistice with the addition of 3,842 graves from across the area of the Somme. As Howell is buried in Plot III it is likely that his body had been originally buried in one of these smaller cemeteries and brought to Flers later.

He was the second son of Mr W. Roland Howell, an architect. He was born at Reading in April 1897, and educated at Reading School and St. Laurence College, Ramsgate, and had been about a year in his father's office before joining the Army in November, 1915. His cadet training at school and college enabled him to get his commission. He was posted to the King's Shropshires, was ordered to the front at the end of June last, and was in the thick of the Somme fighting for six months. Lieut. Norman Howell came home on his first leave on December 6th and returned on the 16th. Within a week he had made the great sacrifice.

His Commanding Officer wrote to Mr Howell on December 24th:

> *'I deeply regret to report the death of your son, who was serving in my Battalion. Whilst going up to the front line trenches in charge of a party last night an enemy sniper shot him through the head, killing him instantly. This morning his body was buried by the Chaplain near where he fell, with military honours, officers and men attending.*
>
> *I had trench mortars and rifle grenades on the sniper's post, patrols had reported 8 to 10 Huns there, none there now! On behalf of his comrades, officers, N.C.O.s and men, I wish to convey to you our profound sympathy. He was loved and respected by all of us, and we mourn the loss of a very gallant officer and gentleman. To all of us he was known as recklessly brave and a fine example of cool courage, devoted to his duties, which he discharged most cheerfully under the most trying conditions.*
>
> *I placed him in charge of the Lewis Gun detachment, on which he had set his heart and soul. He belonged to my own Headquarters' Mess, and I took particular interest in him. A cross has been put up on the grave near Les Boeufs'.*
> (January 1917 Magazine)

* The 6th (Service) Battalion was formed in Shrewsbury in 1914 as part of Kitchener's 2nd Army. In September it was attached to the 60th Brigade, 20th (Light) Division. As part of this Division Howell would have seen action at the Battle of Delville Wood (July 15th - September 3rd 1916).

## IREMONGER Hubert Roxby

OR 1902-08

Pte. 81435. 8th Battalion Canadian Infantry. (Manitoba Regt.)*

Killed in action on Tuesday 25th January 1916. Aged 24.

Son of Mortimer West Iremonger and Ellen Iremonger of Aldermaston.

CEMETERY: Berkshire Cemetery Extension, Ploegsteert, Comines-Warneton, Hainaut, Belgium. Panel: III.A.51.

This cemetery was used from June 1916 until September 1917. This would suggest that Iremonger had originally been buried elsewhere and his body brought to this site during these dates.

The Canadians offered to send an Infantry Division to the Western Front on August 6th 1914. It was expected that this would comprise 60,000 members of the Canadian militia, but the then Minister of Militia and Defence, Colonel Samuel Hughes, decided to organise the volunteers into new consecutively numbered battalions.

The first contingent of the CEF, which sailed on October 3rd 1914, was comprised of the 1st – 17th battalions plus the Princess Patricia's Canadian Light Infantry in which R.H.H.Biddulph (OR.1901-03) served. P. O. Payze (OR 1895-7) also served in the Manitoba Regiment. He died on the first day of the Somme.

According to Canadian Military records, the 8th Battalion was called the 'Black Devils/90th Winnipeg Rifles. There is no mention of the Manitoba Regiment until the second wave of troops contained the 32nd Infantry Battalion Manitoba and Saskatchewan and the third wave 45th Infantry Battalion Manitoba Regiment. In all Canada sent 260 Infantry Battalions to the war zone.

## JAMES Joe Conquest

OR 1891-95

Captain. 5th Battalion Royal Berkshire Regt.*

Died at Boulogne on Friday 14th July 1916 of wounds received on the 3rd.

CEMETERY: Wimereux Communal Cemetery, Pas-de-Calais, France. Grave Ref. III.K.2.

During the war Wimereux was the headquarters of the Q.M.A.A.C and it became the General HQ of the British Army in 1919. From October 1914 it was also the site of a major hospital complex and until June 1918 those who died of wounds, or were dead on arrival were buried in the Communal Cemetery.

Among those buried in this cemetery is Lt-Col John McCrae who wrote the poem 'In Flanders Field' while working at a Casualty Clearing station at Essex Farm near Boezinge in the Ypres salient. He died on the 28th January 1918.

Captain Joe Conquest James, Royal Berkshire Regiment, only son of William Joseph James, Wellington College Hotel and dearly beloved husband of Connie James (40). The following notice is from the Reading Mercury:

*'Deep regret is felt in Berkshire that Captain Joe Conquest James, Royal Berkshire Regiment, proprietor of the Wellington Hotel, Wellington College Station and son of Mr. W.J.James has died of wounds. Captain James was wounded by shell in the great push on July 3rd, while leading his company, and taken to Boulogne Hospital where, after an operation, he died on July 14th. His wife was too late to see him before he died. The deceased was extremely popular with all who knew him. He was educated at Cranleigh and Reading School. He went to South Africa and joined the British South African Police. In the South African War he served as a trooper in Thorneycroft's Mounted Infantry, and received the Queen's and King's medals with four clasps. In September, 1914, he joined the Berkshire Royal Horse Artillery as a gunner, and was a great favourite with the Battery. In December of that year he received his Captaincy in the Royal Berkshire Regiment. He went to the front last May. He was forty years of age. The deceased was a Freemason, being a member of the Downshire and Heather Lodges. He was extremely fond of horses'.*

*The 5th Battalion was heavily involved during the Battle of the Somme and James was wounded on the 3rd day of the campaign.

---

**MAJOR Cyril Bisdee**

OR 1908-1909

2nd Lieutenant. 7th Battalion. East Yorkshire Regt. *

(Reported as 'Missing' in the Magazine of April 1917)

Killed in action on Sunday 5th November 1916. Aged 19.

Not Commemorated on the War Memorial but instated in 2001.

MEMORIAL: Thiepval Memorial, Somme, France. Panel: Pier and Face 2C.

* The 7th (Service) Battalion was formed at Beverley in Yorkshire on September 16th 1914 as part of Kitchener's 2nd Army. Later in the same month it was attached to the 50th Brigade, 17th (Northern) Division. Its early days were very chaotic because there were very few trained officers and NCOs to look after the volunteers. Neither was there any equipment or billets. However, the Division was transferred to France during the 12-17 July 1915.

Major would have seen action during early February and March 1916 and at the Battle of Albert July 1–13 1916 as the 17th Division captured Fricourt during which it suffered severe casualties.

## PAYZE P.O

OR 1895-97

Listed Private 426063 (but later 2nd Lieutenant). 16th Battalion, Canadian Infantry, Manitoba Regt.

Killed in action on Thursday 20th July 1916. Aged 36.

CEMETERY: Military Cemetery, Poperinge, West-Vlaanderen, Belgium. Grave Ref. VIII.C.36A.

The rail line between Hazebrouck and Poperinghe and the Poperinghe-Ypres road provided the main communication links between military bases and the battlefields in the area and was an obvious location for a casualty clearing station as it was just beyond the range of the German guns. Between June 1915 and November 1918 it became the second largest British war cemetery.

Son of Percy Owen Payze and Charlotte Payze of Selsdon, Henley-on-Thames, England. Native of Whitchurch, Oxon, England.

## PENSON A.R.

OR 1902-1907

Pte.2655. 1/4th Battalion, Oxford and Bucks Light Infantry. *

Killed in action on Sunday 23rd July 1916. Aged 30.

CEMETERY: Pozieres British Cemetery, Ovillers-La Boisselle, Somme, France. Grave Ref. I.A.37.

The village of Pozieres was attacked on the 23rd July 1916 by the 1st Australian and the 48th (South Midland) Divisions, during which Penson was killed. It was captured on the 24th. However, it was later lost to the Germans in March 1918 before being recaptured later in the same year on August 24th.

Son of Richard and Clara Penson, 32 Alexandra Road, Reading.

* The 1/4th Battalion was raised in Oxford in August 1914 and became part of the South Midland Brigade, South Midland Division. On March 30th 1915 it landed at Boulogne and proceeded to the Western Front. On May 15th 1915 the formation became the 145th Brigade, 48th Division. Before being killed at the Battle of Pozieres, Penson would have seen action during the Battle of Albert July 1st-13th and the Battle of Bazentin July 14th-17th where the Division captured Ovillers.

## PROCTOR James Claude Beauchamp

OR 1900-03

Captain. 10th Battalion, Royal Inniskilling Fusiliers.*

Killed in action on Saturday 1st July 1916. Aged 31.

CEMETERY: Mill Road Cemetery, Thiepval, Somme, France. Grave Ref. IX.D.9.

Proctor died when the German lines around Thiepval, garrisoned by the 160th Regiment of Wurttembergers, were attacked unsuccessfully by the 36th (Ulster) Division on the 1st July 1916. The 18th Division attacked again and took the garrison on the 26th September.

The cemetery was created in the spring of 1917 after the battlefield was cleared. The Divion Road Cemetery No.1, 400 metres south of St-Pierre-Divion, originally contained the graves of 29 soldiers who were killed between July and September, before being reburied at Mill Road. One can assume that Proctor was among this group.

Son of James Edwin and Frances J.Proctor, of Tullydoey, Moy.Co. Tyrone. Native of Limavady, Co. Londonderry.

Had been a House Prefect and member of the 1st XV 1901-02.

* The 10th Battalion was formed at Omagh in September 1914 from the Derry Volunteers. (A group which had been in a high state of readiness in August 1914 as a result of heightened tension because of the Home Rule debate). Later in the

month it was attached to the 3rd Brigade Ulster Division until it was renamed on November 2nd as the 109th Brigade 36th Division. It was disbanded in France on January 21st, 1918.

## PULLEN-BURRY Cyril Arthur

OR 1910-13

Sergt. Duke of Cornwall's Light Infantry.

Killed in action on Monday 10th April 1916. Aged 22.

CEMETERY: Faubourg D'Amiens Cemetery, Arras, Pas-de-Calais, France. Grave Ref. I.A.31

Arras was attacked by German forces at the end of August 1914 and it was occupied, albeit briefly, by the Germans during the end of September. Although the target of fierce fighting in October it remained in control of the Allies until the end of the war. The Faubourg Cemetery was started in March 1916 and remained open until November 1918. It was used by various field ambulances and fighting units throughout the period. It was enlarged after the armistice by bringing to the area bodies from two smaller cemeteries and other places across the Arras battlefields.

Letter to father from Lt. Col. Stokoe:

*Dear Sir,*

*It is with the very greatest regret that I write to tell you of your dear son's death killed in action. He was a great friend of mine and every night in the trenches he used to bring me his intelligence report and have a cup of cocoa and some cake with me. I have several times wanted him and asked him to take a Commission but he used to say he thought he was more useful as he was.*

*He was so fearless that I have several times heard the remark that Pullen-Burry was asking for it. His splendid pluck and intelligent work was so well known in the Brigade and Division that directly his death was reported both Generals wired to me, a thing I think without precedent in the case of a Sergeant.*

*Only two nights before he was nearly killed by gas-poisoning from a coke-stove in his dug-out. I carried him into my dug-out and had to pump his arms and pour stimulant down his throat as he was absolutely pulseless. It was some time before we got him round and at one time thought him dead. His first remark on regaining consciousness was 'Well, Sir, I had better get back to the telephone'…a wonderful spirit of devotion and duty, others who were in a similar state were asking for the doctor and brandy.*

*He had absolutely no suffering and although he breathed for several hours he never regained consciousness.*

*I know what this loss must mean to you, but you must have great consolation in knowing what a splendid work he has done in his short life and must be very proud to have such a son.*

*On behalf of every Officer and man and myself in the Battalion please accept our very deepest sympathies.*

*Yours very truly*

*W. Stokoe. Lt Col C/86/D.C.L.I.*

Pullen-Burry had been a School Prefect and member of the 1ˢᵗ XV in 1911 and 1912.

'Full-Back. Has not come on as well as was expected. Slow at fielding the ball, frequently misjudging and fumbling it. Tackles well however, and is fairly safe at touch finding'.

**SADLER Hereward Pattison**

OR 1908-1913

2ⁿᵈ Lieutenant. 6ᵗʰ Battalion. Royal Berkshire Regiment.*

Killed in action on Wednesday 19ᵗʰ July 1916. Aged 20.

CEMETERY: Carnoy Military Cemetery, Somme, France. Grave Ref. K.32

The cemetery at Carnoy was started in August 1915 when the village was immediately south of the British front line. It continued to be used by fighting units in the area until July 1916 and then by field ambulances which were established, together with a camp, to the north of the village. It was closed in March 1917.

Son of William and Jane Sadler of 'Oakdene', 4 Hillside Gardens, Wallington, Surrey.

He left school in 1913 and had been a member of the 1ˢᵗ XV 1912.

Described in the magazine as 'Forward. A good all-round player who has done several good things, especially in the loose. Dribbles and follows up well'.

* The 6ᵗʰ Battalion, Royal Berkshire Regiment, was heavily involved during the Battle of the Somme resulting in heavy casualties.

**SHIRLEY F.L.J.** Yorkshire Regt.

OR 1908-1914

Left school in 1914. He was a Prefect. In the 1ˢᵗ XV from 1911-1914, 1ˢᵗ XI 1912-14 and 1ˢᵗ XI Hockey 1912-13.

Gentleman cadet R.M. College to be 2ⁿᵈ Lieut. in Yorks Regt (Regular Forces), attached to the Royal Flying Corps.

1ˢᵗ XI 1914          1ˢᵗ XV 1911

'A left-handed bat with a powerful drive on both sides of the wicket, who can deal satisfactorily with loose bowling. He has been rather apt to lose his wicket by playing a cross-bat shot at the wrong moment, but towards the end of the season has learnt to watch the ball much more closely. A fair catch in the deep'.

Also 1ˢᵗ XV. 'Forward. Has been a good leader of the front rank, working hard in the scrums and good in the line-out. His place kicking has been very useful on several occasions.' April 1914.

Letter to Magazine July 1916:

*'Dear Mr Sylo-Jones*

*We have at last arrived in France after many false alarms as to when we should really go. My trip was not without excitement. We started from Rugby on July 15ᵗʰ and after following the L & N.W.R. as far as London, through a number of storms which cut one's face about, when over Wormwood Scrubs my engine began to spit and splutter, and as I was wet through I thought it best to come down and have my engine seen to, before attempting the Channel. I had a very good trip to France, but could see very little at 5,500 feet over the Channel as the clouds and mist were very thick......I went over the lines for the first time yesterday afternoon and could plainly see the guns working their havoc. The Huns seem to have a mania for shelling certain woods close round here; trying to cut up many of our army of pursuit or reserves, I suppose.*

*....We are living in stables, about as crammed in as we could be, with a fair amount of comfort...The Hun airman seems to be thoroughly afraid of us. He only comes up when he sees a stranger, and then there are five or six at a time....'*

Shirley gave a lecture on November 30th 1918 in Big School on 'War in the Air' in connection with the War Savings Association.

Captain Shirley M.C. died on November 30th 1919 of enteric dysentery.

**TAYLOR Cedric Charles Okey**

OR 1909-14

Lieutenant. 3rd Battalion attached Trench Mortar Battery. The Buffs (East Kent Regiment).

Killed in action on Sunday 3rd December 1916.

CEMETERY: Faubourg D'Amiens Cemetery, Arras, Pas-de-Calais, France. Grave Ref. I.J.58.

'Lieut.C.C.O.Taylor of the 3rd Buffs, attached to the Trench Mortar Battery Z/14, 14th Division, British Expeditionary Force, France, fell in action on Sunday, December 3rd, 1916. (East Kent Regt. attached to Trench Mortar Battery). He was not quite 22 years of age, and the only son of Mrs Taylor of 31, Weltje Road, Ravenscourt Park, London W., and the late Charles Warmsley Taylor of Reading. Much sympathy is expressed for his mother, sister, and aged grandfather, and for the many friends who mourn the loss of this young officer. He was educated at Reading School, and was in the midst of a successful course at the Central and Technical Engineering College, Kensington, when war broke out. He received a Commission March 1915, was promoted in April 1916, and showed a devotion to duty and enthusiasm in the field which only ended with his life, laid down for King and Country. He was in constant action for 15 months, at Ypres in 1915 and on the Somme in 1916'.

His Captain writes:

*'It is with deep regret that I have to convey the sad news that your son, Lieutenant C.C.O. Taylor, was killed in action yesterday, the 3rd instant. He was at a gun position with his men when the dug-out was blown in. His death must have been instantaneous, and two of his men were killed with him. We have recovered his body, and he will be buried tomorrow, and as many of his brother officers that are available will attend. I need hardly say how deeply sorry all his friends are, and to me it is a personal loss, since he has been associated with me longer than any other officer, and we have been together since he joined the Expeditionary Force. One cannot speak too highly of his ability, his devotion to duty, and the keen interest he took in all his men and their welfare. It is a sad loss which we all feel, and offer you our deepest and heartfelt sympathy.'*

## WILKEN Alan Gillies

OR 1898-1904

1st XV 1903
'Plays very keenly and follows up hard. Must learn to dribble more'.

1st XI 1904
'A fairly fast bowler. As a bat he has a good reach with a nice forward stroke'.

'Capt. Brigade Chaplain in Canadian Force, eldest son of Major John Wilken, late R.H.A., Dagmar. Alexandra Rd. Reading. Missing after the engagement at Hooge on June 2nd'.

Since the above notice appeared the following letter from Capt. Wilken announces that he is a prisoner of war in Germany. He is apparently being well treated.

*'Offizier gefangenenlager,*
*Gutersloh*
*June 12th 1916*

*We came over here into the camp on Friday, June 9th. We are really very comfortable. I share a nice bright room with one of the 1st C.M.R.Majors. All the British Officers live in a big house, and French, Russians and Belgians in other houses. There are about 1000 all told. We have good grounds, plenty of tennis courts and two playing fields. A few have small gardens. We have a good library with nearly 2,000 English books.*

*Now you will like to know something about our food. We get three good meals a day and are allowed to supplement these with food from home. Enormous quantities of tinned goods come here. We have to provide our own afternoon tea. They have a system here of supplying newcomers with tinned goods for six weeks, the time it takes to get back a reply for this purpose and we must pay back. I bought a nice pair of boots from the canteen as mine were blown up and I was captured in rubber boots.*

*Friday, June 2ⁿᵈ, was a nightmare, and how I am alive to speak of it God alone knows. I should not have thought it possible to live under such a bombardment. I do not think there were 100 left alive. About 50 were taken prisoners including wounded, and the rest of my regiment are dead.*

*Offizier gefangenenlager*
*Gutersloh*
*June 26ᵗʰ, 1916*

*You ought to have heard by now from me and know that I am no longer 'missing'. You may have got the first news from the Bank as I got a draft through this week for £10. We are allowed to have only a certain amount of money (up to 100 marks) but I had bought quite a few things at the Canteen. We have to pay for our messing.*

*I am pretty busy here. There is plenty to do and really the time is not wasted. For me it is a time of intellectual activity which has been denied me during the last few years of missionary wanderings over the prairie and the last nine months at the Front. I am working hard at French and German. It is really a rare opportunity to study them first hand. Four languages are spoken in this large camp.*

*A little while ago I had a letter from the British Chaplain at Berlin. He visits all the Prisoners' Camps and was due here when he heard I was here. He looked me up in an old 'Crockford'. He was at Cambridge and Cuddesdon and then at my old parish, St Mary's, Bromley-by-Bow, E.*

*Last Sunday we had a splendid open-air concert by the Camp Orchestra. It is chiefly composed of Russians. There is a fine bandstand erected by money from the Canteen.*

*We had a very heavy rainstorm last evening but it dries up quickly on this sandy ground and we shall be able to play tennis this afternoon. We have just finished an International Hockey League, French, Russian and British, the British winning easily. But the Russians play very well, they are wonderfully quick at learning the game; although the French too are good.*

*All here divide up into little parties of three for messing. An ordinary tin of meat or fruit is a meal for three, not enough for more and too much for one.*

*We don't live without the world's news here. We can, of course, get all the German papers. Some enterprising officers started what is called the 'Daily Journal'. One, as Editor, chooses the best news, the various official reports from the warring nations. He and others translate, he writes the editorial as well, and the whole is then typewritten and put in the Common Room'.*

### WISE Frederick Mortimer

OR 1907-1913

2nd Lieutenant. 13th Battalion York and Lancs.*

Killed in action on Tuesday 5th September 1916. Aged 22.

CEMETERY: St.Vaast Post Military Cemetery, Richbourg-L'Avoue, Pas de Calais, Calais, France. Grave Ref. II.W.5.

Even though the village of Richbourg-L'Avoue was only a mile or so from the front line, it remained under British control from the autumn of 1914 until April 1918 when it was captured by the Germans. It was retaken in September of the same year. The cemetery, which takes its name from the local hamlet of St. Vaast, lies in an old orchard between two farm buildings where a trench tramway had its terminus. A dressing station was established on the site in May 1915 during the Battle of Festubert and it was used by fighting units and field ambulances until July 1917.

'It is with deep regret that a wide circle of friends will learn of the death of 2nd Lieut. F.M. Wise, while serving his country in France. The gallant officer was the younger son of the late Mr. W.E. Wise and Mrs Wise. He was educated at Reading School, and only attained his majority on May 21st of the present year.

Of an enterprising turn of mind, he set out for Canada some three or four years ago, and when war broke out he was in British Columbia, where he had taken up fruit farming. The call to arms sounded, and he at once responded by joining the

Canadian Highlanders. In an incredibly short time he received his baptism of fire, for in March of 1915 he was in the thick of the fighting on the French front. Constantly in action, he received a bayonet wound in the early days of the fighting, and was in hospital in France for a month. On his recovery he rejoined the Canadians, but quite recently he had been given a Commission in the York and Lancaster Regiment. Unfortunately he was killed in action on September 5th, and was then cut off at the commencement of what would no doubt have proved a brilliant career. Much sympathy is felt with the widowed mother and other members of the family'.

* The 13th (Service) Battalion (1st Barnsley) was formed on September 17th 1914, by the Mayor and the Town. In May 1915 it was attached to the 94th Brigade, 31st Division. This Division was originally part of Kitchener's 5th Army and was numbered 38 but the 4th New Army was broken up in April 1915 and the Division was renumbered the 31st.

Wise would have seen action at the Battle of Albert July 1st–13th, 1916 before being killed on September 6th.

Letter from Oxford, April 1916:

> *Dear Sir,*
>
> *To write a letter for the Reading School Magazine about events in Oxford and the doings of the O.R.s there, is not an easy matter when no events happen in Oxford and when the only OR surviving is myself. However, I will do my best.*
>
> *Oxford is about as unlike its former self as it could well be. The streets are in almost total darkness at night and the passages and staircases are little better. The scores of empty rooms present a most melancholy spectacle. The striking of bells, which was such a familiar feature of Oxford life, has ceased and we no longer hear the regular chiming of the quarters, nor midnight pandemonium. Big Tom moreover rests from his nightly labours at 9.5 pm and altogether the place is like a tomb.*
>
> *One incident served to break the monotony of the term, and that was the Zeppelin alarm of Sunday night, February 27th. No airships appeared, but the scare provided some welcome excitement for those who were awake....'*

# 1917

*'The war has been a great experience, and what has helped me out here has been a sound school training at Reading and always having taken part in any games going.'*
Capt.J.E. Corry. MC. Wounded at Passchendaele.

On August 9th 1917 the Belgian Government signed an agreement in the Le Havre with Britain whereby the land on which the British War Cemeteries and graves in Belgium were located was 'conceded in perpetuity' to Britain. A similar agreement had been signed with France in 1915.

Overview:

| | |
|---|---|
| **April 9 – 14** | Arras |
| **April 9 – 14** | Vimy Ridge |
| **April 9 – 14** | Scarpe |
| **April 23 – 24** | Scarpe |
| **April 28 – 29** | Arleux |
| **May 3 – 4** | Scarpe |
| **May 3 – 17** | Bullecourt |
| **June 28** | Oppy Wood |
| **July 31 – November 10** | Ypres |
| **July 31 – August 2** | Pilckem |
| **August 10** | Westhoek |
| **August 15 – 25** | Hill 70 |
| **August 16 – 18** | Langemarck |
| **August 22 – 27** | St Julien |
| **September 20 – 25** | Menin Road |
| **September 26 – October 3** | Polygon Wood |
| **October 4** | Broodseinde |
| **October 9** | Poelcappelle |
| **October 12,26, November 10** | Passchendaele |
| **November 20 – 27** | Cambrai |
| **November 20 – 21** | Gouzeacourt |

## BATTLES OF ARRAS AND VIMY RIDGE

### April 9th–14th 1917

On April 9th 1917 British and Canadian forces launched simultaneous attacks at Arras and Vimy Ridge. The first British attacks were successful with the Hindenberg Line being breached and around 5,500 Germans taken prisoner. By nightfall both of the German front lines, and part of the third had been taken. This was in part due to a new tactic of 'rolling barrage' which was tried out for the first time. The artillery would move forward with the infantry following behind to take advantage of the effect on the opposition trenches.

On the second day the attack was resumed after many of the men had had to sleep in freezing conditions out in the open. On the 11th, General Allenby ordered the cavalry to be sent in to exploit the gaps but they were forced back by machine gun fire and wire which had remained intact.

The weather got worse and the men were at the limit of their endurance. Three Generals called on Haig to cease the attack because of mounting casualties in both sectors. On the 15th April the offensive officially ended.

In Arras cemetery there is a British memorial which contains the names of 35,928 soldiers killed who have no known grave. There are also 2,395 named grave markers.

## THIRD BATTLE OF YPRES (Passchendaele)

### July 31st–November 10th 1917

Haig's plan was to break through the German lines, sweep behind them and push them back into Belgium. Churchill, who had been brought back into the Cabinet in July 1917 as Minister of Munitions, had already suggested to Lloyd George that before launching any attack, Haig should wait until American forces had arrived in France in order to tip the manpower balance in favour of the allies. He warned that:

*'If anything the Germans are stronger, they have larger reserves, and ample munitions. An endless series of fortified lines with all kinds of flooding possibilities, and great natural difficulties of ground, constitute insuperable difficulties'.*
*(Ref Gilbert op cit. p350).*

His advice was ignored.

The attack began on July 31st with a 3,000 gun barrage. The first objective was to take the village of Passchendaele a distance of around 4.5 miles from the British front. During the first two days all went well and the troops advanced as much as 2.5 miles in some areas of the line, taking in the process some 5,000 German prisoners.

A renewed attack on August 6th was hindered by very heavy rain and on the 16th the Germans regained the ground around Langemarck. Casualties on both sides were mounting. On August 22nd an allied gain of half a mile along the Menin Road resulted in 3,000 casualties.

The battle recommenced on September 20th with Passchendaele still being the objective. It was to take another seven weeks. During the first days of October the British lost 162,768 dead and wounded and even Haig's most senior commanders, Gough and Plumer, were advising him to call a halt because of high casualties for little gain. He ignored them and the attack continued on October 9th to be stopped again on the 13th because of heavy rain.

It was not until October 30th that a Canadian detachment entered Passchendaele, only to suffer heavy casualties and be forced to withdraw.

The battle finally ended on November 10th. The Allies had gained their 4.5 miles but at a cost of 244,897 casualties, with around 66,000 killed - 8 killed for every yard gained! The Germans lost around 400,000. Because of the weather and the condition of the area over which the armies fought, many of the wounded drowned in shell holes or where they lay in No Mans Land.

The area around Passchendaele would be lost to the Germans on April 15th 1918 during the German counter offensive on the Western Front.

**BATTLE OF CAMBRAI**

**November 20th– 27th 1917**

250,000 British troops took part in the battle of Cambrai along a six-mile front. For the first time in History the main thrust of the opening attack was carried out by 324 tanks. Although they were effective during the opening phase, breaking their way through the barbed wire defences and reaching some of the German trenches, they became vulnerable to mechanical faults. Also, unknown to the British, despite the use of 300 reconnaissance aircraft, there were German artillery batteries at Flesquieres which destroyed 39 tanks in that area, bringing the attack to an abrupt halt. However, in other sectors the infantry had advanced five miles behind the tanks and in the process taken over 4,000 German prisoners.

On the second day the Germans deployed a new division on the St Quentin Canal. On the 23rd November 62 tanks were lost at Bourlon Wood.[1] On November 27th the British tried to take the village of Fontaine by driving tanks through the narrow streets, which made them very vulnerable to enemy fire while at the same time restricted their own capacity to retaliate. German machine gunners swept the village and those tanks which did manage to get through were withdrawn.

The battle ended on November 27th. Casualties: 44,000 Canadian and British dead and wounded, 53,000 Germans.

## AVELINE Alec Pendock

OR 1909-1915

2nd Lieutenant. Royal Berkshire Regiment.

Prefect. Captain 1st XV. 1913,1914,1915:

'Forward. Captain of the team; a hardworking forward, sometimes displaying considerable dash, but appeared fonder of the open than of scrum work. Played a splendid game against Emanuel School'.

April 1915
Forward. Captain of the team. Has improved very considerably this term, playing with greater dash in the open and working harder in the scrums. Was the best forward on the field against Whitgift School'.

Shooting Colours 1915. Captain of the Corps 1915. Entered RMC Sandhurst in1915.

April 1916: '2nd Lieut. A.P. Aveline. Gentleman cadet of the Royal Military College'.

January 1917: Awarded Military Cross.

'He led a raid against the enemy's trenches with marked ability and succeeded in capturing 52 prisoners. He has at all times set a fine example'.

July 1917: 'Wounded in the foot and in hospital in England'.

---

1    On November 28th the Germans fired 16,000 high explosive and gas shells on the British positions in Bourlon Wood. They advanced three miles taking over 6,000 prisoners and a great deal of materiel.

## BARDSLEY R.C.

OR 1909-1914

Captain. Manchester Regiment, elder son of Mrs Bardsley, of 72, Addington Rd. Reading.

Wounded severely in the right arm and hand on October 8th 1917

Capt. Bardsley was educated at Reading School, where he distinguished himself in all athletic pursuits.

1st XI 1914

'Has been rather disappointing as a bat, except on two or three occasions. Has many good strokes but plays them half-heartedly. Has bowled well at times but is apt to sacrifice length to pace. A good field.'
July 1914.

## BIDDULPH R.H.H.

OR 1901-03

Pte. 487521. No 2 Coy., Princess Patricia's Canadian Light Infantry (Eastern Ontario Regt.)

Killed in action on Thursday 5th July 1917. Aged 27.

CEMETERY: La Targette British Cemetery, Neuville-St.Vaast, Pas de Calais, France. Grave Ref. I.E.3

La Targette British Cemetery is at the cross-roads at Aux-Reitz, behind which is the French National cemetery at La Targette. It was established at the end of April 1917 and used by field ambulances and fighting units until September 1918.

Son of R.F.S. Biddulph, late of London, Ontario, and G.L. Biddulph BSc. McGill University, Montreal.

## CARTER D.W.

OR 1907-14

'The funeral took place on Monday at Caversham Cemetery, of Mr Donovan Carter, only son of Mr and Mrs A.W. Carter, of 'Maubeuge', Church Road, Caversham, who was drowned while bathing last week at Peterborough, where he was stationed with the R.N.A.S

Carter was educated at Reading School and spent three years in the OTC., passing the School Leaving Certificate in 1913. He passed the London Metriculation in 1914, and was studying for a B.Sc., with a view to taking up research work in a Belgian chemical works in which his father was interested. He was passed for a commission in the A.S.C. in January 1915, but, eager to serve his country at the earliest possible moment, he would not wait for the commission and enlisted in the R.N.A.S. as a driver in June of that year. Most of the time he spent at an R.N.A.S. station at Felixstowe, afterwards training at the Crystal Palace as an engineer.

All the naval ratings and officers turned out to do him honour when he was brought home from Peterborough'.

## COLVIN Russell Alexander

OR 1894 -1898

Captain. 10th Battalion, Argyll and Sutherland Highlanders.*

Killed in action on Tuesday, 1st May 1917. Aged 36.

CEMETERY: Athies Communal Cemetery Extension, Pas-de-Calais, France. Grave Ref: G.37.

The area around Athies was captured in April 1917 and remained in British control until the end of the war. The cemetery was used by field ambulances and fighting units until May 1918 and then again from September 1918.

Son of Russell Pakenham Colvin, I.C.S. and Emily Mary Colvin, husband of the late Mary Harvey Elwyn Colvin. Left School in 1898 while in the fourth form. Had been in the 1st XI Football, 2nd XI Cricket and Fenced Sabre in 1898.

* The 10th (Service) Battalion was formed at Stirling in August 1914 as part of Kitchener's 1st Army. Later in the same month it was attached to 27th Brigade, 9th Scottish Division and on May 6th 1916 it was transferred to 26th Brigade. On February 17th 1918 it became part of the 97th Brigade, 32nd Division.

Before his death in May, Colvin would have seen action at the First Battle of the Scarpe which took place between the 9th and 14th April 1917. The Division was in action again on May 3rd which casts some doubt on the listing of Colvin's death as happening on the 1st.

## COOPER W.M.

OR 1909-16

2nd Lieutenant. 2nd Battalion Worcestershire Regiment.*

Killed in action on Sunday 17th February 1917. Aged 19.

CEMETERY: Peronne Communal Cemetery Extension, Ste Radegonde, Somme, France. Grave Ref: V.O.4.

Peronne was captured by the Germans on the 24th September 1914. It was recaptured on the 18th March 1917 but then retaken by the Germans on the 23rd. An Australian division eventually took it back on September 1st 1918. The cemetery extension was first used in March 1917 then by the Germans and finally the Australians. It was later used to bury others who had died in the battlefields to the north and east of Peronne and had been buried in small cemeteries.

1st XI. 1914
'1915. Captain. Has been a hardworked Captain, but has always set his men an excellent example in the field. His bowling has been more effective than last year; the responsibilities of Captain have had an injurious effect on his batting in spite of his persistent efforts to make runs'.

1st XV. 1915
'Outside half. Has a very effective swerve, but was not quite so successful at 'giving the dummy'. Has a good knowledge of the game and both kicks and tackles well'.

Only son of Mr and Mrs John Cooper, 107 London Road, Reading.

'Cooper was only 19 years of age and went out to the front in the Worcestershires about the middle of last December, shortly after completing his course at the Royal

Military College, Sandhurst. He was educated at Reading School, where he gained a Council Scholarship in 1909. His school career was unusually distinguished. In 1914 he gained a School Certificate followed the next year by a Higher Certificate. In response to his country's call, he decided to take a Commission, and in the entrance examination for the Royal Military College, Sandhurst, held in February 1916, he came second on the list, gaining a Prize Cadetship. At Sandhurst his success was no less pronounced than at school, and he gained the position of Sergeant in his cadet unit, the highest position a cadet can obtain, before he left the College. Not only had he considerable intellectual gifts, as his record shows, but he was a fine athlete as well. He was an excellent all round cricketer, and his natural powers as a bowler would have enabled him to make his mark in really good company. As a rugby player he showed great promise, and before he left school he had the distinction of being Captain of Football, Captain of Cricket and Captain of School. Yet he was never elated by his success and perhaps it was more than anything else his modesty which made him so popular with boys and masters alike. Those who have watched his career for the last two years, and marked the way in which his development always seemed to keep pace with his new responsibilities, feel a special grief that a young life so full of promise should have been brought thus prematurely to a close'.

Speech Day. Weds. August 1st. 1917
Headmaster's Speech, one other name he felt bound to mention......
'*2nd Lieutenant Cooper who only left in April of last year. While at school he captained the cricket and football teams, and was of splendid promise, and had considerable ability both as a scholar and athlete, and it was a matter of deep regret that death should have cut short a very promising career. What always pleased him (the Headmaster) was the way in which he always seemed to develop so as to be able to take new responsibilities as they came along. Cooper's record emphasised the importance of all boys forming an ambition early in life, and of having a definite object in life.....*'

* The 2nd Battalion was raised in Aldershot in August 1914 as part of the 5th Brigade, 2nd Division. It transferred to the 100th Brigade, 33rd Division on December 20th 1915.

## DAVIES D.J.

OR 1909-14

2nd Lieutenant. Machine Guns Corps attached 'C' Battalion Tank Corps.

Killed in action on Tuesday 31st July 1917 when in command of a tank.

MEMORIAL: Ypres (Menin Gate) Memorial, Ieper, West Vlaanderen, Belgium. Panel 56.

1st XV.
'Forward. Has improved but is still rather faint-hearted about the scrum. Is playing better in the open, but is inclined to kick too hard'.

*'A bequest to the Governors of Reading School. My Liddell and Scott's Greek Lexicon to be given in the October next following my death to the best First Year Greek Scholar.*

*Thirty shillings to purchase a prize for the best English Essay of not more than 1,500 words (time unlimited) open to boys under 15 years of age upon 'The meaning of the War'. Style, depth of thought and originality are all to be taken into consideration. This prize is also to be given in the October following my death'.*

*These prizes will be presented next Speech Day as this would, under the altered conditions of Speech Day, be no doubt the wish of the Donor'.*

(The prize was awarded to R.Childs, Vc)

2nd Lieutenant D.J.Davies.
'By the death of Second-Lieutenant D.J.Davies, the only son of Mr and Mrs Davies, of the Market Place, Reading, Reading has lost one of the most distinguished of its young men and Reading School one of the most brilliant of its old boys.

Davies' record at Reading School was a remarkable one. When he left in the summer of 1915 he was Captain of the School, the highest honour which a school can confer on any boy, and the holder of a Draper's Scholarship and an Open Classical Scholarship at Trinity College, Oxford. He joined the OTC on the outbreak of war in 1914, and in the Spring Term of 1915 he was in the Rugby XV, and won his 1st XV colours. He was a prominent member of the Literary and Debating Societies. On the occasion of the school holding a debate in French, Davies opened the debate.

He never failed in a public examination and passed the Higher Certificate Examination of the Oxford and Cambridge Board in 1913 with one distinction, in 1914 with four distinctions and in 1915 with five distinctions, coming out at the head of 1,700 candidates. He competed regularly in the school sports and won several prizes in the under 15 events. Latterly, however, intellectual pursuits were more to his inclination, though he always took a very keen interest in all the school activities. He combined great ability with a real capacity for thoroughness and hard work, and had he lived would have gone far. He died, his tank being struck by a shell, on July 31st, the day before his 20th birthday. His loss is greatly to be regretted'.

His Commanding Officer, writing to his father, says:

> *'The death of your son is a great loss to us all; he was very popular and was an exceedingly gallant officer. Up to the time of his death his tank did exceedingly good work'.*

December 1916
Written by DJD otherwise anonymous. Likely to be D.J. Davies who was a tank commander:

## THE 'TANK'

*There it lay in its fallen majesty as I approached it in thick fog, my landmark, the 'Tank'. I heaved a sigh of relief; whereas I had been lost I now knew my bearings. Have you ever tried crossing a field cut up with trenches and pitted with shell holes in a thick fog without a compass? I can assure you it is not an easy job. And when I struck this monster in the battlefield I was naturally glad, for I knew that from this point I could work from place to place till I reached my objective. I was too pleased at the time to think of the poor wretch which had served as my guide; but later I pictured the scene. This mighty engine of destruction pounding along over the trenches and shell holes, and spitting fire as it went; and then just as it reached the ridge and could look down upon the village of.........(in which, by the way, I afterwards found one live tree, an evergreen), just there the hand of fate was stretched out. 'Thus far shalt thou go and no further.' Fritz had scored a direct hit on its 'prow' and the shell had pierced clean through the armour plate and exploded inside. And that was the end of its story; duty well done, but cut off, as it were, in the prime of its life. And of the gunners inside, who shall ask? There it still lies, a hulk on the skyline; and there it will lie, I presume, till the end of time. First to be shown to tourists from America and the home country, then to be neglected and left to decay. And perchance one day someone will point a finger of scorn at it. 'Look at it, and learn; twenty, thirty, forty years ago it started to plough its double furrow across the field; but it exceeded in pride and offended the Gods; so the hand of fate intervened and it was blasted as it went. Look at it, and learn the lesson of the Gods; think not*

*thyself too great. Boast not thyself so that men talk of thee; thou wilt perchance be cut off in the midst of thy mad career, and men will say of thee, 'This man began to build, and was not able to finish.' Take heed I say, and learn to be moderate in all things; and fear the vengeance of heaven when men talk of thee'.*
*DJD.*

**EPPSTEIN. Maurice William Wallis**  b.8.11.96

OR 1905-6

Flight Sub-Lieut. Royal Naval Air Service.

Killed in action on Saturday 12th May. 1917. Aged 20.

CEMETERY: Dunkirk Town Cemetery, Nord, France. Grave Ref: V.A.16.

Throughout the war Dunkirk was a British seaplane base and later an American Naval Air Service base. This would account for the reason why Eppstein was buried here as his body was washed up on shore in an unknown location.

Magazine July 17
'Reported 'missing' after the raid on Zeebrugge on May 12th, and now officially reported 'killed'. Was the younger son of the Rev. Dr. Eppstein, Rector of Lambourne, Essex and formerly Headmaster of Reading School and Mrs Eppstein. He was educated at Cheam School, the R.N.C. Osborne, into which he passed third, and the R.N.C. Dartmouth, where he became cadet captain and chief whip of the Britannia Beagles. Both at his preparatory school and at Dartmouth he showed unusual powers as a runner. At the outbreak of the war he was a Midshipman on H.M.S. 'Hibernia' and was gazetted as Flight Officer in the R.N.A.S. in September 1916. He came out first in the examination for his Sub-Lieutenant's Examination in March 1917 and obtained 10 weeks seniority. He was a keen and fearless flier'.

His commanding officer wrote:

*'Your son was an exceptional officer, skilful and daring in his air work, and adding to this a power of organisation and management which made him invaluable in the squadron routine work. There is no need for me to say anything of the personal qualities that made him such a general favourite, and the loss of which has made so great a void among even us, who are, of necessity, accustomed to sudden voids......You may at least feel the consolation that he was lost in the execution of brave and gallant service'.*

Eppstein was a Probabtionary Flight Officer at Crystal Palace in September 1916 and then posted to Chingford in the October. In March 1917 he attended the Cranwell Gunnery school and in April 1917 was posted to Dover. He was promoted to Flight Sub-Lieutenant in 1917.

He had left the base at Dunkirk on May 12th and was reported missing. Gear from a wrecked aeroplane bearing his name was found by a French destroyer. The Commanding Officer informed the French Commodore and asked for a search to be carried out in the area where the wreckage was found. On May 22nd No.10 Squadron reported the total loss of the aeroplane N5456 (Sopwith Triplane Scout) on May 12th and they informed Dunkirk of this on July 1st.

His body was washed up on the French coast at Guydecoot on July 1st and was buried the next day. *(Ref. Fleet Air Arm Archive. RNAS Yeovilton.)*

## FRANCIS Oswald

OR 1913

'Lieut. Royal Berks Regt. has been awarded the Military Cross for conspicuous gallantry and devotion to duty in the recent fighting in Belgium and also had the honour of being personally congratulated by Sir Douglas Haig.

He left Sandhurst in September 1915 and has served for the last 15 months in France and Belgium, for the greater part of the time on the Somme Front'.

**O.S. Francis, M.C.** (Gazetted October 18th 1917)

April 1918. Bar to Military Cross.

'As forward observing officer to the brigade he occupied a shell hole in an exposed position during an advance and sent back valuable information throughout the day. Later, when a withdrawal became necessary, he helped to rally the troops and organise the defence under heavy fire, moving about in the open with absolute disregard of danger. When the line was established he took command of part of it, and by his example and precept inspired all his men.'

Official Statement:
*'He marked out the assembly positions for the whole brigade before an attack and guided forward companies of two battalions over very difficult ground and under heavy fire'.*

**FROST A.**

OR 1903-05

Captain. 28th Battalion, London Regt. Artists' Rifles attached to 259th Company, Machine Gun Corps (Inf.)

Killed in action on Wednesday 17th October 1917. Aged 28.

CEMETERY: Dar es Salaam War Cemetery, Tanzania. Grave Ref. 5.M.2.

Son of Ralph Frost, 13 Wandle Road, Wandsworth Common, London, England.

During the war Dar es Salaam was the capital of German East Africa. After persistent shelling from Royal Naval vessels from mid-August 1916 the city surrendered on the 4th September. Later in the month the No.3 East African Stationary hospital was located there and as the site was the main port of entry for supplies and the evacuation of sick and wounded it is obvious that any casualties in this area would be brought here. The dead were originally buried in the Dar es Salaam Ocean Rd Cemetery. However, in 1968, during a road building programme, 660 bodies were moved to the Dar es Salaam War Cemetery.

**HARRISON J.**

OR 1908-1909

Lieutenant. 3rd Dorset Regiment attached to Royal Flying Corps.

'Son of G.W. Harrison, Chemist of 'Ramsbury', Shinfield Rd, has met with an accident while flying in the New Forest, resulting in his leg, hands and face being burned. The accident occurred on Saturday, April 7th 1917 when he was flying at Beaulieu, Hants.

His engine caught fire but fortunately the machine was not far from the ground and he was strapped in, with the result that when his aeroplane fell to earth he was able to get free from it. He was then conveyed to Brockenhurst Hospital where he is now progressing favourably. Lieut. Harrison joined up in the early days of the war and has seen service in France and Mesopotamia. He has twice been invalided home, on one occasion with fever'.

**HATT Charles Todd**

OR 1896-1901

2nd Lieutenant. Royal Berkshire Regt.

Killed in action on Friday 12th October 1917. Aged 33.

MEMORIAL: Tyne Cot Memorial, Zonnebeck, West Vlaanderen, Belgium. Panel: 105, 106, 162.

Son of Mr and Mrs Richard Todd of Englefield, Reading. Husband of Elsie Anne Todd of Lotmeade, Warnborough, Swindon.

**JACKMAN George Radcliffe**

OR 1896-99

2nd Lieutenant. 17th Battalion Welsh Regt.*

Died on Saturday 21st April 1917. Aged 34.

CEMETERY: Fins New British Cemetery, Sorel-le-Grand, Somme, France. Grave Ref. IV.L.1.

The villages of Fins and Sorel were taken in April 1917 during the German retreat to the Hindenburg line. They were lost in March 1918 but were regained in the September. The New British Cemetery was not used until July 1917 so this would suggest that Jackman had been originally buried elsewhere. There is a possibility that he was first interred in the Fins Churchyard which contained the bodies of nine soldiers buried in April 1917 which were subsequently moved to the New British Cemetery when the former was closed.

* The 17th (Service) Battalion (1st Glamorgan) was formed at Cardiff in December 1914 as a Bantam Battalion. These battalions had a mixture of regulation height and shorter men. Weeding out of very undersized or unfit men delayed the training programmes and it did not go to France until June 1916. It was attached to the 43rd Division and in July 1915 transferred to the 119th Brigade, 40th Division and was disbanded in France on February 9th 1918. From the dates this Division was in action it would seem that Jackman was wounded during the German retreat to the Hindenberg Line which took place between the March 14th and April 5th 1917. The 40th was not in action again until the Battle of Cambrai at the end of the year.

**KEEBLE Arthur Theodore**

Elder son of Headmaster. 2^nd Lieutenant. Royal Engineers.

Killed in action on Thursday 28^th June 1917.

CEMETERY: Lijssenthoek Military Cemetery, Poperinge, West-Vlaanderen, Belgium. Grave Ref: XIII.A.II.

The rail link between Hazebrouck and Poperinghe and the Poperinghe-Ypres road provided the main communication links between military bases and the battlefields in the area. Lijssenthoek was an obvious location for a casualty clearing station as it was just beyond the range of the German guns. Between June 1915 and November 1918 it became the second largest British war cemetery.

Editorial
*'We should like to express our deep sympathy with Mr and Mrs Keeble on the loss of their elder son who died of wounds in France on June 28^th.*

*A most promising career has thus been cut short, though in a deeper sense, in the things that really matter, we know that there was not only promise but a large measure of fulfilment. Keeble was a boy of unusual and varied abilities. To these he added the yet more precious gifts of energy and industry and the crowing grace of a happy Christian disposition. His career at Kendrick School was one of unusual brilliance and usefulness. He passed the London Matriculation (1^st Division) at a very early age and, while still at school, also passed Inter. B.Sc. Examination. Nor were his activities confined to the classroom. He excelled at all games, and in all the departments of school life he was equally interested and successful. Keeble's long tenure of the Captaincy of the school, the duties of which office he conscientiously carried out, must have left a deep and abiding mark on his generation, and his memory will live in the hearts of hundreds of Kendrick boys who were privileged to know him.*

*From School he went on to University College, Reading and it was amidst the full tide of College life that the call came for him to serve his country. He received his commission in the Royal Engineers last summer and went out to France in November. He was attached to Divisional Headquarters, and was in charge of a party of men laying cable to the front line trenches in the early morning of June 27^th when he was mortally wounded by shrapnel. He was carried to the casualty station and underwent an operation, but died the next day without recovering consciousness'.*

**KILBY Tom Wheatley**

OR 1898-1903

Pte. 181204. 88th Battalion, 3rd Canadian Pioneers.

Killed in action on Tuesday, 27th March 1917. Aged 30.

CEMETERY: Ecoivres Military Cemetery, Mont-St.Eloi, Pas de Calais, France. Grave Ref. IV.H.23

This cemetery is an extension of the Communal Cemetery where the French buried over 1,000 men. The dead from various attacks and battles were brought from the front line to the site via the French Military tramway and from the first row to the last buried them in date order. It contains the graves of many Canadians.

Son of Edward and Annie Kilby of Greenwich, England and Yokohama, Japan.

**KNOWLES Walford Vernon**

OR 1909-16

2nd Lieutenant. 3rd Battalion, attached 2nd Battalion. Royal Berkshire Regt.

Killed in action on Monday 31st December 1917. Aged 20.

CEMETERY: Poelcapelle British Cemetery, Langemark-Poelkapelle, West-Vlassnderen, Belgium. Grave Ref. XIII.E.1

1st XI 1916: 'His lack of batting abIlIity is to some extent compensated for by his energy and keenness in the field'.

1st XV 1915: 'Forward. A much improved forward; played an excellent game at Windsor. Works hard and is becoming very useful in the open'.

The village of Poelcapelle was captured by the Germans in October 1914 and remained in their control until October 1917, evacuated by the British in April 1918 and retaken by the Belgians in September 1918. The cemetery was constructed after November 1918 and bodies from other cemeteries and other battlefields were brought to the site. The vast majority of those buried here were killed during the latter half of 1917.

Editorial 1918
*'Knowles entered the school in 1909 with the brightest promise of success, and left us only in December 1916, with that promised fully realised.*

*He had just been elected to a Classical Exhibition at New College and we had been hoping to congratulate him after the war on further successes in his Oxford career. Nor was he merely a scholar. He was a prominent member of the XI and of the XV and a Sergeant in the OTC, and in every department of school life he showed the greatest interest and activity. He was so near a neighbour and was so lately a member of the school that his death affects us all, to quite a peculiar extent, as a personal loss. We should like to express to Mr and Mrs Knowles the sympathy of the whole school with them in their great sorrow'.*

'2$^{nd}$ Lieut. Walford Vernon Knowles, Royal Berkshire Regiment who was killed in action on December 31$^{st}$ 1917, was the elder son of Mr and Mrs Vernon Knowles of Kendrick View, Reading. Born in January 1898, he was educated at Reading School into which he took an open Scholarship in 1909, one of the first scholarships offered by the Reading Town Council. In 1916 he passed the Higher Certificate Examination with distinction in French and German. During his last year at School he won the Laud Scholarship, the blue ribbon of Reading School, also an exhibition at Worcester College, Oxford, and was further awarded the Ewelme Exhibition. Later he gave up the Worcester College Exhibition in favour of an open Classical Exhibition at New College Oxford.

It was not only in his studies that he did well, but in every side of school life he made his mark, becoming a member of the Rugby football and Cricket teams, a Sergeant in the OTC and finally Captain of School. Of those who have in recent years held this coveted position he is the third to make the supreme sacrifice during the war, the other two being W.M. Cooper and D.J. Davies.

On reaching military age he carried his characteristic energy into the sterner school of war, passing with credit through his cadetship at Gales and afterwards Portsmouth. He went out to France early in October as Second Lieutenant in the County Regiment, and in his all too brief period of service had already won the affection and esteem of his comrades and superior officers;'

'It is with deepest regret,' writes Lieut-Colonel C.M.H Stirling, Commanding his Battalion of the Berkshire Regt., to his parents. 'that I have to tell you of the death of your son in action on December 31$^{st}$. His loss has made us all most sad, as everybody liked him and he was such a good officer'.

**LONG Harry Ireland**

OR 1897-1901

Cpl. 1054256. 24th Battalion, Canadian Infantry (Quebec Regiment).

Killed in action on August 15th 1917. Aged 31.

MEMORIAL: Vimy Memorial, Pas de Calais, France.

This memorial, the most impressive Canadian memorial on the Western front, overlooks the Douai plain from the highest point on the Vimy Ridge. The land around the memorial was given by the French government to the Canadians 'the free gift in perpetuity of the French nation to the people of Canada'.

The names of more than 11,000 Canadians who were 'missing presumed dead' are inscribed on the panels.

Son of William and Anna Long; husband of Isabel Clendinnen Long. 139, Wentworth Road, Golders Green, London, England

Long was in Canada at the outbreak of war and joined the Canadian Forces. He fell on August 15th 1917 during the attack on Hill 70 by the 24th Canadian Infantry Battalion.

**LOWSLEY S E**

OR 1889-1892

Air Mechanic 1st Class. F/35435. HMS 'President', RNAS. *

Killed in Action Thursday 27th September. 1917.

Enlisted 13th August 1917.

The RNAS records show that he was a Civil Engineer by profession and he enlisted as a Draughtsman. According to the entry in 'Airmen Died in the Great War 1914-18', by Chris Hobson, he died in the UK. This would suggest that he was killed while on basic training.

CEMETERY: Harrogate (Harlow Hill) Cemetery, Yorkshire, England.
Grave Ref. H.190

This led to an interesting research problem. The cemetery is located on the Otley Road and is now in a state of reconstruction due to minor subsidence which is causing headstones to fall. However, there was no headstone for Lowsley. The local vicar, the Rev. Martin Soar of All Saints in which part of St. Mary's incumbency lies, was contacted. He provided the address of the bereavement services who were very helpful. Derek Thacker visited the location with maps and burial details etc. but no one of the name Lowesly could be located from either these documents or by reference to War Grave burials.

H190 had the name Allen written in on the maps although nothing was visible at all. The adjacent grave was Harrison. Having checked all the War Grave tablets at Harlow Hill the conclusion was reached that Lowsley was no longer buried there, even if he had been at one time. However we do know that Lowsley enlisted at Harrogate and his address was 11 Wensley Rd, Harrogate.

(We are indebted to Colin Brooks, Pickering, for carrying out this research on our behalf).

* HMS President was, and still is, a shore base in London. All Naval personnel are required to be attached to a ship for payment purposes so although Lowsley was killed in action he would not have been on HMS President as such. All the 'President's' are listed in Shore Establishments of the Royal Navy (ed. Lt.Cdr. Warlow. Maritime Books). as 'Accounting Bases' and since May 1878 all officers serving in the Admiralty have been borne on the books of the 'President'. (ref British Warship Names. Capt. T.D.Manning & Commander C.F.Walker. pub. Putnam. 1959). It is worth noting that by the end of the war 25% of all squadrons on the Western Front were naval.

**RAKE Henry Stansfield**

OR 1899-1902

Pte. 693186. 43rd Battalion, Canadian Infantry (Manitoba Regt).

Killed in action on Friday 26th October 1917. Aged 32. Son of the late Herbert Rake, Denefield, Tilehurst, Reading.

MEMORIAL. Ypres, Menin Gate, Ieper, West-Vlaanderen, Belgium.
Panel 24,26,28,30.

## SMITH L. Victor

OR 1892–97

July 1917.
'2<sup>nd</sup> Lieut. Awarded the Military Cross for gallantry whilst in command of a tank in the Arras battle'.
'Victor Smith has been with tanks ever since they went to France and was with them through the Somme Offensive'.

## SOOLE Seymour Waldegrave

OR 1889-1890

Gunner 199044. 3<sup>rd</sup> Reserve Brigade, Royal Horse Artillery.

Died on February 3<sup>rd</sup> 1917 of Cerebro-Meningitis at Portsmouth Hospital.
Aged 39.

CEMETERY: Reading Cemetery, Berkshire. Grave Ref. 46. 7627

The Reading Cemetery contains 204 war graves. Those which are no longer marked are commemorated on a Screen Wall near the Cross of Sacrifice in the right hand corner at the rear of the cemetery.

Son of Laura Sophia Soole of 3, Castle Crescent, Reading and the late Rev. S.H. Soole.

## WARNER Bertram

OR 1902-06

2<sup>nd</sup> Lieutenant. 1<sup>st</sup>/5<sup>th</sup> Battalion. London Regt. (London Rifle Brigade) formerly Worcestshire Regt.

Killed in action on Thursday 12<sup>th</sup> April 1917. Aged 28.

MEMORIAL. Arras Memorial, Pas de Calais, France.
Panel: Bay 9

The Arras memorial commemorates almost 35,000 soldiers of the British, New Zealand and South African forces who were killed between the spring of 1916 and the 7<sup>th</sup> August 1918 and have no known grave. It does not include those killed at Cambrai in 1917. It is situated in the Faubourg-d'Amiens Cemetery.

1<sup>st</sup> XV. 1905-6
'Has pace and kicks and tackles well. Should combine more with the other three-quarters'.

'We much regret to record that Mr John Warner of Waddon House, Croydon, has lost his third son in the war. Mr Warner gave three sons to the London Regiment and all have sacrificed their lives for their country.

On April 12<sup>th</sup> , 2<sup>nd</sup> Lieut. Bertram Warner led his platoon in a bombing attack against the enemy, and was shot down.

After his education at 'The Limes' School, Croydon, and at Reading School, Lieut. Warner was engaged in agriculture at Evesham, and immediately on the outbreak of war joined the Worcestershire Regiment. He reached the rank of Acting Quartermaster Sergeant and after a year's work was offered a commission in the London Regiment. He accepted it, and was gazetted in September, 1916, proceeding to the front again in November. A glowing tribute is paid to the memory of the fallen officer, who was 28 years of age, by his Major, who stated:

> *'We have lost one of our best officers, one who was beloved by his men, always reliable, and at all times cool, courageous; an example to everybody, cheerful in all circumstances and universally popular. We all know, of course, how much our regiment owes to your sons and so can all the more sympathise with your additional grief'.*

⚬

### WELLS Douglas Henry MC

OR 1906-12

2<sup>nd</sup> Lieutenant. 5<sup>th</sup> Battalion, Yorks and Lancaster Regt.

Killed in action on Thursday 3<sup>rd</sup> May 1917.
Aged 24.

MEMORIAL: Arras Memorial, Pas de Calais, France.
Panel: Bay 8

14<sup>th</sup> March 1915
From Pte. D.H. Wells of the Canadian Contingent.

*'This is Sunday evening, a mild Spring night, and there is a fearful bombardment going on. For a couple of hours there has been a regular storm of thunder from hundreds of guns and there must be a terrible scrap going on somewhere.*

*There is an air of hope and expectancy about, you can feel and see it everywhere. We know we are top dogs now and it is a question of a week or two. There are going to be heavy casualty lists, but it is the price of advance, and it is a damned sight better to go down advancing than retreating.*

*I got a pass out yesterday and went down town for a shave and good feed. An English band was playing in the Square and the enthusiasm was great when the 'Marseillaise' was played. As we listened, round the corner came an endless stream of Paris motor-buses, and then transports of all sorts. There were despatch riders tearing through, Staff Officers strolling around, cavalry trotting through in twos and threes, ambulance wagons, London General omnibuses, and so in spite of the music you knew it was WAR, WAR, WAR everywhere about you.*

*I wish you could have been in that square for a few minutes, and have seen the little groups of French soldiers, and their blue serge and red pants, in strange contrast to our dull khaki; or a group of civilians excitedly discussing the latest news and commenting upon the future; or the little boys in their 'kepis' and cloaks, eyeing you as though you were a fresh animal at the Zoo.*

*Last night a brigade of cavalry passed through in a seemingly endless stream, smoking and whistling as though nothing much was wrong, and yet they had been through the whole weary seven months of it and been through hell in that time.*

*By the bye, its going to be a great time for the cavalry soon and they won't have to go into the trenches much longer.*

*I was talking to a fellow in the...........who has been right through everything. I was speaking about reports in the paper of men simply longing to get back to the war, and expressed my doubts as to the sincerity of these reports; and he said:*

*There are 25 left out of my regiment and I got five days leave some time ago, and if I had thought I was going back to the trenches I should never have gone back'.*

Wells was one of a permanent Guard for Headquarters. He stated that the only men that might want to get back to it were the ASC men and the RAMC men.
*(Letter sent by Doris Higgs, Alexandra Road, Reading)*

1st XV 1908
'Right wing. Has not fulfilled expectations owing to weak tackling and lack of dash when running. Kicks well. Has played at full back in the last two matches'.

'We regret to announce the death in action of 2nd Lieut. D.H.Wells. M.C., Yorks and Lancs. Regiment, which occurred on May 3rd. 1917. He was the son of the late Mr.G.H.Wells and Mrs Wells of 237, Oxford Rd. Educated at Reading School, where he greatly distinguished himself at athletics, he went out to Canada and enlisted on the first day of the war. He was wounded at Ypres in May 1915, and afterwards gained his Commission. A short time ago he was awarded the Military Cross for conspicuous gallantry and devotion to duty when in command of a patrol. He carried out a difficult reconnaissance and obtained most valuable information. Later he rendered invaluable service when in command of a company. His Commanding Officer writes of him:

> *'During an attack on the German trenches he led his platoon forward. Although under heavy shell fire and intense machine gun fire, he rallied his men, and was last seen leading a bomb attack down a German communication trench, where he was shot in the head and killed instantly. I need hardly say we, miss him very much. I think your son was one of the most gallant officers I have met; he had already won the M.C. and I considered him particularly capable and efficient as an officer and leader of men. His men speak of him in the highest terms, and say his conduct was beyond all praise'.*

A brother officer writes:

> *'Among the officers and men in this battalion, especially the latter, he was worshipped, and it is by a man's followers you can judge him best. His death has been felt deeply from the Colonel downwards. Our objective was being resisted strongly, and so after a first and hopeless attempt we withdrew and had another attempt. 'Duggie' was wounded in the first, but would not leave his men, he was again wounded in the second attempt and reached the trench with only five men, but undaunted he led a bombing attack with his few and was killed attempting to capture a German machine gun at hopeless odds. He has again been recommended, which goes to prove that he was undoubtedly one of the best soldiers in the battalion, and certainly quite the best friend one could wish for'.*

**WHEELER John Piggot MC**

OR 1900-1902

Major. 'D' Battery, 82nd Brigade, Royal Field Artillery.

Killed in action on Tuesday 30th October 1917. Aged 25.

CEMETERY: Vlamertinghe New Military Cemetery, Ieper, West-Vlaanderen, Belgium. Grave Ref. IX.E.23.

The area around Vlamertinghe was just outside the range of enemy gunfire for the major part of the war. The first Military Cemetery used primarily by Artillery units and field ambulances, contains the bodies of those killed between 1914 to the early part of 1917. There was not enough room to extend the graveyard so the New Military Cemetery was built in June 1917 and by December twelve plots were almost full.

Son of Samuel and Elizabeth Wheeler, 30 Craven Road, Reading.

'On the first Sunday of term, September 18th, a window was dedicated in the Chapel to the memory of Major J.P. Wheeler. The window, which is at the East end of the North side, represents St. Barbara, and was given by Major Wheeler's relatives. The dedication service was conducted by the Rev. Piggott Smith, St Aidan's, New Cleethorpes, formerly Curate of St. Giles' Reading'.

The inscription is as follows:

'In memory of John Piggot Wheeler, M.C., Major R.F.A. who fell at Langemarck, October 30th 1917, aged 25'.

**WILD Lionel Tudor**

OR 1903-06

Captain. 'B' Company, 7th Battalion Somerset Light Infantry.*

Killed in action on Friday 30th November 1917. Aged 29.

MEMORIAL: Cambrai Memorial, Louverval, Nord,. France. Panel 4 and 5.

The Cambrai Memorial stands in the Louveral Military Cemetery in the village of Louveral.

The memorial inscription, in both French and English, is as follows:

*'To the Glory of God and to the enduring memory of 7048 officers and men of the forces of the British Empire who fell at the Battle of Cambrai between 20th November and the 3rd December 1917, whose names are here recorded but to whom the fortunes of war denied the known and honoured burial given to comrades in death'.*

July 1918

'Lionel Wild was the second son of Mr and Mrs Aubrey S. Wild, of 21 Canning Rd. Addiscombe, Croydon and was born in 1888. Educated at St. Winifred's, Kenley, and Reading School, he was for a short time in the service of the London and Westminster Bank, but afterwards turning his attention to motor engineering, he took up an appointment with Messrs. Argylls (Limited) in Dundee, and was subsequently manager of the company's branch at Aberdeen. For several years before the war he was a member of the Surrey Yeomanry, and attained the rank of Sergeant, being one of the best rifle-shots in his squadron. On the oubreak of war he was mobilised with his regiment, and after some months' training obtained a commission in the Somerset Light Infantry, proceeding to France with his battalion in July 1915. In 1916 he was appointed Brigade Staff Captain, but eventually returned to his regiment, and was given the command of a company. He was reported 'wounded and missing' on November 30th 1917, and it has now been established that he was killed on that date, in an attempt to save the remnants of his company during the German counter-attack near Cambrai, and was buried by the enemy at Masnieres.

\* The 7th (Service) Battalion was formed in Taunton in September 1914 as part of Kitchener's 2nd Army. Later in the month it was attached to the 61st Brigade 20th Light Division.

## WRIGHT R.F.

OR 1909-1916

Captain of School.

1st XI Hockey 1915/16 and 1st XV Rugby 1914/15/16.

'Forward. A steady hardworking forward, always doing well in the tight scrums. Is not fast enough to be very effective in the open'.

Royal Naval Air Service in Russia.

Wright sent the following letter to Mr Diemer in April 1917.

*'The weather conditions may interest some people. When we were right in the Arctic Circle it was 2 days less cold than England. This I believe was partly due to the influence of the Gulf Stream. Once North Cape was passed the real cold began. The sun was above the horizon for only 5 hours, and the masts, decks and rails began to have ice on them. There is no glare about the sun when it rises. One can look right at it without hurting one's eyes. All the colours too of the sunrise are softer than in England.....In some ways the most beautiful sight we saw was the Aurora which we saw one very fine starlit night. The light is quite white and very soft and is moving all the time....On land the sleighs are sometimes drawn by a team of reindeer. They are quite small, grey deer, but they can move faster than the horses that seem to be more generally used. Some of the dogs look very much like foxes'.*

December 1919
*'R.F.Wright (St John's) has safely passed through Armistice Night as well as the 'glorious 5$^{th}$' which is no small achievement.'*
Oxford O.R.

---

**From France.**
*April 1917.*
*Anonymous.*

*'The French seem to love enormous trains with as many engines as possible. By yesterday ours had attained a great length, and rests by the wayside were quite frequent. At one of them we ran across a ripping little wood. It was a glorious sunny day and we had a splendid shave and general clean up, all in a cup of hot water borrowed from the engine. It is quite usual to get out and walk if one gets cold and fed up with things. A brisk walk soon improves matters and the train is sure to catch up if one waits long enough.*

*We have quite a good billet, well ventilated but comfortable. It is possible for shells to pop in, hence we sleep in the cellar which beggars description. My servant has improvised a bed from a door supported on a pair of steps, and an orange box with a couple of small barrels to prevent it from collapsing in the middle. The ground floor of the house is fairly well furnished. Our table is composed of old planks varying in thickness, while the 'Morning Post' of November 14$^{th}$ makes an excellent tablecloth. The fireplace is a work of art. A few bricks firmly bound with mud make a graceful exit for smoke through what was once a window, but which is now obliterated with packing case lids. At the top of the brickwork is balanced a piece of stove pipe and the back draught is immense. Our coal limber has gone astray but the Bosche has turned the roof of a barn into firewood, so we do not worry. There is an upper* *floor to the billet, but only one of the four of us is hard enough to spend the night there. From here a splendid view of the stars can be obtained. The servants talk of rats and hence the real reason for my dive into the cellar. Today I had an excellent bath in a disused brewery and feel civilised again.*

*One poor misguided aunt of one of our subs packed two eggs in hay in a tin. This was meant to be a treat, I suppose. The parcel arrived when we were resting and for two days the Mess was uninhabitable. If he gets any more such gifts there'll be much trouble'.*

## HEADMASTERS SPEECH 1st August 1917

*'Another contribution which the school had made to the war was in the workshops, from which they had turned out requisites for the hospitals such as splints, crutches and bedrests. In the way of assisting food production the boys helped last Easter on the allotments and during the summer holidays all the boys of about 16 would be helping in farm work of some kind....'*

The School had not been affected too much, if at all by the complicated laws governing pupil attendance and child employment. Children under 11 were not allowed to sell articles on the street and boys under 14 could not work in the mines. Local Authorities might, although few did, forbid all children under 14 to work. By the end of the first year of the war the Board of Education was under pressure from many Local Authorities who wished to suspend the school attendance by-laws. Magistrates were particularly keen that children should be released for war-work or 'national work'. It was a fact that there was a great deal of economic pressure placed on those families who had a least one member of active service. In August 1917 H.A.L. Fisher, the Minister responsible for Education admitted that for the first three years of the war 600,000 children had been put to work prematurely. This was the official figure and did not take into account those who had worked illegally.
*(Ref. House of Commons Debates 10 August 1917)*

## EXPERIENCES OF AN O.R.

Magazine July 1917. Anon.

*'What awful tramp is that coming?' exclaimed the lady as she was approaching her house a young fellow weirdly attired in most incongruous clothing, including a very old coat, an officer's boots, a Trilby hat and wearing no collar. But her alarm was quickly transformed to joy when she recognised her son whom she had not seen for 18 months and who, as a cadet in the Mercantile Marine, had had some thrilling experiences.*

*He was having a rest one Sunday afternoon somewhere on the high seas when his ship was torpedoed. Four boats were lowered, but he, an old Reading School boy, was left standing with the others on the poop. A second torpedo was fired at the ship but missed its mark, and then a third struck the engine room, hurling the ship's funnel into the water and scattering the coal about in all directions. A boat containing three men was blown into the air, but men were 'landed' safely into the water. The Germans refused to allow the small boats to approach the ships to rescue the men remaining, and so they had to plunge into the sea and swim about a quarter of a mile before being picked up.*

*When the ship went down the flag staff came out of its socket and floated on the water. A pathetic sight was the pet monkey clinging to a piece of wood as it was tossed about by the waves, and an attempt to rescue the poor creature proved in vain.*

*After the ship had sunk, the submarine officer ordered the Chief Officer of the ship to go on board their boat. He only had on a vest. He was in a dazed condition owing to the experience he had just passed through. The Germans could get little out of him and so, after photographing him, they sent him back and eventually took the Second Officer a prisoner. When the boats containing the cadets looked like becoming swamped they asked the Germans for a bailer, but the Germans seem as though they would rather spit in their faces and refusing went on their way beneath the waves.*

*The small boats then shaped their course for a lighthouse 43 miles away and, after being on the water for seven hours, were picked up by a French destroyer. The French were the embodiment of kindness and a real French Admiral congratulated the cadets on having come out of the ordeal safely, telling them that they had worthily upheld the honour of Great Britain'.*

# 1918

*'They do send some funny people over here nowadays. I hope we are lucky and get a youngster straight from school. They're the kind that do best'.*

(Osborne. Responding to the fact that they were expecting a new officer in March 1918 from *Journeys End. R.C. Sherriff. p3*).

Overview:

| | |
|---|---|
| March 21 – April 5 | Somme |
| March 21 – 22 | Fontaine-les-Clercs |
| March 21 – 23 | St. Quentin |
| March 23 | Cugny |
| March 24 – 25 | Bapaume |
| March 26 – 27 | Rosieres |
| March 28 | Arras |
| April 4 | Avre |
| April 5 | Ancre |
| April 9 – 29 | Lys |
| April 9 – 11 | Estaires |
| April 10 – 11 | Messines |
| April 12 – 25 | Hazebrouck |
| April 13 – 15 | Bailleul |
| April 17 – 19 | Kemmel |
| April 18 | Bethune |
| April 22 | Pacaut Wood |
| April 24 – 25 | Villers-Bretonneux |
| April 25 – 26 | Kemmel |
| April 29 | Scherpenberg |
| May 27 – June 6 | Aisne |
| June 6 | Bligny |
| June 6 | Bois des Buttes |
| July 4 | Hamel |
| July 20 – August 2 | Marne |
| July 20 – 31 | Tardenois |
| July 23 – August 2 | Soissonais-Ourcq |
| August 8 – 11 | Amiens |
| August 8 | Harbonnieres |
| August 21 – 23 | Albert |
| August 21 – 23 | Chuignes |
| August 21 – September 5 | Somme |
| August 26 – September 3 | Arras |

| | |
|---|---|
| **August 26 – 30** | Scarpe |
| **August 29** | Mont Vidaigne |
| **August 31 – September 3** | Bapaume |
| **August 31 – September 3** | Mont St. Quentin |
| **September 2 – 3** | Drocourt-Queant |
| **September 12 – October 9** | Hindenberg Line |
| **September 12** | Havrincourt |
| **September 18** | Epehy |
| **September 27 – October 1** | Canal du Nord |
| **September 28 – October 2** | Ypres |
| **September 29 – October 2** | St Quentin Canal |
| **October  3 – 6** | Beaurevoir |
| **October 8 – 9** | Cambrai |
| **October 14 – 19** | Courtrai |
| **October 17 – 25** | Selle |
| **October 17 – 18** | Le Cateau |
| **October 31** | Tieghem |
| **November 1 – 2** | Valenciennes |
| **November 4** | Sambre |
| **November 4** | Le Quesnoy |
| **November 4 – 11** | Pursuit to Mons |

## OPERATION MICHAEL

### March 21st–April 5th 1918

The Germans planned a surprise attack to take place in March-April 1918 with the aim of capturing the area around Amiens and dividing the French and British armies. This was particularly important because of the extra man-power provided by the newly arrived American forces.

A total of 63 German divisions attacked over a 60-mile front held by 26 British divisions. The latter were overwhelmed and pushed back westwards. Within 5 days the Germans had retaken all the land they had lost in the Somme area over the previous two years and they were very close to the strategic rail network at Amiens and only 50 miles from Paris.

A gap did develop between the French and British positions but this was filled by Australian and American troops.

The assault finished on April 5th by which time the Germans had taken around 90,000 British prisoners and inflicted 164,000 casualties on the British and 70,000 on the

French. However, their own costs were high. During the 40 mile gain there were 160,000 casualties and 70,000 had been taken prisoner. All German divisions were exhausted and because the breakthrough had not been achieved the morale of the troops was very low.

## BATTLE OF LYS

### April 9th–29th 1918

Despite the set back of Operation Michael, the Germans continued their offensive in other areas. On April 9th fourteen German divisions attacked on a ten-mile front, driving the British back and creating a 3 mile gap in the line. Around 2,000 tons of mustard gas and phosgene was used against the British and Portuguese forces in the area causing a great deal of injury and blindness. The following day the allies were driven out of the Messines area where German gas had also been used to great effect. The Allies held out for six days behind the river Lys.

On April 15th the allies withdrew from the Passchendaele ridge and on the 20th the Germans launched a massive gas attack in an area just south of Ypres. However, the Germans were being forced back in many sectors and on April 29th Ludendorff called off the assault. This was to have a devastating effect on German morale.

## THIRD BATTLE OF THE AISNE

### May 27th–June 1st

After an early bombardment the Germans drove through the French lines in the area to a distance of 12 miles. They reached the River Aisne in less than six hours. By the next day a 15 mile deep wedge had been created in the Allied line over a 40 mile wide front. By June 1st the Germans were only 40 miles from Paris. American troops joined the line and held it. The Germans were exhausted and the speed of their advance meant that they had 'outrun' their supply lines.

London

ENGLAND
Dover

English
Channel

Ostend  Zeebrug
Nieuport
Dunkirk
Calais
Hazebrouck
Passchendaele
Ypres
Messines
Armentières
Neuve Chapelle
La Bassée
Loos
Vimy
Arras
Boulogne
R.Scheld

Cambrai
Bapaume  Le Cateau
Albert  Péronne

R.Somme

Dieppe
Amiens  St Q

June 1918
Furthest
German Advance

Barisis

Le Havre
Rouen  FRANCE  Compiègne
Soissons

R.Seine  R.Oise  R.M

Meaux
Paris

# The Western Front, 1918

HOLLAND

Antwerp

BELGIUM

Cologne

Aachen

Brussels

Bonn

R.Rhine

Liege

R.Maas

GERMANY

Namur

Charleroi

Koblenz

R.Sambre

LUXEMBOURG

Sedan

Reims

R.Aisne

11 November 1918
Armistice Line

R.Moselle

Verdun

Epernay

R.Meuse

March 1918
Front Line

**AUST Henry Ernest**

OR 1908-14

Lieutenant. 1/4th Battalion, Yorkshire Regt.

Killed in action on Wednesday 18th September 1918. Aged 22.

MEMORIAL: Vis-en Artois Memorial, Pas-de-Calais, France. Panel 5.

This memorial contains the names of more than 9,000 soldiers who were killed between August 8th and November 11th in Picardy and Artois, between the Somme and Loos who have no known grave.

Son of Thomas and Mary Ann Aust, of 'Carn Brea', Northcourt Ave., Reading.

1st XV 1913
'A light but hardworking forward, always on the ball. Played as a reserve in several matches'.

* The 1/4th Battalion was established in August 1914 at Northallerton as part of the York and Durham Brigade, Northumbrian Division. It landed at Boulogne in France on April 18th 1915. On May 14th 1915 the formation became the 150th Brigade, 50th Division. On July 16th 1918 it was reduced in strength and moved to lines of communication. On August 16th it was transferred to the 116th Brigade, 39th Division. It was finally demobilised on November 6th 1918.

As part of this Division, Aust would have seen action at the Battle of St Quentin March 21st-23rd 1918 and the crossing of the Somme, March 24th-25th, before being killed in action in September.

**BRAIN Francis Sydney**

OR 1901-1907

Captain. Royal Berks Regiment attached 1st Battalion Dorsetshire Regt. *

Killed in action on Thursday 3rd October 1918. Aged 24.

CEMETERY: Cerisy-Gailly Military Cemetery, Somme, France.
Grave Ref. III.K.14.

Gailly was the site of 2 Casualty Clearing Stations during early 1917 and a Field Hospital from May 1917-March 1918. The area was then captured by the

Germans but retaken by the Australians in August 1918. After the end of the war bodies were brought from various other cemeteries including: Maricourt Military Cemetery, Ste. Helene British Cemetery, Beaufort British Cemetery and Buigny-les-Gamaches Communal Cemetery.

'The sympathy of the whole town will go out to Mr and Mrs Sydney Brain in the loss of their second son, Captain Francis Sydney Brain, Royal Berkshire Regiment, who was killed in action on 3rd October 1918.

Born in 1893, he was educated at Reading School and Leighton Park School, and in 1912 he obtained a scholarship at Trinity Hall, Cambridge. At the outbreak of war he joined the Cambridge University OTC and on February 26th 1915, was gazetted 2nd Lieutenant, being promoted Lieutenant on July 29th, 1918. He proceeded to France in June 1916, and was attached to the 1st Battalion Dorset Regt., with which he served to the time of his death. He saw much service in France and was recently promoted Captain. The news of the death was received by his parents on Wednesday, and was contained in a letter from the Chaplain of the regiment, who wrote as follows:

> *'I am grieved to have to tell you of the loss of your gallant son in action on 3rd inst. He was hit on the head by a shell during the course of our brilliant advance and died instantly. I hope it will be of some little consolation to know that he died gloriously doing glorious deeds. He is a great loss to the regiment, as he was one of our most promising officers. In him I, too, had a friend, and more than a friend, for we were both of the same Varsity, and had mutual friends. I was able to get his body and bring it back to a little cemetery which we started here, where he lies with others of his regiment. We had the service of the Church of England, the Last Post and a funeral party. My prayers go up that the Almighty will give you strength to bear your sorrow'.*

* The 1st Battalion was actually established in Belfast in August 1914 as part of the 15th Brigade, 5th Division. On December 31st 1915 it transferred to the 95th Brigade, 32nd Division and from January 7th 1916 was part of the 14th Brigade, 32nd Division.

As part of this Division, Brain would have seen action at the First Battle of Albert July 1st-13th 1916, the Battle of Bazentin July 14th-17th 1916, the Battle of Ancre November 13th-18th 1916, the German retreat to the Hindenberg Line March 14th-April 5th 1917, and the Second Battle of Albert August 21st-23rd 1918.

## CLARKE A. FIELDING

OR 1911-1914

April 1918
'On Wednesday in last week Captain Fielding Clarke of Ampthill, Craven Rd, Reading, received a telegram intimating that his second son, Second Lieutenant A. Fielding Clark, RFC, was missing. The previous Saturday he had been with his squadron carrying out a bombing raid on and around Metz, and his machine was the only one which did not return. Lieut. Clarke whose age is 18 years and 6 months, was educated at Reading School and Bradfield College, and he joined the RFC at the age of 17 years and four months. He had been in France about three months and had just returned from his first furlough. It is supposed that the cause of his failing to return must have been engine trouble, for on the occasion of the raid there was particularly little German anti-aircraft fire'.

Later: 'Lieut A. Fielding Clark is now known to be a prisoner of war interned at Karlsruhe'.

Post War: 'A.F. Clarke (St John's) still carries his pocket violin (as at school) and proves to all that 'music hath charms to soothe the savage beast. e.g. Ruskin Hall'.

## COOK Howard Mortimer

OR 1903-06

Lieutenant. 12th Battalion Machine Gun Corps.

Killed in action on Friday 9th August 1918. Aged 28.

CEMETERY: Contay British Cemetery, Contay, Somme, France.
Grave Ref. IX.B.22.

The site of the cemetery was chosen in August 1916, for the 49th Casualty Clearing Station which arrived at Contay at the end of August. It was used until March 1917. The German withdrawal in the area meant that other medical units could be brought in from the east and it was not until April 1918, when the Germans advanced to Albert, that the cemetery was used again. The last burials took place in August 1918 and Cook was among this group.

Son of Mr and Mrs John R. Cook, Reading. A Commoner of St.Edmund Hall, Oxford.

'Lieut. Howard Mortimer Cook, who was killed on August 8-9th 1918, would have been 29 on September 1st had he lived. He was the elder son of Mr John R. Cook, late of Lloyds Bank, Reading and Mrs Cook and grandson of the late Town Clerk of Reading (Mr Henry Day). He was educated at Reading School and St Edmund Hall, Oxford, where he rowed in the eight. Although his original intention was to take Orders, at the outbreak of war he was on the point of leaving for Holland to take up teaching in schools, and his passport bore the date August 4th 1914. He applied for a Commission at once, having in the meantime joined the Public Schools Battalion as a private, and in November 1914, he was gazetted to the 6th Royal Berkshire Regiment. He went to the front in February 1916, being attached to the 5th Battalion, and shortly afterwards was wounded in the head by shrapnel; but after a few months at home he returned to the Front. He and two other officers were specially mentioned in certain orders of the day as having accomplished some very good work at Cambrai, in which he was transferred to the Machine-gun Corps. He was killed by the explosion of a mine when taking his section into action during the night. His commanding officer wrote that although he had only been in the battalion a short time he was very popular and his death meant a sad loss to the regiment'.

## CUNNINGHAM F.J.

OR 1895-1906*

2nd Lieutenant. Royal Flying Corps.

July 1918.
'On Saturday the death occurred at 'Westdene' Early, the home of his parents, of Second Lieut. F.I. (Frank) Cunningham after illness contracted on active service. The deceased was educated at Reading School, from which he entered the City and Guilds Engineering College, London and after going through the three years' course he obtained a diploma in civil and mechanical engineering. In 1910 he went to Canada, and was assistant engineer on the Grand Trunk Railway. When war broke out he enlisted on August 14th, 1914, as a private in the Royal Highlanders of Canada. He was at Valcartier and Salisbury Plain, and in 1915 went to the front. At Ypres he was wounded in the foot, and after recovery was attached to the C.A.M.C. until 1916. He then obtained a commission in the R.F.C., which he held up to February 3rd of this year, when he was invalided out of the service and granted honorary rank of Second Lieut'.

'The funeral took place at St. Peter's Early, on Thursday April 11th. The officiating clergy were Rev. W.S. Mahony, Vicar of Linslade, the Rev.Capt. A. Gillies Wilken

(O.R.) Chaplain of Canadian Forces, lately prisoner of war in Germany, and the Vicar (Canon Fowler). The coffin was draped with the Union Jack'.

\* This span of dates seem to be incorrect but they are the ones listed.

## CUNNINGTON E.C.

(Originally listed on the Chapel War Memorial as E.C. CUNNINGHAM).

OR 1908

Captain. 95th Field Ambulance, RAMC.

Killed in action on Saturday 23rd March 1918. Aged 28.

1st XV 1905-6
'Inside Half. Fearless in tackling and in saving from a forward rush. Collars low. Much improved at opening the game out'.

Son of Benjamin Howard Cunnington of 33, Long St. Devizes, husband of Maud Edith Cunnington.

CEMETERY: Cabaret-Rouge British Cemetery, Souchez, Pas-de-Calais, France. Grave Ref: VIII.R.6.

The area around Souchez was captured by the French in September 1915 and then taken over by the British in March 1916. The cemetery was then established and used at various times until September 1918. After November 1918 it was used for the re-internment of over 7000 bodies from battlefields around Arras and from 103 small cemeteries in the Nord and Pas-de-Calais regions.

## DEADMAN Robert Methven

Left School in 1916.

Wireless Operator on the S.S. 'Romeo' (Hull). Mercantile Marine.\*

Killed in action on Sunday March 3rd 1918. Aged 17.

Son of Ernest Bezant and Helen Deadman of 28 Manchester Road, Reading.

CEMETERY: Tower Hill Memorial, London.

This memorial commemorates men of the Merchant Navy and Fishing Fleets who died in both World Wars and who have no known grave.

*The 'Romeo' was built in 1881 and was a 'screw' steamer of 1,840 tons gross. She was fitted out for carrying 3rd Class passengers in three compartments and was used in the late 19th Century by the Ellerman Wilson Line for carrying emigrants from Scandinavia to Hull. Records indicate that it was used for this purpose up until 1906.

She was sunk of the coast of Galloway in March 1918 with the loss of 29 lives.

## EPPSTEIN W.R.

OR 1906-09

Lieutenant. Durham Light Infantry.

Wounded on July 16th 1915 at the Dardenelles and transferred to the Anglo-American Hospital, Cairo suffering from a wound in the groin. He was the nephew of Dr. Eppstein and was a pupil under him at Reading School.

Captain 20th Battn. Durham Light Infantry.*

Killed in action on Sunday September 4th 1918. Aged 27.

CEMETERY: Lijssenthoek Military Cemetery, Poperinge, West Vlaanderen, Belgium. Grave Ref: XXIV D.22.

1st XV 1908
'Changed over this season from right wing to left centre and was very successful in this position. Runs well and hard and usually goes straighter than the other threes. A good defensive player. Runs well'.

Son of Maurice Reginald and Lucy Jane Eppstein, of Smyrna, Asia Minor. Educated at Reading School. Volunteered for service at the outbreak of war at the British Consulate, Smyrna.

* The 20th Battalion was formed in Sunderland on July 10 1915 by the Mayor and a committee. In January 1916 it was attached to the 123rd Brigade, 41st Division and

on March 17th 1918 was transferred to 124th Brigade, 41st Division. As part of this Division Eppstein would have seen action at the Battle of Flers-Courcelette September 15th-22nd 1916, the Battle of Messines 1917, the Battle of Pilkem July 31st to August 2nd 1917 and the Battle of the Menin Road September 20th-25th 1917.

It moved to Italy in November 1917 returning to France in March 1918.

The Division was then involved at the Battle of St.Quentin March 21st-23rd 1918, the First Battle of Bapaume March 24th-25th 1918, the First Battle of Arras March 28th 1918 and finally the advance into Flanders August 18th to September 6th during which Eppstein was killed.

## FARRANT Archibald William

OR 1906-1912

Lieutenant. Machine Gun Corps (Infantry).

Killed in action on Wednesday November 6th 1918. Aged 23.

Son of William and Emily Farrant, The Grange, Mortimer.

CEMETERY: Stratfield Mortimer (St.Mary) Churchyard, Mortimer, Berks.

## HAIGH R.

OR 1907-1914

Captain. M.C.

1st XV 1911,12.
'Right Wing. The most prolific scorer in the team. Runs with great determination, but has an unfortunate propensity for 'bullocking' through the thick of his opponents, instead of trying to get round, has improved in this respect latterly. Generally effective in defence, but must learn to collar low'.

April 1918

'We are now in a position to publish news of a great honour which has been conferred upon Capt. Richard Haigh, M.C. Tanks Corps….Captain Haigh has been selected from all the officers of 'His Majesty's Land Ships' to take charge of the tank which has been touring Canada and the United States to help boom the U.S. Liberty Loan. He and his crew all of whom, by the way have been wounded, have been touring the chief cities of the Republic for the past three months popularising the great loan which our Allies have been raising. Such work is, of course, of the highest responsibility and the fact that the gallant officer has been entrusted with this duty speaks well for his ability and for the confidence which the authorities place in him.

Educated at Reading School, where he distinguished himself in every form of athletics, particularly long distance running and football, Capt. Haigh obtained a Commission in the Royal Berkshire Regt. just after the outbreak of war. He was wounded at Loos in 1915 and again on the Somme in 1916. In January of last year he was awarded the Military Cross, and for the last twelve months he has been attached to the Tank Corps'.

## HAWKES Septimus James

OR 1909-12

Captain. (formerly 25th Light T.M. Battery) Royal Berks Regt.

Died on Wednesday 10th July 1918. Aged 23.

CEMETERY: Reading Cemetery, Berkshire. Grave Ref. 66.14431.

Son of Eliza Laura Louise Hawkes, 49, London Road, Reading, and the late John Hollingworth Hawkes.

Dec 1918 Magazine

'At St Bartholomew's Church Reading, on Monday afternoon, a very large congregation assembled to pay their last tributes to Capt. Septimus J. Hawkes, Royal Berkshire Regt, who died suddenly in his barrack quarters at Dublin on the previous Wednesday. The Rev. T.J. Norris was the officiant clergyman, being assisted by the Revs. A.T. Gray, B. Mead and H. Elton Lury, C.F., the latter reading the lesson. The deceased officer was before the war, greatly interested in the boys of St. Bartholomew's Church, and held position as Scoutmaster of the St Bartholomew's Troop. Educated at Reading School, where he was a member of the Officer's Training Corps and of the Rugby XV, he joined the University and Public Schools Brigade soon after the commencement of hostilities, and subsequently transferred to the Military College, Sandhurst, where he obtained his commission in the Royal Berks. Regt. He soon went to France, and after serving there for some time was wounded and returned to England, and later, with the rank of Captain, went to Ireland. As recently as last month Capt. Hawkes was on leave in Reading on the occasion of the wedding of one of his brothers, at which ceremony he performed the duties of best man. A short time ago Capt. Hawkes successfully passed the difficult examination for the Royal Air Force to which he had transferred just prior to his death'.

### HEDGCOCK Frederick Leslie

OR 1907-13

2nd Lieutenant 'D'Company. 57th Battalion, Machine Gun Corps (Inf).

Killed in action on Sunday 29th September 1918. Aged 20.

CEMETERY: Anneux British Cemetery, Nord, France. Grave Ref. II.A.8.

The village of Anneux, together with Havrincourt and Graincourt was captured in November 1917 but was retaken by the Germans in December of the same year. It was then recaptured by the British in September 1918. The cemetery originally contained 131 graves but after November 1918 875 bodies from smaller cemeteries in the area were reburied at Anneux. Out of these only one corresponds with the date of Hedgcock's death, the Nieuwe Kruiseecke Cabaret Cemetery, Gheluvelt, on the Menin Road, where 21 soldiers were buried in October 1918.

Son of Mr and Mrs E. Hedgcock, 'St.Margaret's' 4, Shinfield Road, Reading.

December1918 Magazine
We regret to record the death of Second Lieutenant Frederick Leslie Hedgcock, M.G.C., who was killed in action on Sunday 29th September 1918 at the age of 20, and after having served with his Regiment in France over seven months. He was educated at Reading School and Brighton College, and was the youngest son of Mr and Mrs Hedgcock of St Margarets, Shinfield Rd, Reading. Mr Hedgcock has two other sons serving in the Army, the eldest, Captain S.E.Hedgcock, now on the Staff in Mesopotamia and Lieut. S.D.Hedgcock, recently gazetted to the R.E. Both have been on active service, the eldest at Suvla Bay and the second son twice in France.

A brother officer writes:

> *'We were fighting in a very important sector, and had done very well. Your son was shot through the heart, and was therefore instantly killed'.*

His Major writes that he was killed while leading his men into action.

*'On behalf of the officers and men of the company I would tender you our heartfelt sympathy in your sad bereavement. We have lost an excellent officer and you have lost an excellent son'.*

---

## KINGTON Percy Francis

OR 1916-17

Rifleman 554923. London Regt., (Queen's Westminster Rifles).

Killed in action on Saturday 16th March 1918.

CEMETERY: Maroeuil British Cemetery, Pas-de-Calais, France. Grave Ref. IV.H.II.

The cemetery was started in March 1916 when the British took over in the Arras Front. It remained in use until 1918. It remained unobserved by the enemy because of a hill behind it and, because of this, bodies were brought from the front line to the site by way of the French Military tramway.

Son of John Francis and Marian Kington of 1 Hamilton Road, Reading.

---

## LAWES Frederick Compton (Eric)

OR 1911-1912

Pte. 814293. 4th Battalion, Canadian Infantry, (Central Ontario Regt.)

Killed in action on Thursday 8th August 1918. Aged 21.

CEMETERY: Caix British Cemetery, Somme, France. Grave Ref. 1915.I.F.2.

The village of Caix was captured by the British in March 1917, lost exactly one year later and recaptured on the 8th August 1918 by the Canadian Corps. It would seem that Lawes was killed during this advance.

The cemetery was built after November 1918 and contains those killed mainly between March and August 1918 who had been buried in other sites. Lawes could have originally been buried at Caix (Old) British Cemetery because 91 Canadian soldiers who were killed in August 1918 were removed from there and re-interred at the new cemetery.

Eldest son of Mr. Frederick J. and Florence C. Lawes of 116, Hamilton Road, Reading.

⚙

## LOVE H.C.

OR 1894-1901

Corporal. Despatch Rider R.E.

July 1918
Military Medal for conspicuous gallantry during the retreat March 23rd-30th 1918.

⚙

## LOVERIDGE J.L. M.C.

OR 1908-09

2nd Lieutenant (Acting Captain). Royal Berks.

December 1918
A Bar to his Military Cross.

'He made a reconnaissance under heavy enemy barrage, and the next day led his section to the starting point, in spite of the fact that his Tanks had been observed by the enemy and were submitted to heavy fire. Throughout he showed great coolness and initiative'.

⚙

## MATTHEWS John Waldron

OR 1900-07

Captain. 206 Squadron Royal Air Force. *

Killed in action on Thursday 1st August 1918. Aged 28.

Had been a member of the 1st XV in 1906 and the Shooting VIII in 1905 and 1906.

'A most useful forward and an excellent tackler. Inclined at times to do too much out of the scrum'.

CEMETERY: Hooge Crater Cemetery, Ieper, West-Vlaanderen, Belgium. Grave Ref. II.H.9.

The Hooge Chateau on the north side of the Menin road witnessed fierce fighting throughout the war. The Hooge Crater cemetery lies in the remains of a crater left by a mine detonated by the British in July 1915. The cemetery was started in October 1917 and it originally contained 76 graves in Plot I. It was increased after November 1918 when bodies from the cemeteries at Zillebecke, Zantvoodre and Gheluvelt were reburied there. Although the main cemeteries providing the extra bodies are mentioned in the official records no RAF personnel are listed. All refer to soldiers of the United Kingdom. One can only assume that Matthews was previously buried elsewhere.

December 1918
'Previously reported missing, now known to have been killed in action on the 31st July 1918. Captain John Waldron Matthews RAF of San Julian, Patagonia, elder son of E.J. Matthews and Mrs Matthews, Brockly Combe, Weybridge, aged 28'. (August 1st was the official date of his death).

Before the war Matthews had been employed by the San Julian Sheep Farming Co.Ltd. He joined the Royal Flying Corps on March 12th 1917 and served with 'A' and later 'D' squadrons at the Central Flying School, Upavon and at Waddington. After having joined the RFC he flew with No. 6 Squadron (Corps) for eight months as an observer on BEs., No 55 Squadron (Reprisals) for eight months as Flight/Flying Officer/Observer on DH4s. He joined 206 squadron on his appointment as Captain Flying A & S on DH9s. As an observer and pilot he had completed 550 flying hours in a wide range of aircraft. He also did an aerial gunnery course at Turnberry on May 17th 1917. It was reported that he had a fair knowledge of Spanish.

On the day of his death there had been a bombing operation in the Menin area. He was reported missing at 8.40 am. There was an unconfirmed 'DH4' claim in combat at Ypres at 8.45am by Ltn. L. Beckmann (Ja56) and an unconfirmed 'possible' DH9 at 8.40am by Ltn.K.Seit (Ja80). *(Ref. 'The Sky Their Battlefield' Trevor Henshaw).*

Either of these could have been Matthews.

*206 Squadron RAF was originally part of the RNAS and formed on November 1st 1916 using Nieuport Scout and F1 Camel aircraft. It was disbanded in August 1917 and reformed on January 1st 1918 as a bomber squadron using DH4 aircraft in training and DH9 on active service.

## PAUER W.L.

OR 1909–(not listed)

July 1918
'Corporal, a sniper in the Munster Fusiliers has been awarded the Military Medal and also the Medaille Militaire. He has been twice wounded. During the retreat in March he was made King's Sergeant on the field and he has since been awarded a Bar to his Military Medal'.

Awarded Distinguished Conduct Medal.

1st XV 1914
'Forward. A very hardworking forward, playing with dash throughout the game. A good place kick and useful in defence'.

## RUSSELL N.J.G

OR 1908-1914

2nd Lieutenant. 'A' Battery, 26th Brigade, Royal Field Artillery.

Killed in action on Friday 27th September 1918.

1st XI 1912

CEMETERY: Duisans British Cemetery, Etrun, Pas de Calais, France. Grave Ref: VII.A.23.

Duisans and the surrounding area was occupied by British forces from March 1916. The site for the cemetery was chosen by the 8th Casualty Clearing Station in February 1917 and the first burials took place there during the following month. It grew very quickly because of casualties during the Battles of Arras in 1917 and the trench warfare going on in the vicinity. During the autumn of 1918 the 23rd, 1st Canadian and 4th Canadian Casualty Clearing stations remained in the area adding to the number of graves.

Son of Mr. W.H.Russell of Pitville House, Cheltenham. (Royal Fusiliers.)

Russell had been a School Prefect, Captain of the 1st XV and a member of the Cricket and Hockey 1st XIs.

Rugby: 'Has this year played in the stand-off half position. Has some idea of making an opening and passes fairly well. Is a good dribbler and tackles resolutely. As Captain has set a good example to the side. His absence was a great loss to the team in the last three matches'.

Cricket: 'Is really a much better bat than last year, but has not had much opportunity of distinguishing himself. A very sound field'.

---

## SHORE Leonard Charles

OR 1910-1914

Pte. 52075. 2nd Battalion, Lincolnshire Regt. *

Killed in action on Monday 19th August 1918. Aged 19.

CEMETERY: Bagneux British Cemetery, Gezaincourt, Somme, France. Grave Ref. IV.F.7.

The Bagneux cemetery was started in April 1918 after the end of the German campaign in Picardy. By the end of April four Casualty Clearing Stations had been established in Gezaincourt and they remained there until September. One can only assume that Shore was taken from the front line to one of these CCSs.

December 1918
'Died on August 19th of wounds received in action in France, was the son of Lance-Cpl Shore and Mrs Shore of 51,Francis Street, Reading and was 19 years of age. He was educated at Central School and Reading School, having won a scholarship to the latter. Prior to joining up in April 1917, he was in the office of the surveyor of taxes in Richmond, Surrey. His father, an old soldier, is serving with the Rifle Brigade in Egypt, where he has been for the past three years'.

* The 2nd Battalion had originally been raised in Bermuda in August 1914 and returned to England in October 1914. On October 3rd it was attached to the 25th Brigade, 8th Division and on February 4th 1918 was transferred to the 62nd Brigade, 21st Division. Shore would have seen action at the Battle of the Aisne May 26th to June 6th, 1918. He may well have been wounded during this battle because the Division did not see action again until the Battle of Albert, August 21st-23rd 1918.

## WAKEFORD Owen MC

OR 1908-11

Major. 76th Siege Bty., Royal Garrison Artillery.

Killed in action on Thursday 21st March 1918.

MEMORIAL: Arras Memorial, Faubourg-d'Amiens Cemetery, Arras, France. Bay 1

December 1918: Awarded Military Cross

'For consistent good work, especially as Officer Commanding Battery, during the operations in the Ypres Sector, from July to December 1917; where he maintained the efficiency of his Unit, under very heavy fire'.

## WELLS Arnold J.

OR 1898–(not listed)

July 1918
'Captain. A.S.C. T.F.(Territorial Force) has been awarded the Military Cross for meritorious service in Egypt. He has served in Gallipoli, Egypt and Palestine'.

## WILKEN A.G.

(See also page 247)

OR 1898-1904

Captain.

April 1918
'We must congratulate Capt. Rev. A.G. Wilken, Brigade Chaplain, Canadian Force, on his return from Germany. He has been a prisoner of war for a year and eight months, during which time he has hade the acquaintance of no less than six prison camps, Gutersloh, Minden, Crefeld, Schwarmstedt, Holminden and Freiburg.

We understand that some of these were comfortable enough, others very much the reverse. We hope one day perhaps Capt. Wilken will tell us of some of his experiences'.

December 1918
The following article appeared in 'Chevrons to Stars' the official paper of the Canadian Training School, Bexhill during World War One. Written by Capt. Rev. A.G.Wilken and was reproduced in the December 1918 Magazine.

*THE UNSPEAKABLE HUN*

*A TRUE INCIDENT*

*It was Thursday morning, February 16$^{th}$ of last year, and intensely cold, the thermometer registering 10 degrees below zero. At 9 a German soldier came to tell me that I was wanted at the camp hospital. I was there met by the British doctor, Captain Frank Park, C.A.M.C., who told me that sixteen British prisoners had just newly arrived from the station seven kilometres away. With him I went to Ward 2, and there saw 16 specimens of humanity. That is all I could call them, 16 frozen, hollow cheeked wrecks, the remnants of hundreds and hundreds of once strong healthy men, who had been taken prisoners and kept to work behind the lines. Their comrades were dead.*

*Now these men were captured in September, October and November, 1916, and kept to work close up to the front working in preparation for the big German retreat then planned to take place in February and March, 1917. Their work was demolishing houses, bridges, felling trees, making roads and digging trenches, those called the Hindenburg line. This line and others were built by prisoners of war. We praised German engineering skill and paid silent tribute to the endurance and work of the German working parties, but it was not the work of the German parties, but the work of prisoners, Russians and Rumanians in thousands, tens of thousands, and of British. They worked under appalling conditions, brutal treatment, blows, kicks, death if they refused, with housing and quarters not fit for pigs and food not enough to keep even body and soul together. What did it matter if they died, there were plenty more where they came from? Germany numbered her prisoners by millions. Prisoners they were, not prisoners of war; slaves, yea worse than slaves.*

*These details these poor wretches told us with tears in their eyes when they spoke of some poor dear friend and pal who died beside them at work, died of exposure, starvation, or our own shell fire. They told us of the clothes they had to wear. There was no need to tell, we saw it for ourselves when we undressed them. Here is the list, and think of the temperature and cold as you read it: Thin Service tunic and trousers, old cotton shirt, socks and boots and old cap. That was all, no warm underclothing, no great coat. All these the Boche had stolen under the plea that they had to be fumigated. But they were never returned.*

*And what did the outside world know of this or care? It may have cared, it must have cared, but it knew nothing. Germany took good care of that. These men were reported in British Casualty lists as 'missing' and missing they will remain until the end of time. But they were not missing, they were once strong healthy men, prisoners of war. They were not allowed to write to their relatives, Germany did not want the world to know where they were, or of their existence. Amongst the sixteen who reached Minden were men who had been prisoners four to five months. This I found out as a fact when I wrote home to their relatives. They told me of pals who had died beside them and I reported them to the Record Office of their Regiments and my letters never got home. It was always a mystery to us that these sixteen and other little parties later ever got back into Germany. They attributed it to the fact that, being men of fine physique and health, they didn't succumb as quickly as their comrades, went into hospital suffering chiefly from dysentery, recovered a little strength, and the Germans, seeing it was no good sending them back to the line, put them on a train and back they came into Germany.*

*This is just one isolated instance of many that might be quoted. What one must realise in relation to these crimes is that while primarily they may be said to be the work of the system and spirit inculcated throughout the German Army by 'Prussian Militarism', yet nevertheless they were perpetrated by the Boche generally, and that right down to the very last German soldier this devilish brutality is to be expected and looked for. This is not generally realised, and only those who have lived amongst the Boche can fully appreciate what it means to be at the mercy of a brutal bully. You have no possible redress, no chance of even making your conditions known to the outside world, and you have only your own British spirit to carry you through.*

*If you can realise what this means, perhaps you then can appreciate what the ex-prisoner feels when he tells you that never again can he hold out his hand in friendship to a German.*

*Capt. Rev. A. Gilles Wilken (Late British Prisoner of War).*

Wilken addressed the school in July 1919 (see page 307).

## WILLIAMS E.C.P

OR 1909-1910

T/2nd Lieutentant. Middlesex Regiment.

December 1918
Awarded Military Cross.

'When the enemy attacked in great force, driving a line and endeavouring to cut off the retirement of the battalion, this officer remained as a rearguard with a small party of men and a Lewis gun, inflicting heavy casualties on the enemy and gaining time for the battalion to withdraw in good order. On previous days he had been out with patrols securing prisoners and bringing back valuable information.

## WILLS A.N.

OR 1901-04

Captain. 1/5th Battalion, King's Own Yorkshire Light Infantry.*

Killed in action on Thursday 7th March 1918. Aged 30.

CEMETERY. Lijssenthoek Military Cemetery, Poperinge, West-Vlaanderen, Belgium. Grave Ref. XXVII. E. 21.

Son of Henry and Katherine Wills, 8 Cleveland Place West, Bath and of Colwyn Bay. Born Loughborough, Leicestershire.

* The 1/5th Battalion was raised in Doncaster in August 1914 as part of the 3rd West Riding Brigade, West Riding Division. It landed in France at Boulogne on April 12th 1915 and on May 12th the formation became the 148th Brigade, 49th Division. On February 2nd, 1918 it transferred to the 187th Brigade, 62nd Division absorbing the 2/5th and was renamed the 5th Battalion.

## THE ARMISTICE

There were a number of battles and skirmishes throughout the rest of 1918. But continued defeats and unrest at home eventually brought about the German surrender at Compiegne on November 10th. The delegates worked through the night and signed the document at 5.00 am on November 11th 1918. By this time the British Empire had lost over 908,000 men. Many more were affected physically, emotionally and psychologically. France had lost 1,357,000 dead which equated with 10.5% of the total male population. The USA lost 126,000. Germany's deaths totalled 1,773,000 while Austria-Hungary lost 1,200,000, Italy 650,000, Turkey 325,000 and Japan 300. Civilian deaths were not counted in the war casualties but these would have run into millions. It is estimated that the Russians lost around 39 million.

# 1919

*Lambourn Rectory.*
*Romford*
*December 4th 1918*
*To the Editor of the School Magazine.*

*Sir,*

*I shall be glad if you will kindly give me the opportunity of using your pages to acknowledge the receipt of a cheque from C.D.Balding, which, he informs me, is what the Old Boys collected on my resignation as a Testimonial.*

*Deeply as I appreciate this mark of their regard, it was hardly necessary that I should have any assurance of their affection. I gave the best years of my life and much of my thought and energy to the Old School, and its alumni will always hold my most cherished memories. I have been proud, even in the midst of deepest personal sorrow, of the readiness with which so many of them gave their all for England, proud that the lessons they learnt at Reading helped them to play the game in the hardest of life's combats.*

*Yours faithfully*

*W. Chas. Eppstein.*

## COLE R.N.

OR 1911

Gunner 16308. 10th Armoured Battery. Machine Gun Corps (Motors).

Died on Sunday January 5th 1919.

MEMORIAL: Kirkee 1914-1918, India. Grave Ref. Face 11.

Kirkee, also known as Khadki is a Military area close to the University Town of Poona on the plateau above Bombay. The Memorial commemorates more than 1,800 servicemen who died in India during the First World War, who are buried in cemeteries in India and Pakistan where their graves can no longer be properly maintained.

## COLLIER H.E.

OR 1903-1908

Captain. RAMC attached to 1st Gloucesters.
Awarded Military Cross, July 1919.

Captain of School 1907.

1st XI Cricket 1906/7/8
'A good bat though without any powerful shots. A fine deep field'.

1st XV Football 1906/7
'Full-back. Was tried at the beginning of the term but failed; on his second trial was a great success. Tackles well and kicks with judgement. Should not wait for the ball to bounce'.

1st XI Hockey 1906/7/8. Captain in 1908.
'Captain. Left Back. Has proved a capable and energetic captain. A safe and hardworking back with sound defence. In the match with USC undoubtedly saved his side from defeat'.

Won the Earl Roberts Prize in 1908 for 'Best All Round Boy'.

## DE VOS Gaston

OR 1914-1916

Gaston de Vos left the school in 1916 from Form VI M. He was in the 1st XV in 1914 and 1915 described as 'Right Wing-threequarter. The most prolific scorer in the team, using weight and pace to great advantage in attack. Kicks well and tackles magnificently'

He was also 'Champion of Sports' in 1915. 'We congratulate De Vos on his excellent performance in winning the individual Championship with 17 points..... When it is remembered that the maximum points obtainable by a boy is 22, it will be seen what an all round display this was. In only one event did he fail to obtain a point'.

He was awarded colours in both Rugby and Running and was a member of the OTC.

Writes from France (December 1916):

> 'He is in a training camp of about 6,000 men where, in addition to the hard work, plenty of recreation seems to be provided. He says that he finds his OTC training at school of real use to him'.

December 1919

*October 18th 1919*

*Dear Mr Keeton,*

*It is already a long time I have not written you, but don't think I have forgotten all about Reading School. No, for my greatest pleasure is when I am at home to look at the old Reading School Magazine again. It reminds me of my former English teachers whom I never will forget, the boys and the School where I had such a happy time.*

*Since I wrote to you last time a lot of things have happened and the big war is over. Let me tell just what became of me. In the beginning of 1918, about the month of April, they sent me to the Belgian Sub-Lieutenant School near Treport (along the coast). I stopped there for six months, when the offensive broke out. We were cadets so they sent us at once to the Belgian front. I came too late for the first push, but the second was mine. On the 6th of October I was at the front at Roulers. On the 14th at 5.35 our artillery began and we pushed forward. My battery was with the English people. After about three hours firing everything became quiet. Our troops were advancing and I went to a British ambulance near by, to help carry the wounded.*

*The next day I had to move again, this time to Iseghem, where the French came to take our positions. Later on we came down to Thourout for two day's rest. Hearing that our troops had entered Ostend I asked one night and day's leave and went walking to Ostend where I arrived at night. You could never imagine what a sensation you have to enter your birthplace again after having left it for five years, not knowing anything about it and fearing not to find anything but ruins. Luckily for me I found everything back, except for the small pieces of furniture and copper they took away. I stopped in Ostend till the next day, when I met my brother, then came back to the Battery. They had just received orders to move. We had to go by Bruges to a small village called Ursel, to the north of Ghent. We did not stop long, for we were trying not to give the Germans time to breathe. On the 31st of October we made an attack but we could not pass the Canal de Derivation. We tried again the same morning, but again we could not get through. That day we had rather heavy losses. Two days later, on the 2nd of November, we heard the Germans had left their positions in front of us and were retreating. At once the cavalry began to chase them as far as Ghent. Our artillery pressure had become useless there and we moved to the South of Ghent. Everything was ready to make our big push on the 13th November early in the morning. We had seen the infantry going up to the line in order to start at daybreak. Our guns and munitions were ready, at that time I had to look out for the munitions of my battery, even the men were already at the guns, when the order came that we had to return to our quarters for the Armistice was signed. Luckily for Fritz! For his worst was coming, especially now because we had French and English reinforcements behind us.*

*From Ghent I went to Brussels and stopped there for about two months. Then we had the re-opening of our Universities. I went in for Mechanical Engineering at the Brussels University, and I have just finished my first year. I have still three other years to do...........*

*I hope that the list of casualties of the Old Reading School Boys is not too heavy.*

*Yours very sincerely*

*G. Devos*

## GIMBLETT Thomas Fairbairn

Driver 6125. Royal Canadian Horse Artillery.

Died on Saturday 11th October 1919. Aged 36.

CEMETERY: Mapledurham (St. Margaret) Churchyard, Oxon.

'The death occurred at Sutherlands Hospital Reading of Mr T.F.Gimblett son of Mr T.W.Gimblett of New Farm, Mapledurham, at the age of 36'.

*'Mr Gimblett, who was an old Reading School boy, was a native of Mapledurham, and after leaving school entered the auctioneers profession, spending time in the office of Messrs. Gales of Wallingford. He was a keen member of the Reading Rowing Club, and for a number of years was one of the best coxes the Club had. Many are the oarsmen who can remember the familiar and popular figure of 'Tommy' Gimblett as he was generally known on the river. He was a capable horseman, and used to follow the South Berks. Hounds.*

*Some years before the war he went to Canada, and within a week of the outbreak of war enlisted in the Royal Canadian Horse Artillery. He came over to England with the forces exactly five years ago to a day, before the day of his funeral. Throughout the war he fought in France, and took part in all the heaviest engagements, escaping any casualties. Two months after the armistice, however, he was taken ill and was brought home some few months ago. After several months at Orpington he was brought to Sutherlands Hospital, where he died from Heart disease'.*

## NELIGAN M.R.

Right Rev. Bishop (late Auckland. N.Z.)

'*19th April 1919*

*Dear Sir,*

*I see from my last Reading School Magazine that you wish to know of ORs who may have tried to do their bit in the War. My case is almost, alas!, a prehistoric peep! Anyhow I served last year as Bishop and Chaplain of the Forces, 4th Class in the N.Z.E.F.*
*My time at Reading must be some forty years ago.*

*Yours faithfully*

*M.R.Neligan*

*Bishop.*

## WILKEN A.G.

Rev. Major

July 1919

'*On Wednesday July 16th, Major The Rev. A.G.Wilken (O.R.) 3rd Canadians, gave his long promised address to the School. The audience were seated on the ground in the shade of the trees. Major Wilken was captured, with seven survivors of his unit, at Zillebeeke in June 1916 and he spent 21 months as a prisoner of war in Germany. He had experience of no less than eight prison camps, both officers' and mens' and he had therefore exceptional opportunities of observing the treatment our prisoners received. He told us of some of the sights that he himself had seen, and impressed upon all who might have been inclined to doubt that decent treatment was quite the exception, even in officer's prison camps. It was only at Aachen, in the repatriation camp there, that any attempt was made, officially, to provide comforts, or even the rudiments of proper nursing, for our men. The Boche, a name that the German loathes, whereas at times he rather prides himself on being called a Hun, was actually simple enough to declare openly that he wished our men to take home a good impression. Our men naturally replied that this effort came a good deal too late. The impression was already made. It was satisfactory to hear of the abject terror inspired in the frontier towns by our air raids, though sad to think that our own poor fellows were too often deliberately exposed, in reprisal camps such as Freiburg, to the awful destruction. These deadly air raids of ours, drawing nearer and nearer, were a great factor in bringing the war to a speedy conclusion. We heard with pride how our men constantly refused, often at great risk of death, to work at munition-making for the enemy. And then there was that blackest crime of all, which cost the lives of thousands of our men and which only so lately, almost accidentally, came to light, the treatment of our prisoners behind the Western Front. These men, never reported as prisoners of war, were forced to work at Trench-making under our own fire, and their deaths from this cause and from the brutal treatment they received go to swell that appalling list of 'missing' which is one of the greatest tragedies of the war. Such was the nation against whom we fought, men who have put themselves, as Major Wilken said 'beyond the pale of civilised intercourse', self-confessed as breakers of every solemn obligation, and ready to make war in the same way tomorrow if they see the slightest chance of success.*

*Major Wilken concluded by saying that it was not his object to fill our ears with tales of horror, but that he felt it his duty to make us, who would so soon have to carry on the work of the Empire, realise what manner of men we had to deal with'.*

---

## THEY ALSO SERVED

A selection of others mentioned in the School Magazine.

**BUTLER Adrian Illingworth**

2nd Lieutenant. Royal Field Artillery.

'Awarded Military Cross for 'Conspicuous gallantry and devotion to duty'. This Officer fought his section in the open, engaging enemy infantry and tanks until they got within 50 yards, scoring a direct hit on a tank at this distance. He rallied the infantry and only withdrew at the last moment, having himself to drive in a gun team when the driver was killed'.

---

## CHURCHILL M.C.

December 1918
'2nd Lieut. R.F.A. son of Mr and Mrs H.A.Churchill, of Eldon Square, Reading has been awarded the Croix de Guerre by the President of the French Republic'.

## DYMORE-BROWN Hugh Patterson

OR 1907-1913

Fifth son of family who ran the Royal Albert Brewery. Lived on Queen's Rd. Reading and was educated at Marlborough House before entering Reading School.

Keen sportsman at school and outside. Played for Berkshire Wanderers RFC, Reading Cricket Club and was a member of Sonning Golf Club. In 1913 he was a Sgt. in the OTC. He was also a Prefect.

As a member of the 1st XV he was described as:

'Forward. Was tried at centre three-quarter first but not satisfactory. Displays dash in the open, but must work harder in the scrums. Unable to tackle'.

April 1915
'Forward. Another player who has shown improvement, but is still rather faint-hearted about the scrum. Is playing better in the open, but is inclined to kick too hard'.

December 1915
'Forward. The best forward in the team, displaying great energy throughout. Tackles in poor style, but very effectively'.

Awarded XV Colours.

And of the 1st XI:

July 1915
'On some occasions has bowled really well, but must be careful about loose balls on the leg. As a bat, he has improved, and can hit hard as long as he remembers to choose the right ball. A good field'.

When he left school in 1913 he joined Barclays Bank.

On August 5th 1914 he was mobilised with the Berkshire Yeomanry and Commissioned in the Royal Berkshire Regiment in January 1915. In October of the same year he was attached to the 5th Battalion in France.

On January 17th 1916 he was in charge of a party attacking with rifle grenades at Givenchy and was seriously wounded in the eye and removed to the hospital at Boulogne where his recovery was only slight. He never regained his sight in his left eye and in December 1917 he was declared 'permanently unfit' and medically discharged from the Army. He returned home.

In 1919 he caught influenza and died of septic pneumonia on February 21st aged 22. He is buried at St. Peter's Church, Earley, Reading.
*(Ref. Appendix II. 'Responding to the Call'. Chapman, Cull, Croucher,Fox, McIntyre,Webb University of Reading 1995).*

## EGGINTON D.

OR 1880-1886

Honorary Major. 4th Battalion Royal Berks Regt.

April 1915
'Became Director of Recruiting for Reading in 1916'.

## FAIRBAIRN G.G.

OR 1901-1909

Lieutenant. Royal Flying Corps.

Only son of the Rev. R.G.Fairbairn, Pastor of King's Road Baptist Chapel.

'Wounded in the scalp for the second time, now in hospital at Regent's Park. The casualty occurred while Lieut. Fairbairn was flying over German Lines, his machine being caught in the telegraph wires and falling to the ground. Fortunately the nature of his wounds is not severe'.

School Prefect.

1st XI 1909
'A useful but ugly batsman. Rather too much inclined to hit across the ball. A moderate deep field'.

Also outside right in the Hockey XI. ' A very persevering forward. Waits rather too long before centreing but improved in this respect towards the end of the season. Not very neat with his stick'.

## FULLBROOK-LEGGATT C.St.Q.O

OR 1897-1905

Joined 1st Battalion. Berkshire Regt. 18th September 1909. Promoted Lieutenant. August 17th 1911. Mentioned in Despatches for bravery at Maruilles.

Promoted to Captain. Awarded the DSO and then the Military Cross.

December 1914.
'Lieut. C. St.Q.O Fullbrook Leggatt has been appointed adjutant in the Royal Berks. Regt. He is at the front with the 1st Battalion and apparently succeeds Lieut. A.H. Perrott who was killed in the retreat from Mons'.

Awarded DSO 1915.

'For gallant conduct during an attempt to regain a bridge over the Sambre, near Maruilles, on the night of August 25-26th'.

'The brave Berkshire men, led by their gallant Lieutenant dashed at night along a bullet-swept road on either side of which was a ditch 15 feet broad and 5 feet deep, towards a bridge held by the Germans. By their heroic conduct, under a deadly fire, they delayed the advance of the Germans at one of the most critical stages of the war. Awarded the Military Cross'.

December 1915.
'Captain and Adjutant. He was invalided home last spring, and in August he sprained his ankle through the falling off a sandbag in a mine explosion. On September 28th he was hit in the left thigh. He is still quite an invalid but is progressing favourably in a London hospital whither he was taken on October 10th'.

July 1918.
'Fullbrook-Leggatt, Capt. C.St.Q.O. DSO. MC. Royal Berks Regt. Mentioned in Despatches. Also promoted to the rank of Brevet Major'.

His Brothers:

**FULLBROOK-LEGGATT L.E.W.O.**

OR  1895-1907

Captain of School. 1907.

Member of the 1ˢᵗ XV 1906
'Right Wing. Was most prominent in the House Matches. Kicks well but is weak in defence. Inclined to slow up when tackled'.

and 1ˢᵗ XI Hockey 1906-07
'Right-half for the first part of the season. Was inclined to leave the wing unmarked. As a forward he showed considerable pace and shooting power and played a fine game in the last two matches'.

December 1918
'The Bar to the Military Cross has been awarded Lieutenant (Acting Captain) L.E.W.O.Fullbrook Leggatt. MC. Oxon and Bucks L.I. Special Reserve for:

*Conspicuous gallantry and devotion to duty while attached to brigade headquarters. Headquarters suddenly came under heavy rifle fire, and this officer at once organised an emergency company of personnel stragglers and all available officers and men on the spot and formed a line of resistance about 100 strong. He sent out patrols to locate the enemy and our own troops, and himself collected much valuable information. His promptitude did much to clear an obscure situation and strengthen the line.*
*MC Gazetted February 18ᵗʰ 1918'.*

## FULLBROOK-LEGGATT A.K.O.

OR 1901-1910

School Prefect and Member of the 1ˢᵗ XV.

'A thoroughly reliable forward, working hard in the scrum, dribbling well in the loose rushes and a determined tackler. Has improved wonderfully since last year'.

1ˢᵗ XI

'Has the appearance of a good bat, but inclined to hit widely across the ball. Improved greatly towards the end of term. Rather uncertain in the field but hampered by eyesight'.

'3ʳᵈ Battalion Royal Berks. Regt. A.K.O. Fullbrook Leggatt is appointed Second Lieutenant (on probation). He later joined the Machine Gun Corps and was wounded'.

## GRANT D.F.

OR 1902–(not listed)

Captain (Acting Major). R.F.A.

Son of Mr. W.J.Grant of 12 Glebe Road, Reading. Awarded Military Cross.

'Major Grant was educated at Reading School, and quite recently lost his eyesight in France, but has since regained it'.

## HOLBROOK Vincent S.

OR 1904

2ⁿᵈ Lieutenant.

'Formerly member of the Inns of Court Officer's Training Corps and Reading School Cadet Corps, on probation Special Reserve of Officers, Royal Flying Corps, E.O. 3ʳᵈ Class, is confirmed in rank'.

## HUTCHINGS C.E.

'Army Cyclist Corps. Temporary 2nd Lieut. From the 8th Battalion Royal Berks. Regt. has been appointed temporary Lieutenant'.

## IREMONGER R.G.

Lieut-Col. South Lancashire Regiment. Killed in Action.

Although on the Chapel War Memorial there is no record of his death at the Commonwealth War Graves Archive and no indication of where he was killed.

## KILBY Herbert Frank Shaw

OR 1908-1912

*'We regret to announce the death of Frank Kilby who was killed whilst flying in Japan on August Bank Holiday 1920. Kilby joined the RNAS in 1915 and continued on service until the end of 1919. In March 1920 he sailed for Japan as a flying expert to organise a new department for Messrs. Sale and Frazer, taking with him one mechanic for erection purposes. After assembling the machine and making several flights he went up for an exhibition flight on August 3rd at the request of the Japanese flying authorities, but on returning to land and at only 500 feet the machine suddenly dived to earth....'*

## LUNN A.C.P.

'A.C.P. Lunn 2nd Lieut. Royal Berkshire Regiment has been wounded. July 1916'.

## RICE S.M.

OR 1882-87

New Years Honours List 1917
'Lieut-Colonel S.M. Rice received the C.I.E. for meritorious work in connection with the war'.

## REES R.A.T.

'Major Lancashire Regiment attached to South Staffs Regiment has been wounded.

He was formerly classical master at Reading School where he held a Commission in the OTC'.

## SAXBY C.O.

'(St John's and 3/4th Berks) is prospering and has been appointed machine gun officer'.

July 1919
'C.O. Saxby (St John's) devotes the major portion of his energies to oar and splash worship and is not worried by Mathematics'.
Oxford O.R.

December 1919
'Assured us on the night of the dinner that 'he was the man who won the war' and that 'he felt wonderfully well', in which he was lucky as well as unique'.
Oxford O.R.

## STEVENS W.A.

'2nd Lieutenant Berks. R.H.A appointed temporary Lieutenant January 23rd 1916'.

## TEMPLAR C.F.

Colonel Indian Army. Gazetted Brigadier-General. January 1917.

**TURNER H.A.**

OR  1892-1898

December 1916
'We have received a cheery letter from H.A. Turner who is in Alexandria. Defective eyesight has kept him out of the army, much against his will, but he is doing useful work in the Egyptian Customs.

Turner had been a Prefect in 1894 and Captain of School 1897-8. He was Captain of Cricket in 1898 and also in the 1st XV 1895-98'.

**WAKEFIELD O.**

Appointed 2nd Lieutenant. January 8th 1916.

## THE MEMORIAL

*July 1919*
*'It is proposed to open a subscription for the purpose of providing a permanent memorial to those ORs who have fallen in the War. The form the memorial will take of course depends on the amount subscribed. A meeting of the ORs to discuss the subject will be held later on. As we go to press no Treasurer has yet been appointed, but meanwhile any subscriptions sent to J.Ll. Sylo-Jones Esq, Reading School, will be gratefully acknowledged'.*

*December 1921*
*'It has now been decided what form the OR War Memorial is to take. After considering many proposals, and having due regard to the amount of money collected, the O.R. Committee have decided to place the Memorial in the School Chapel. The scheme finally adopted is to erect oak panelling at the East End, on either side of the reredos. This panelling is to be continued for some distance along the North and South Walls. The names are to be placed on specially designed panels on the South side. The work is already placed in the capable hands of Mr. Harold S. Rogers of Oxford and early next term we hope the Memorial will be ready for unveiling'.*

Magazine April 1922.

# Chapter 9

## CONCLUSION

### THE AFTERMATH

*'You are asked to be silent for two minutes today, to be silent and
pause in your labours, to remember this day and this hour last year...
What will you remember and what will you forget?
You will remember, mothers, the sons you have lost;
wives, you will think of the husbands who went out in the mist of
the winter morning - the mist that sent cold chills round the heart -
never to come back. And brothers will think of brothers and friends
of friends, all lying dead today under an alien soil.
But what will you forget? The crime that called these men to battle.
The war that was to end war and in reality did not?...
Make the most of this day of official remembrance. By the sacred
memory of those lost to you, swear to yourself this day at 11 o'clock,
that never again, God helping you, shall the peace and happiness of the
world fall into the murderous hands of cynical old men'.*

Front page of the Daily Herald. 11th November 1919.

The death toll amongst the young men from public schools in the Great War was disproportional and it goes without saying that those ORs returning from the Front at the end of the war were affected in one way or another by what they had experienced. Some would suffer from 'survivor syndrome' and question why they had been spared, others from 'Shell-shock', 'nerves', battle fatigue and some from a total disbelief in what they had seen and experienced. As a family member they would have been affected by loss[1], and as soldiers at the front would also have witnessed the death of friends and comrades. To make matters worse they had also

---

1     It has been estimated that 3 million people, out of a total population of the time of 42 million lost a close relative during the war. This figure only includes what are called the 'Primary bereaved', immediate family. If one adds the 'Secondary bereaved', cousins, uncles, friends etc the figure becomes enormous.
(Ref. Silence of Memory. Adrian Gregory. Berg. 1994.  p29)

been caught at a time of transient attitudes to death. According to Gregory 'Their affective state was miserable, a combination of the worst of Victorian grief and modern sense of loss, but without access to the defensive strategies of either period, extravagant public mourning or denial of death'. *(Ref. Silence of Memory op.cit p22).* The need for wartime morale and keeping up appearances prevented the former and the latter was not effective for at least another generation.

A great deal has been said in other books about the devastation caused by the raising and subsequent annihilation of the various 'Pals' Battalions on local communities and on the small number of survivors who returned. However, apart from the fact that few of the younger ORs had wives or children and they were not linked to a specific geographical area, similar long-term emotional concerns could apply equally to those who had had their formative years in institutions like Reading School, where pupils had eaten, drank, lived and socialised with each other and formed bonds and friendships which would have lasted for a long time had the war not intervened. It is not insignificant that many of the letters from individuals contain references to their peers who had been killed or wounded.

> *'I am awfully sorry to see that Harold Edwards and Billy Haynes have fallen in this last attack. With the deaths of Trewman and Hawkins, both of whom were great friends of mine, this makes a big gap in the circle of school friends that mean so much'.*
> P. Sharp OR. 1915.

How much this post-war trauma affected them is extremely difficult to research or quantify especially as their education had trained them to display little emotion and 'keep a stiff upper lip'. In a way some of them had been in an emotional straitjacket for the duration of the war. Many observers would consider that the exemplary behaviour of young 2nd Lieutenants leading their men over the top, sometimes knowingly to certain death, was necessary. Their spirit and example, under such extreme pressure, was required in order to motivate the men under their command. The vast majority led by example at a time when soldiers of all ranks could be shot for 'cowardice' and disciplined for displaying any semblance of 'nerves' or 'backsliding' (in reality there was a very thin line between the former and the latter!) and, in addition had shouldered the problems of men under their command, some of whom were a good deal older. There were no counsellors to help them come to terms with their experiences. They had to get on with their lives as best they could.

So, having lived on the edge for so long how did they cope with life after the war? One could say that their education had provided them with the support and experience they needed, but this would be too much of a generalisation. We see a whole generation of ORs coping, but we know little about the effect on them as individuals. (It is unfortunate that, because of the desire to get back to normal as quickly as possible and to a great extent the nature of the editing of the School Magazine, we will never know how much some of the ORs suffered, both mentally and physically.)

The memories of war simply did not go away, and it needs to be remembered that even after the Armistice there were still conflicts going on in which ORs were involved. The IRA was conducting a guerrilla campaign in Ireland, the RAF was bombing Kurdish tribesmen, Germany was being blockaded in order to prevent the movement of raw materials to her heavy industry and allied forces were involved in the civil war in the Soviet Union and in Turkey. There was also a military presence in Germany and China. The Afghans took the opportunity to exploit possible British weaknesses in India and many parts of the Ottoman Empire; Egypt, the Sudan, Cyprus, Mesopotamia and Palestine came under British control. In the end Britain was to look after forty Crown Colonies and Mandated Territories with a combined population nearing fifty million. There was also a great deal of uncertainty in Europe, where mutinies in France and extreme politics in Germany could easily have been replicated in the UK.

What were they coming back to? Some simply took up where they had left off before call up. The Oxford and Cambridge letters provide us with an indication of this...

July 1919
*'J.C.Johnstone. (St. Johns) sounds an aspirant philosopher, but seems to find rowing a more congenial object of study. What he was doing with that tennis racket remains unexplained'.*

*'H.B.F.Kenney (All Souls) navigates a punt the name of which (Sans peur, sans chaperone) suggests Parisien antecedents. History is believed to absorb part of his spare time'.*

December 1919
*'J.C. Johnstone plays a good hand at Auction Bridge\* with a strong partiality for 'No Trumps'.*
(\*the forerunner of Contract Bridge which was introduced in the 1930s).

*'Kenney has started work but has found time for a few other pleasures!'*

July 1919
'W.C. Costin (St. John's) is enthusiastic about mediaeval history, judging by his voluminous tomes and still more voluminous personal expositions with which he is constantly seen walking about. His athletic activities have been confined to punting, though he can still run a mile with undiminished vigour'.

Dec. 1919
'W.C. Costin has devoted himself most keenly to the foundation of the O.U.O.R. Club; has been seen on the track and occasionally leaving a lecture room'.

Some ORs returned to school to speak about their exploits or on related issues.

Capt. F.L.J. Shirley MC. gave a slide show and lecture in November 1918 on 'War in the Air' and many others just returned for a visit. Lists of these appeared in post-war editions of the magazine into the mid-twenties. In 1919, the Debating Society discussed 'This House is in favour of the ex-Kaiser being hanged' (27-19 in favour), and the school itself spent a great deal of time immediately post-war combating the effects of the 'flu epidemic.

At Speech Day, postponed from October 1918 to January 1919, the Headmaster referred predictably to the war. However, he made general, slightly patronising, comments such as:

'The British soldier, with no thought of detracting from our allies, was entirely different from the soldier of any other country. The British soldier was never so cheerful as when he was hopelessly and miserably uncomfortable. When things were at their worst he was the most cheerful person one could find but as soon as things were happy and comfortable, he started grousing'.

He made no mention of the individual ORs who had been killed, or even participated in the war except in an oblique way:

'….he would advise young hearers to imitate those men who had been through four and a half years of war. Let them imitate the high sense of duty and the high sense of patriotism and determination which had characterised all their actions, he was sure that in civil life as they had done in military life, there would be no doubt as to the future of the nation'.

It was not until the Memorial Service, held at St Luke's Church, Reading on February 1st 1919 that we get a more jingoistic approach to commemoration and exhortations reminiscent of those made pre-war. During his sermon, the Bishop of Wakefield said:

'They went smiling with open brow and steadfast face, with the love of life strong in them, yet the love of duty stronger. They went to save our homes, to save the women *and children from unspeakable horrors, to save the name of honour and freedom and to crush the spirit of hatred, cruelty and wrong.........And to us they have left a heritage of imperishable glory. The traditions of such a Public School as this.....are crowned with a new light these last four years. The country has lost some of its best of a whole generation. There is a gap which time will never fill. The School will fill up quickly enough; the torch will be passed from hand to hand as of old. But we shall have need of new leaders in the Church and State. In the new Empire, in the new England, God is calling boys and men to fill the ranks of the fallen'.*

In terms of being 'educated for Empire' it was as if nothing had changed although a great deal had. Many of the young officers who died were considered to be the cream of their generation. Out of 14,561 'Oxford Men' who joined up, 2,680 were killed and, as Professor Marwick says, 'Society, very hesitantly, was turning towards the idea of choosing the occasional leader elsewhere than from the University Officer class, but there is no doubt that much of the political weakness of Britain in the inter-war years can be attributed to the paucity of young talent of quality'.
*(Ref. The Deluge. A.Marwick. MacMillan. 1965. p291)*

However, there was a need for such comments and before being critical of them we should view them in the context of the time for the simple reason that, in order to justify what had gone on before in terms of the killing, devastation and loss, it was necessary to eulogise about the values which had been fought for. They also reinforced the concept of nation and in doing so suppressed those who may have wished to speak out against it. Britain had fought a war under the banner of decency and fair play, in the same way as the country played its sport, and there was no escaping the fact that such sentiments did not disappear once the war had ended. It is rather a paradox, however, that these comments were made at a time when Britain was still controlling an Empire and class division in this country was still very much apparent, even though somewhat diluted.

There are plenty of people who argue that the Public School system was (a) divisive and (b) responsible for the decline and eventual fall of the British Empire. They argue that it discouraged intellectual curiosity and encouraged and perpetuated social barriers between the British rulers and the ruled. We are at odds with the first two contentions and cite evidence of the Reading School curriculum and the lively writing and observations of many of our contributors. With the latter charge we must largely agree and cite personal experience in our support. It is our view however, that the products of the Public School system had both the capacity to set up and stand by standards of conduct, and had a readiness to accept responsibility which to a large extent offset their faults.

There was a general revulsion for jingoism and a gradual rise of regimentation within the magazine which can be seen demonstrated in the style of the comments and articles which appeared immediately post war and well into the 1920s. Surprisingly there was no evidence of pacifism although the lack of it may have been a conscious censorship decision on the part of the editors.

In the meantime boys were still being educated to take their place in the services, both Civil and Military and there was still the expectation that they should remember and uphold the standards of their forebears. In this respect nothing had changed!

## POSTSCRIPT

There was one rather bizarre postscript to the war in regards to the OTC. This extract was contained in a letter sent from the War Office to the school early in 1919:

> '*I am directed to inform you that in consequence of the work of the OTC at Reading School during the war, representations were submitted to the War Trophies Committee that a distribution should be made to recall to future generations the part played by both officers, cadets and contingent in preparing candidates for commissions in the Great War. I am to inform you that the War Trophies committee has allotted a German Machine Gun to your school*'.

It would have been interesting to know what the returning infantry officers thought of such a gift!

And where is it now?

*Floreat Redingensis*

# Chapter 10

## CEMETERY AND MEMORIAL LOCATIONS
### (Mentioned in the text)

**A.I.F. BURIAL GROUND.** This can be found 2km north of the village of Flers. (Somme). Go south-west from Bapaume on the D929 towards Albert for 6km to the village of Le Sars. Turn left, eastwards, on the D11 in the direction of Geudecourt for 3.5km to the D74/D197 junction. Continue along the D74 in the direction of Geudecourt for 500m. A signpost indicates the cemetery down a track on the right.

**ANNEUX BRITISH CEMETERY.** The village of Anneux is south of the main road from Cambrai to Bapaume. The cemetery is 200m from the junction of the N30 with the D15.

**ARRAS MEMORIAL.** The Arras Memorial is in the Faubourg-d'Amiens Cemetery. (For directions, see page 327).

**ATHIES COMMUNAL CEMETERY EXTENSION.** The village of Athies is approximately 5km west of Arras. The Cemetery is on the north side of the road from Arras to Fampoux and the Extension is on the north-east side of the Communal Cemetery.

**BAGNEUX BRITISH CEMETERY.** This can be found in the village of Gezaincourt (Somme) situated 2km to the south-west of the town of Doullens, and Bagneux British Cemetery lies to the south of the village.

**BANCOURT BRITISH CEMETERY.** The village of Bancourt lies approximately 4km due east of Bapaume on the north side of the Bapaume to Bertincourt road (D7). Bancourt British Cemetery is situated east of Bancourt village, 300m off the D7 on the north side.

**BERKSHIRE CEMETERY EXTENSION.** (See directions for Ploegsteert Memorial).

**BOIS-CARRE MILITARY CEMETERY.** This can be found in Haisnes, a village just south of La Bassee. The Military cemetery is approximately 2km south of the village, south-west of the village of Hulluch. From Lens take the D947 to La Bassee. At Hulluch turn left at the roundabout and take the D39 towards Vermelles. The cemetery is on the left hand side of the road in the middle of fields.

**BRANDHOEK MILITARY CEMETERY.** The cemetery is located 6.5km west of Ypres town centre on the Branderstraat, a road leading from the N308 (Ypres to Poperinge). From Ypres town centre the N308 is reached via Elverdingsestraat then directly over two roundabouts in the J. Capronstraat. The N308 is a continuation of this road and begins after a prominent level crossing. 6km along the N308, after passing the village of Vlamertinge and just after the Brandhoek Church, is a left hand turn to Grote Bransderstraat. The Cemetery is 300m on the left beyond the N38 dual carriageway.

**CABARET-ROUGE BRITISH CEMETERY.** The village of Souchez lies 3.5km north of Arras on the main road to Bethune. The cemetery is about 1.5km. south of the village on the west side of the D937 Arras-Bethune road.

**CAIX BRITISH CEMETERY.** The village of Caix can be found 28km south-east of Amiens, midway between the N29, Amiens to St Quentin road, and the D934 Amiens to Roye road. The Cemetery is south of the village.

From the centre of the village take the D28 in the direction of Beaucourt en Santerre, turn left at the D41 in the direction of Le Quesnel. Approximately 200m along can be found the local Communal Cemetery. Turn left just before it and the British Cemetery will be found on the right.

**CAMBRAI MEMORIAL.** This is located in the village of Louveral which is on the north side of the N30, Bapaume to Cambrai road, 13km north east of Bapaume and 16km south-west of Cambrai. The Memorial stands in the Louveral Military Cemetery which is situated on the north side of the N30 south of the village.

**CARNOY MILITARY CEMETERY.** Carnoy is a village north of the D938, Albert to Peronne, about 10km east-south-east of Albert. The military cemetery is on the south side of the village on the north side of the road to Maricourt.

**CERISY-GAILLY MILITARY CEMETERY.** The village of Cerisy is approximately 10km south-west of Albert. From Albert take the D42 in the direction of Morlancourt and Moreuil. After passing through Morlancourt you arrive at Sailly-Laurette. Continue until reaching the cross-roads where you turn left onto the D71 in the direction of Cerisy. Continue on the D71 until you approach a group of bungalows on your left. Turn left at the end of this group when you will then approach the Cerisy-Gailly Military Cemetery.

**DAR ES SALAAM CEMETERY.** Is located on the right (eastern-coastal) side of the Bagamoyo Road which follows a north easterly direction along the coast from the centre of Dar-es-Salaam. It is about 5km from the city centre. A direction sign on the road indicates the turn off to the cemetery.

**DIVE COPSE BRITISH CEMETERY.** The village of Sailly-le-Sac is approximately 20km east of Amiens. The cemetery is just over 1.5km north-east of Sailly church.

**DUNKIRK TOWN CEMETERY.** This is situated at the south-eastern corner of the town of Dunkirk, immediately south of the canal and on the road to Veurne (Furnes) in Belgium.

Plots IV and V (First World War) are found by going through the columns of the Dunkirk memorial.

Plots I, II and III are in the main cemetery to the right of the entrance.

**DUISANS BRITISH CEMETERY. Etrun. Pas-de-Calais.** Duisans and Etrun are villages in the Department of the Pas-de-Calais, about 9km west of Arras. The Cemetery lies in Etrun but takes it name from the nearer village of Duisans. It is one kilometre north of Duisans on the D339 road off the Route Nationale N39 (Arras-St Pol), in the angle of the Arras Habarcq road and a track leading to Haute-Avesnes.

**ECOIVRES MILITARY CEMETERY.** This can be found near the village of Mont-St Eloi (Somme). Ecoivres is a small hamlet lying at the foot of the hill to the south-west and approximately 1.5km from Mont-St Eloi. The cemetery is on the D49 road.

**FAUBOURG D'AMIENS CEMETERY.** This can be found in the western part of the town of Arras in the Boulevard du General de Gaulle, near the citadel, approximately 2km due west of the railway station.

**FINS NEW BRITISH CEMETERY.** Fins is a village on the Cambrai-Peronne road. The Cemetery is to the south-east of the village in the district of Sorel Le Grand on the right-hand side of the road to Heudicourt.

**HAUBOURDIN COMMUNAL CEMETERY.** This is in the Nord District of France.

**HAZEBROUCK COMMUNAL CEMETERY.** Hazebrouck is 56km south-east of Calais. The Communal Cemetery is on the south-western outskirts of the town. From the Grand Place in the town centre, follow the D916 Bethune road. Cross the first set of traffic lights and the Communal Cemetery will be found 200 m along on the right hand side. The War Graves lie immediately inside the entrance.

**HEBUTERNE MILITARY CEMETERY.** The village of Hebuterne is situated 15km north of Albert (Somme) and 20km. south-west of Arras. Take the D919 from Arras to Amiens and drive through the villages of Bucquoy, Puisieux then Serre Les Puisieux. On leaving this village turn right after 3km along the D919 and follow the signs to Hebuterne. The Military cemetery lies to the west of the village and is signposted from the village green.

**HOOGE CRATER CEMETERY.** Can be found 4km east from Ypres town centre on the Meenseweg, N8, connecting Ypres to Menin. The Cemetery is located 3.6km along the Meenseweg on the right hand side of the road. Directly opposite is the Hooge Crater Museum and Café.

**KIRKEE 1914-1918 MEMORIAL. POONA. INDIA.** The cemetery is located almost at the crossroads of the Mula Road with the Bombay-Poona Road. It is on the right hand side.

**LA FERTE-SOUS-JOUARRE MEMORIAL.** This is situated in a La Ferte-sous-Jouarre 66km to the east of Paris. The Memorial is situated in a small park on the south bank of the River Marne.

**LANCASHIRE COTTAGE CEMETERY.** This is located 13.5km from Ypres. Leave the town via the Lille Gate and take the N365. On reaching the village of Ploegsteert take the first left hand turn into Rue de Ploegsteert. The Cemetery is situated 1km along this road on the right.

**LANCASHIRE LANDING CEMETERY. TURKEY.** This can be found 1km west of Sedd el Bahr village. It is on a small ridge named Karaja Oghul Tepe, 110 m above the sea overlooking 'W' beach.

**LA TARGETTE BRITISH CEMETERY.** This is located in the village of Neuville-St.Vaast 6.5km north of Arras to the east of the Bethune-Arras road. The cemetery lies to the south-west of the village on the north-west side of the road to the village of Maroeuil (D55).

**LE TOURET MILITARY CEMETERY.** From Bethune follow the signs for Armentieres until you are on the D171. Proceed along this road through Essars and Le Touret village. Approximately 1km after Le Touret and about 5km before the intersection with the D947, Estaires to La Basse road, the cemetery lies on the right hand side of the road.

Also located in this Cemetery is the Le Touret Memorial, commemorating over 13,000 men who died in this area before September 1915 and who have no known grave.

**LIJSSENTHOEK MILITARY CEMETERY.** This is located 11.5km. west of Ypres on the Boescheepseweg, a road leading from the N308 connecting Ypres to Poperinge. On reaching Poperinge the N308 joins the left hand turning onto the R33, Poperinge Ring Road. The R33 ring continues to the left hand junction with the N38 (Frans-Vlaanderenweg). 800m along the N38 lies the left turn onto Lenestraat. The next immediate right hand turn leads on to Boescheepseweg. The cemetery is located 1.5km on the right hand side.

(From Calais: Take the motorway A16 signposted Dunkerque/Lille. At Dunkerque take the motorway signposted Lille/Ypres, the A25. Leave the motorway at Junction 13, the village of Steenvoorde. Follow the D948/N38 signposted Ypres/Poperinge. After approximately 8-10km Lijssenthoek Military Cemetery is signposted on the right).

**LOOS MEMORIAL.** The village of Loos-en-Gohelle is approximately 5km north-west of Lens. The Loos Memorial forms the side and back of the Dud Corner Cemetery where 1,700 officers and men are buried.

**MAROEUIL BRITISH CEMETERY.** Maroeuil lies 6km to the north-west of Arras, between the roads to Houdain and Aubigny. The British Cemetery can be found at the end of a track running north from the road to Bray and Ecoivres.

**MILL ROAD CEMETERY.** The village of Thiepval on the D151 is approximately 8km north of Albert. The Cemetery is 1km north-west of the village on the north side of the D73, the road to Hamel. Access to the cemetery, 500 m from the road is by a track which is suitable for cars.

**NEUVE-CHAPELLE MEMORIAL.** The village of Neuve-Chapelle is 5km north of La Bassee and 20km west-south-west of Lille. The Memorial is 800m south-west of the village on the east side of the road from La Bassee to Estaires.

**PERONNE COMMUNAL CEMETERY EXTENSION.** From Bapaume take the N17 to Peronne. On entering Peronne turn right towards the Hospital. Opposite the Hospital is a small road and the communal cemetery is at the end of the road on the left. The extension is on the south side of the cemetery.

**PLOEGSTEERT MEMORIAL.** The Memorial stands in the Berkshire Cemetery Extension which can be found 12.5km south of Ypres town centre, on the N365 leading from Ypres to Messines (Ieper to Mesen), Ploegsteert and on to Armentieres. From Ypres town square leave through the Lille Gate (Rijselpoort) and directly over the crossroads with the Ypres ring-road. The road name then changes to Rijselseweg N336. 3.5km along the N336 lies a forked junction with the N365. The N365 (the right fork) goes to Messines. The Cemetery lies 3km. Beyond Messines on the right hand side of the N365 and opposite the Hyde Park Corner. Royal Berks. Cemetery. The memorial commemorates 11,000 men who have no known grave.

**PLYMOUTH NAVAL MEMORIAL.** This Memorial is situated centrally on the Hoe overlooking Plymouth Sound.

**POELCAPELLE BRITISH CEMETERY.** This can be found 10km north-east of Ypres on the Brugseweg N313, a road connecting Ypres with Brugge. The cemetery lies 10km along the N313 on the right hand side of the road after passing through the village of Poelkapelle.

**POZIERES BRITISH CEMETERY.** Pozieres is located 6km north-east of Albert, and the cemetery, enclosed by the Pozieres Memorial, is south-west of the village on the north side of the D929, Albert to Pozieres road.

**PUCHEVILLERS BRITISH CEMETERY.** The village of Puchevillers is on the D11 approximately 19km north-east of Amiens. The British Cemetery is a little west of the village. The signpost to the cemetery can be found near the church in the village.

**RAILWAY DUGOUTS BURIAL GROUND.** Is located 2km south-east of Ypres town centre on the Komenseweg Road, connecting Ypres to Komen (N336). Leave Ypres via the Lille Gate and cross the Ypres ring road to Armentieres and Lille. The road name changes to Pijselseweg. 1km along this road lies a left hand turn to Komenseweg. The cemetery is located 1.2km along on the right hand side.

**RUE-DES-BERCEAUX MILITARY CEMETERY.** This can be found in Richebourg-L'Avoue, Pas de Calais. Richbourg is a village to the north of Bethune in the Pas-de-Calais. From the church in Richebourg, head south on the D166. The Cemetery will be found on the right hand side of the road 950m from the church.

**ST VAAST POST MILITARY CEMETERY.** This can be found in the village of Richebourg-l'Avoue, 9km north-east of Bethune. Follow the D171 towards Armentieres and go onto the D166 proceeding to Richebourg. Turn left into Rue de Charbonniers and after approximately 2km the cemetery will be seen on the right hand side.

**THIEPVAL MEMORIAL.** Can be found on the D73, off the main Bapaume to Albert road, the D929.

**TOWER HILL MEMORIAL. 1914-1918.** This memorial is situated on Tower Hill, London, on the south side of the pleasure garden of Trinity Square. The memorial consists of a vaulted corridor of 21.5 metres long and 7 metres wide and 7-10 metres high. The names of the war dead are carried on Bronze Panels, covering eight of the main masonry piers which support the roof. They are listed alphabetically under the name of the ship in which they died.

**VILLERS-BRETONNEUX MEMORIAL. Somme.** Villers-Bretonneux is a village 16km east of Amiens on the straight main road to St. Quentin. The Memorial stands in Villers-Bretonneux Military Cemetery, which is about 2km north of the village on the east side of the road to Fouilloy.

**VIMY MEMORIAL. Pas de Calais.** Situated 8km northeast of Arras on the N17 towards Lens. The Memorial is signposted from this road to the left, just before you enter the village of Vimy from the South. The Memorial itself is someway inside the memorial park but is well signposted.

**VIS-en-ARTOIS MEMORIAL.** Vis-en-Artois is a village on the straight main road from Arras to Cambrai approximately 10km south-east of Arras. The Vis-en-Artois memorial can be found in Vis-en-Artois British Cemetery, which is west of the village of Harcourt on the north side of the main road. The Memorial bears the names of 9,000 men who died in the period 8 August 1918 to the Armistice in the advance in Picardy and Artois, between the Somme and Loos, and who have no known grave.

**VLAMERTINGHE NEW MILITARY CEMETERY.** This is located 5km west of Ypres town centre and to the south of the village of Vlamertinge. The village is located along the Poperingseweg. The Cemetery is can be found after turning left in the village onto the Hugo Verriestraat. This road crosses a railway and the N38 where the name of the street changes to Bellestraat. The cemetery lies 200m on the left hand side after crossing the N38.

**WIMEREUX COMMUNAL CEMETERY.** The small town of Wimereux is located about 5km north of Boulogne. From Boulogne take the A16 to Calais and come off at junction 4. Take the road to Wimereux north, D242 for approximately 2km following the road around the roundabout. Take the first turn on the left immediately after the roundabout and the Cemetery lies approximately 200m down this road on the left hand side. The War Graves are situated to the rear of the Communal cemetery.

**WOBURN ABBEY CEMETERY.** Cuinchy is a village midway between Bethune and La Bassee. Woburn Abbey Cemetery lies to the south-west of the village towards Cambrin. From the church in Cuinchy head south on the D116, after 300m turn left. The cemetery is a further 200m from the junction on the left.

**YPRES. Menin Gate.** The Memorial is situated at the eastern side of the town on the road to Menin and Courtrai. It bears the names of men who were lost without any known grave during the defence of the Ypres salient. At 8pm every day members of the local fire brigade play the Last Post beneath the eastern end of the Gate.

## Appendix 1

### School Chapel War Memorial

The War Memorial in the School Chapel was unveiled on Saturday, February 18th at 3 o'clock, by Lt-Col. Leslie Wilson DSO. M.P. There was a large gathering of friends of the school, amongst whom were Mrs Wilson, Sir G. Stewart Abram, the Mayor and Mayoress (Mr and Mrs W.R.Howell) and many others. The service was conducted by the Rev. Edgar Priestly (Bursar) assisted by the Rev. F.J. Howard, Vicar of St. Luke's and the Rev. H.A.Smith-Masters O.R. (Vicar of Hagbourne).

The service, which was quite short and simple, commenced with the hymn 'Jesus Lives!' followed by a few sentences of the burial service. Then came the 23rd Psalm 'The Lord is my Shepherd' and the Lesson (Wisdom iii 1-10) read by the Head Master. The choir then sang the beautiful and well-known anthem. 'Blest are the Departed' by the late Dr. Haydn Keeton, and after special versicles and prayers, Harwoods fine setting of the Easter Anthem. 'Christ being raised from the dead dieth no more'. Lt-Colonel Wilson then unveiled the Memorial and it was dedicated by the Rev. H.A. Smith-Masters, O.R. Then came the hymn 'Ye Holy Angels Bright' which was followed by the Benediction. Finally the Last Post was sounded'.

## Appendix 2

### Great Britain Casualty Figures

| Mobilised | Dead | Wounded | Missing/POW |
|---|---|---|---|
| 8,904,467 | 908,371 | 2,090,212 | 191,600 |

The graphs below show the age and rank distribution of ORs killed in action or as a result of wounds received between 1914 and 1919. It should be noted that many ORs entered the Army as Privates and were awaiting their commissions as 2nd Lieutenant to come through when they were either killed or wounded.

## ORs - Number of Deaths by Age

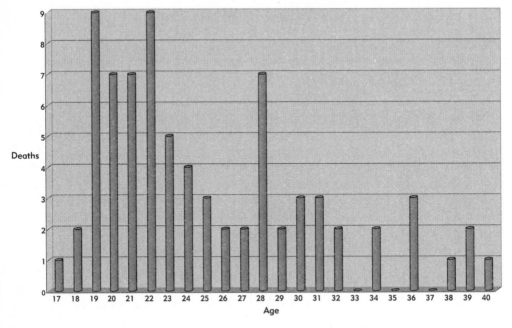

## ORs - Number of Deaths by Rank

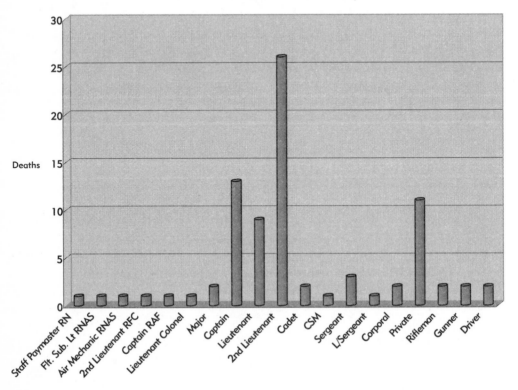

# Appendix 3

## ARMISTICE DEMANDS 10 November 1918

Published in the Kreuz-Zeitung. November 11<sup>th</sup> 1918.

1   To be effective 6 hours after signing.

2   Immediate clearing of Belgium, France, Alsace-Lorraine, to be concluded within 14 days. Any troops remaining in these areas to be interned as prisoners of war.

3   Surrender 5,000 cannon (chiefly heavy), 30,000 machine guns, 3,000 trench mortars, 2,000 planes.

4   Evacuation of the left bank of the Rhine, Mayence, Coblenz, Cologne, occupied by the enemy to a radius of 30 kilometres deep.

5   On the right bank on the Rhine a neutral zone from 30 to 40km deep, evacuation within 11 days.

6   Nothing to be removed from the territory on the left bank of the Rhine, all factories, railroads etc. to be left intact.

7   Surrender of 5,000 locomotives, 150,000 railway coaches, 10,000 trucks.

8   Maintenance of enemy occupation troops through Germany.

9   In the East all troops to withdraw behind the boundaries of August 1<sup>st</sup>, 1914, fixed time not given.

10  Renunciation of the Treaties of Brest-Litovsk and Bucharest.

11  Unconditional surrender of East Africa.

12  Return of property to Belgian Bank, Russian and Romanian gold.

13  Return of Prisoners of War without reciprocity.

14  Surrender of 160 U-boats, 8 light cruisers, 6 Dreadnoughts; the rest of the fleet to be disarmed and controlled by the allies in neutral or allied harbours.

15  Assurance of free trade through the Kattegat Sound; clearance of minefields and occupation of all forts and batteries, through which transit could be hindered.

16  The blockade remains in effect. All German ships to be captured.

17  All limitations by Germany on neutral shipping to be removed.

18  Armistice to last 30 days.

## Appendix 4

# THE A.S. LAWRANCE CASKET

The following document was in a Silver Casket presented to South House, Reading School by Sir Arthur Lawrance. The Casket was originally presented by the merchants of Berbera to Sir Arthur on his retirement as Governor General and Commander in Chief of the British Somaliland Protectorate. It was always brought out with the House Silver on formal occasions but the significance of it was not recognized until this book was commenced. The Casket remains at Reading School. The document is with John Oakes; sometime House Master of South House, for safekeeping and further research.

## THE WORDING OF 'THE PETITION AND FAREWELL' GIVEN TO SIR A.S. LAWRANCE BY THE MERCHANTS OF BERBERA ON HIS RETIREMENT FROM BRITISH SOMALILAND. 14TH NOVEMBER 1938

## TO HIS EXCELLENCY SIR ARTHUR SALISBURY LAWRANCE, K.C.M.G., K.B.E., D.S.O.,

### Governor and Commander in Chief of the Somaliland Protectorate.

MAY IT PLEASE YOUR EXCELLENCEY,

We the merchants of Berbera express our unfeigned regret at your impending departure.

Most of your political career has been spent in this Protectorate and it is a fitting reward of your endeavor and ability that you became the head of its administration, and are now leaving us as the Governor and Commander in Chief of the Somaliland Protectorate.

Changes in the high office you hold are not every-day affairs, and when the change involves the severance of ties with a Governor of Your Excellency's reputation and sympathy, we cannot allow the opportunity to pass without a public expression of our humble appreciation and of all you have done during your service in the Protectorate for the betterment of all communities in Somaliland, for the comfort and well being of its people and for the general interests of the country.

We feel that the Protectorate is in urgent need of deep water berthing accommodation at Berbera, permanent main roads, efficient electric lighting and drainage schemes, and an extension of the present water schemes.

It is a matter of great pride to us that your efforts have been recognized by His Majesty the King Emperor by the conferment on Your Excellency of two high orders of Knighthood, that of the British Empire and that of the Most Distinguished Order of St. Michael and St. George.

In taking leave of Your Excellency we pray that you will commend our earnest attention to Your Successor those many crying needs of the Protectorate which you yourself have so long had at heart, in particular the necessity for improvement of the town area, harbors of Berbera and Zeilah and the encouragement of our transit trade with Abyssinia.

We now respectfully request Your Excellency to accept this Silver Casket as an humble memento of your long and fruitful stay amongst us and bid your Excellency farewell with our earnest prayer that the Supreme Ruler of the Universe may grant you a long life and happiness in your well earned retirement.

We beg to remain,

Your Excellency's most obedient servants,

Berbera 14th November 1938. Signed by members of the Commercial Community.

# Bibliography

Allen. Charles. *Plain Tales from the Raj*. Andre Deutsch. 1975

Amery. L.S. (Ed) *The Times History of the War in South Africa 1899 – 1902*

Baker. Carlos. *Ernest Hemingway. A Life Story*. Penguin. 1972

Bierman. John. *Dark Safari*. Hodder and Stoughton. 1992

Carrington. Charles. *Rudyard Kipling. His Life and Work*. Macmillan. 1955

Carver. Michael. Field Marshal. *Britain and her Armies in the 20$^{th}$ Century*. Macmillan. 1998

Carver. Michael. Field Marshal. *The Boer War*. Sedgwick and Jackson. 1999

Carwell. Colonel C.E. *Lessons from the Tirah Campaign*. London 1897

Chapman, Cull, Croucher, Fox, McIntyre,Webb 'Responding to the Call'. University of Reading 1995.

Collins. Maurice. *Raffles*. Century. 1988

Fox. Colin. *Monchy le Preux. Arras*. Pen and Sword/Lee Cooper. 2000

Gilbert. Martin. *First World War*. Harper Collins. 1995

Gilbert. Martin. *Winston S. Churchill. Companion Vol.IV. January 1917 – June 1919*. Heinemann. 1977

Gregory. Adrian. *The Silence of Memory. Armistice Day. 1919-1946*. Berg. 1994

Hemingway. Ernest. *Green Hills of Africa*. Arrow Books. 1994

HMSO. *The British Invasion of Tibet. Colonel Younghusband*. 1999

Hook. Hilary. *Home from the Hill*. Penguin. 1988

Hopkirk. Peter. *The Quest for Kim*. John Murray. 1996

James. Lawrence. *Raj. The Making and Unmaking of British India*. Little Brown and Co. 1997

Keay. John. *The Honourable Company*. Harper Collins. 1991

MacDonald. Lyn. *1914*. Penguin 1987

MacDonald. Lyn. *1915. The Death of Innocence*. Headline. 1993

MacDonald. Lyn. *Somme*. Papermac.1985

MacDonald. Lyn. *The Roses of No Mans Land*. Papermac. 1986

MacDonald. Lyn. *They Called it Passchendaele*. Papermac. 1984

McNaught. Kenneth. *The Penguin History of Canada*. 1988

Marwick. Arthur. *The Deluge. British Society in the First World War*. Macmillan. 1973

Morris. John. *Farewell the Trumpets. An Imperial Retreat*. London. 1978

Lovell. Mary.S. *A Rage to Live. A biography of Richard and Isabel Burton*. Little Brown and Co. 1988

Packenham. Thomas. *The Scramble for Africa 1876 – 1912*. Abacus. 1992

Packenham. Thomas. *The Boer War*. George Weidenfeld & Nicolson Ltd. 1979

Reader. John. *Africa. A Biography of the Continent*. Hamish Hamilton. 1997

Said. Edward. *Culture and Imperialism*. Chatto and Windus. 1993

Sherriff. R.C. *Journey's End*.

Verrier. Anthony. *Francis Younghusband and the Great Game*. Jonathan Cape. 1991

Wickwire. Franklin and Mary. *Cornwallis and the War of Independence*. Faber and Faber. 1971

Commonwealth War Graves Commission. *Debt of Honour Register*.

## TRAVEL GUIDES

Holt. Toni & Valmai. *Battlefield Guide to the Somme*. Pen and Sword/Lee Cooper 2000

Reed Paul. *Walking the Salient*   Pen and Sword/Lee Cooper  1999

Reed Paul. *Walking the Somme*  Pen and Sword/Lee Cooper  1999

*A Handbook for Travellers in India, Burma and Ceylon*. 12th Edition. John Murray. 1926

Editions of *Footprint Handbooks*. Footprint Handbooks Ltd.

Editions of *The Rough Guides*.  Rough Guides Ltd. Penguin.

## MAGAZINES

Reading School Magazines. 1894 – 1923

Kendrick Boys School Magazines. 1909 - 1915

# Index